PARENT THERAPY

A Relational Alternative to Working with Children

Linda Jacobs and Carol Wachs

JASON ARONSON INC.
Northvale, New Jersey
London

This book was set in 12 pt. Perpetua by Pageworks and printed and bound by Book-Mart Press, Inc. of North Bergen, NJ.

Library of Congress Cataloging-in-Publication Data

Printed in the United States of America on acid-free paper. For information and catalog, write to Jason Aronson Inc., 230 Livingston Street, Northvale, NJ 07647–1726, or visit our website: www.aronson.com

For Jerry, who invented the model—*C.W.*

For Gene, whose abiding love sustains me—*L.J.*

The imperfect is our paradise
—Wallace Stevens
The Poems of Our Climate

Contents

Acknowledgments

First, we would like to thank the many parents who have shared their stories with us; they have done so with the extraordinary openness and generosity and have most obviously contributed to the conception and realization of this work. The material in the book derives from both clinical and non-clinical situations. We have chosen to include vignettes which we feel reflect the significant and common themes that many parents struggle with. Because of this, the cases referred to represent salient issues in composite form, for the sake of clarity and confidentiality. All details of actual cases are altered and embedded in these composites. Friends, colleagues and patients have all contributed so greatly, over the years, to the development of our thinking and we are deeply grateful to all the people who have allowed us to participate in their lives in this most intimate way. They have enhanced our lives in ways we could not have predicted.

Secondly, our own supervisors deserve explicit mention: Neil Altman, Carol Eagle, Linda Taylor, and Gil Trachtman, and certain colleagues who functioned in consultative roles, Nancy Curcio and Karen Lombardi, all contributed significantly to our knowledge of child development and the treatment of children and families. Supervisors from our analytic training have played an invaluable part in our personal and intellectual growth and have been esteemed role models as well. In a variety of ways, the very paradigm of parent consultation is based on the enriching experiences we have had with Phillip Bromberg, Martin Bergmann, Muriel Dimen, James Fosshage, Emanual Ghent, Adrienne Harris, Sue Shapiro, and Warren Wilner. Each, in a distinct way, was present for us throughout this work, which grew out of our own feelings of being held, guided, and supported in all of our endeavors.

I would like to thank my children, Kate Fodaski Jacobson and Elizabeth Fodaski, who have inspired me in everything I do. Sophie Indiana Baker, my granddaughter, has been a constant inspiration for me in my thinking about children.

L.J.

I would like to thank Isabel and Nadine for their tireless efforts in our own collaborative process, and for their earnest attempts to keep their hands off the manuscript. My grandfather, Isadore Wachs, also deserves special mention for his commitment to the belief that every viewpoint deserves "equal time."

C.W.

I
Parent Consultation and Therapy

1

A New Treatment Model

$\mathcal{W}$e are proposing an approach to the treatment of childhood problems that we believe is a useful alternative to individual child treatment and to family therapy. Parent therapy may mitigate some of the problems inherent in more traditional treatment approaches and may be more effective in helping children.

In our culture there is a striking absence of training in how to be a parent. There are no required courses in child development, parent-child relationships, or basic child care. The cultural assumption that, without training, people will become competent parents, however, is belied by the dramatically high rates of child abuse, neglect, and teenage pregnancy. Yet our society continues to privilege parental autonomy over intervention and training. The mental health field contributes to this social condition through the neglect of clinical training in the education of parents to enhance parenting skills and parent-child relationships, even though mental health professionals are often distressed and angered by the perceived failings of parents and by their patients' consequent suffering from the impact of poor or problematic relationships with parents.

Most child treatment approaches are firmly rooted in early psychoanalytic work with adults. In these paradigms the therapist–patient dyad is the primary locus of treatment and the child's behavior is the primary target of change. Current research, however, emphasizes the multiple and complex interactions that constitute parent-child dynamic patterns. Therefore, as we understand more about relational complexities, the appropriate points of entry into child treatment are broadened to include the child *and* the parent. Manifest problems are likely to reflect an intricate system of internal representations and projections. What may be obscured, however, is the substantial impact of the therapist on the relational patterns that have existed between parent and child. The relational context in which both family and therapist become engaged warrants greater attention and exploration.

In individual treatment, the alliance between the patient and the therapist often unwittingly serves to exclude and to vilify the patient's parents. Despite the benefits of such treatments, the stigmatization of the parents, compounded by their exclusion, under the guise of confidentiality, has many negative repercussions. All three parties understand, on some level, that the parent is blameworthy, and may further be seen as underinvolved, neglectful, uninformed, competitive, demanding, or even sadistic.

The premise of our parent therapy model rests on a relational understanding of development and on an exploration of the mutual regulation that exists between parent and child. Consistent with contemporary infant research, the entry points for the treatment process are the parent-child relationship and the self-representations that develop through maternal and paternal histories and projections. The old adage "Give a man a fish, you feed him for a day; teach a man to fish, you feed him for a lifetime" is an apt analogy for this relational alternative to child therapy. Where direct treatment may modify behavioral symptoms, this relational model has the potential for influencing the course of children's development through enhancing the parental experience. This view sees the therapeutic encounter as triadic: parent/child/therapist. In this way the therapist functions as a consultant to the parents, and thus parent therapy is like a consultation. It undertakes transformational experience for the parent through an increase in self-esteem and self-knowledge. In an optimal therapeutic alliance, the corrective emotional experience is aimed not at the individual but at the relationship, which is seen as potentially most mutative and far reaching for the child.

The supervisory model used in psychoanalytic training is an apt analogy in this context. In this model, there is a tacit agreement that the supervisor has particular expertise, greater experience and wisdom, and the capacity to view the analytic relationship unencumbered by pulls from within. The supervisee/therapist has the direct experience in the room with, and in relation to, the patient, as well as an involvement with and attachment to the patient. The collaboration between supervisor and therapist brings together separate spheres of expertise to help the therapist help the patient. Through the process of supervision, there is an internal process of change; the narrative and representational themes that emerge in this encounter are carried into the therapeutic encounter with the patient. In this way the supervisor becomes part of the therapy; he or she is both inside the room, through the supervisee's internalizations, and outside, occupying a transitional space between therapist and patient.

The relational model of child treatment poses a similar paradigm in that the therapist works directly with the parents and, like the supervisor, is poised between the parent and child as a potentially influential force on both. Muriel Dimen (unpublished statement) has said, in reference to the supervisory process, "Psychoanalytic education is, in my view, largely an apprenticeship, both analytic and supervisory. In this old-fashioned, but now vanishing way of transmitting knowledge, learning is so immediate as to be nearly corporeal. My supervisory objective is correlative: to determine where the candidate has yet to grow." She sees her supervisory work as an "intimate project" that is "co-constructed." "Together, supervisor and supervisee figure out what requires work." In the process, Dimen remarks, "I inevitably share the mistakes from which I have learned—this is in part what I mean by 'practice'—as well as what my own teachers have taught me."

These remarks seem especially pertinent for new parents who may have difficulty in traversing bumps in the road of child-rearing. When difficulties do occur, consulting with others who have already had similar experiences can be extremely helpful. In the culturally sanctioned absence of any formal training in parenting, it is reasonable to expect that parents will become insecure when trouble arises. In psychoanalytic training, candidates learn to expect trouble, to anticipate that bumps in the road will inevitably arise. Supervision, therefore, becomes a normal and valued part of the ongoing process of doing treatment. Dimen elaborates this point:

To these ends, I try to keep myself open to the varied perspectives candidates might take or wish to take. . . . What I do not provide is a recipe. I will make it known when an error has been made, and will explore what the supervisee had in mind. What I believe to be the most important is the supervisee's expansion, in ever widening concentric circles, of skill, knowledge and self knowledge. . . . I want to encourage in my supervisees an appreciation for the difficulty, weirdness, and mystery of the unconscious; a deep intense interest in the patient; a feeling for the patient's hidden vitality.

These remarks about the supervisory process most closely resemble the primary thrust of the parent therapy model; it describes a co-creation and a collaboration that is designed to provoke and inspire, and, most importantly, to generate introspective and reflective thought. When supervisors can expand the capacities of the therapist in training, they do a service to the patient; analogously, when therapists can expand the capacities of parents, they not only create the potential for more harmonious parent–child relationships, but also set in motion an ever-unfolding transformational process that potentially ameliorates the tensions and conflicts that permeate troubled relationships.

The supervisory process is both exploratory and supportive. The supervisor is often able to enhance the therapist's confidence while exploring ways in which underlying dynamics may preclude the fruitful progression of the therapeutic process. At times, the therapist enters the supervisory encounter in a state of discouragement, only to emerge with a sense of accomplishment about the therapy's actual progress, the obstacles unearthed, and the insights gained. This effect results from the supervisor's informative suggestions and from the elucidation of transference and countertransference issues not previously recognized. This is one of the most highly valued dimensions of clinical training. Clearly, the solution to therapeutic impasses or difficulties is not to have the supervisor see the patient, which would do irreparable harm to the therapist and the therapist–patient relationship. Analogously, the child with difficulties may not be well served by seeing the "better trained" adult for treatment. Rather, an intervention in which the clinician works with the parents alone provides the opportunity for the parents to develop new capacities as parents.

Although models that are based on systems theory also aim at the contextual issues in the family, the relational model emphasizes the significance and effect of the therapist's involvement in the system. When the child therapist becomes the authority figure, the family is altered by his/her presence, a presence that risks undermining the authority of the parents in their own and their child's perception. With family treatment, the therapist is also privileged: he/she is seen by all participants as a more informed and, perhaps, more benign figure, thereby inviting some of the same stigmatizing beliefs about parents. Thus, while the family therapy approach aims at depathologizing the child's problems, it may perpetuate the parents' unconscious beliefs that they are the root cause of those difficulties. In contrast, the model of parent therapy is designed to address the parents' unconscious conflicts in an atmosphere of collaboration. Implicit in this concept is the belief that one's primary parenting education comes from one's own parents, and, therefore, in the absence of training, mistakes in parenting are handed down from generation to generation.

In the parent therapy paradigm. the parent is helped to assume a more effective role, partly through self-understanding. Mistakes in parenting are detoxified, and the "catching" of mistakes becomes a positive, non-shameful part of a collaborative process. Underscoring this model is the assumption that parents are more amenable to change when they are not overwhelmed with a sense of dissonance or with feelings of shame about their ignorance, anger, or frustration. Moreover, they are more likely to engage with the therapist when they are able to feel collaborative and empowered. When there is a presumption that parents are motivated to improve and enhance their parenting skills, the potential for change increases dramatically.

Often, when a child has been identified as needing some therapeutic intervention, problems arise in the extrafamilial situation that have been given too little attention by the therapeutic community. A relational view of child treatment emphasizes an understanding of the complex intersubjective nature of the family constellation and the ways in which manifest problems reflect an intricate system of internal representations and projections. It is based on the assumption that when a child enters a treatment process, what occurs is a set of projections in which all members—the parents, the child, and the therapist—participate. This model attempts to establish a process through which these projections may be rearranged or reorganized to the benefit of the parent-child relationship. Traditional treatments too often run the risk, through the chronic exclusion of the parents, of being less effective than an approach that would engage the parents in a process of enhancing their skills and parenting capacities. In contrast, parent therapy systematically explores the parents' unconscious projections and the resulting intersubjective experiences that are continually at play in the family's behavior.

The parent therapy model offers a way of entering a relational system in an effort to create shifts not only in the individual's behavior, but also in the relational patterns that have developed through long-standing family interactions and mythologies. What we call mythology is a network of ever-expanding sets of perceptions, intersubjectively developed, through which the child sees himself through the parent's projected self, and the parents see parts of themselves through their experience of the child. In this context the interactions and co-constructed behaviors are seen as the primary locus of the treatment interventions. In this model what is believed to be transformative for the child is a shift in the internal experience of the parent, which leads to a shift in the projections and introjections that are at play in the parent-child relationship.

2

Clinical Vignettes

A young mother and her 2-year-old son are in the waiting room of a busy, inner-city medical center. Angry at her toddler's crying, the mother slaps him across the head. This event does not go unnoticed by the clinic staff, and there is a variety of reactions to the woman's violent outburst. The reactions range from anxious avoidance to glaring judgment and contempt for her lack of self-control and abusiveness. The mother's unrealistic expectations of her child's capacities at a time when he is feeling ill, her belief that he could wait quietly for hours while he is hungry and idle, and her own difficulty in tolerating the frustration of waiting are all potential targets for intervention. Bearing in mind the setting in which she must wait, we can easily imagine that overtaxed staff members may already be predisposed to impatience, and do not care to be reminded that their system may contribute to her behavior.

One physician, also observing this event, approaches the mother and is solicitous of her, asking if she is all right; he never even glances at the child. His exchange is conducted with the mother only, as if she were alone. The mother, prepared for his criticism of her behavior, is startled. Her body quickly shifts from its defensive pose; someone is making contact with *her*, someone is wondering how *she* is faring. The transformation, while minuscule in the enduring life of this mother–child dyad, is nonetheless dramatic and possibly far reaching. When shifts of this nature occur, the child's experience of the parent may also be transformed, and potentially may lead to a self-

experience as the recipient of concern rather than the "bad" child who
has caused mother distress. The young woman tells the doctor of her
long wait, that she and her baby have been there for hours, without
any information about when they will be seen by a doctor. She further
explains that the baby has been sick for two days, and that she had
not realized that the wait would be so long. Therefore, she hasn't
brought food or toys to soothe and occupy him during the waiting
period. In short, her baby is cranky, ill, bored, and hungry. The physician is sympathetic about *her* situation; his approach has almost
instantly reconfigured the psychic climate of this mother–child dynamic experience. He has managed to reframe her role: she is transformed from an abusive, volatile, unskilled parent to a frustrated
but concerned parent. He offers her crackers for the child, and
help in shortening her wait. Through this intervention the mother
is able to turn more considerate attention to her child and, in doing
so, to feel more protective and solicitous herself. Her own distress
and anxiety about not being able to soothe her child could then be
directed outward, not to the child, but to the difficulties to which they
were both subjected. Moreover, the self representation is transmuted
from the inadequate caregiver to the protective and therefore more
loving parent.

This vignette illustrates a salient feature of the parent therapy
model: it circumvents the interaction with the child in order to preserve
the power and preeminence of the parent's direct relationship with the
child. It furthermore seeks to sever the connection between the child and
a hated or disavowed parental self representation. The premise here is that
aggression may be directed toward the child because the child's behavior
resonates with a part of the self that the parent wishes to disavow; the unruly
or distressed child represents an unlovable or incompetent self. If, through
interventions with the parent, the toxic self representation can be transmuted, the projections received by the child can also be modified.

If we were to examine this vignette from the perspective of the
child therapist, we might develop a somewhat different picture. We can
assume that much sympathy would be felt for the child. A potential

transference reaction, in identification with the victim, would be one of negativity and rage toward the abusing parent. However, this focus tragically misses the opportunity to reflect and focus on the internal experience of the parent, and it is this experience, if sensitively addressed, that might be significantly more mutative for her relationship with her child. This vignette illustrates the direction of a therapeutic plan: the therapeutic intervention is seen as an attempt to modify the relational experience of the parent, which, in turn, transforms the intersubjective pattern of the parent-child relationship.

The therapeutic question is simple: What will enable parents to feel and be more protective toward their child? If the therapist is able to make an alliance with the benign part of the parents' self, the relationship with the child will subsequently be enhanced by the parents' perceptions of themselves as a vitally positive force in the child's world. But when the benign protector of the child is the therapist, this potentially invites the emergence or reactivation of the parents' fragile self and sense of inadequacy. The risk exists, as well, that the therapist, or, in this vignette, the clinic staff, may feel responsible for the child's manifest difficulties. Such a countertransferential response may contribute to an escalation of critical reactions toward the parent, which both parent and child are likely to perceive, thus reinforcing the parent's anger at her own incompetence and at the intervening providers. This is the most vital aspect of the parent therapy model: it conceptualizes the therapeutic process as the loosening and reorganizing of negative self representations in order to create a more benign cycle of projective and identificatory processes.

Let us look at another example:

Mr. and Mrs. A. seek therapy for Jonathan, their 11-year-old son, because of his very distressing symptom of bed-wetting. During the preliminary consultation, the therapist identifies not only the obvious concern and anxiety of the parents, but also some mild conflict in their perceptions of their child's problem. Partly to further explore the family dynamics that may underscore some of the child's behavior and partly because of the obvious downside of talking to the adolescent himself about bed-wetting, the therapist decides to continue to see the parents exclusively. At first they are a bit mystified and ask frequently if the therapist wants to meet Jonathan. A clinical assessment of the situation goes something like this: the boy must feel deeply anxious and vulnerable (both as a result of his symptom and as a causal factor in the development of this symptom). He is already described as notably competitive with his sister. The stigma of attending therapy sessions with or without his family seems as if it might exacerbate Jonathan's feelings of humiliation.

The parents agree to see the therapist by themselves; after several sessions they seem intrigued by the work and are eager to continue. They describe their family thus: Mrs. A. feels that Mr. A. is too demanding and puts relatively intense pressure on the children, particularly around academic excellence. Mr. A. was a highly motivated and high-achieving student, and went to prestigious private schools; it has also been his desire to have his children attend his former sleepaway camp for the upcoming summer. Mrs. A. is openly fearful and hesitant about this prospect; she worries that the children will be unhappy without the family, and she would like them to stay at home at the family's country house. It also becomes clear that she is extremely worried that Jonathan would wet his bed at camp. The therapist notes that Jonathan's symptom may perhaps be related to his mother's desire to keep him close by, at home, under the protection of the family.

It is important to pause here to explore the connections between this youngster's behavior and the anxieties and projections of his mother. If we began treatment with the boy alone, we might miss the opportunity to clarify the complex motivational systems that are at play in his relationships with his parents and sibling, of which he is largely unaware, and that therapy might bring to the conscious level at the expense of his self-esteem. If, as is generally the case, we are dealing with the interplay of unconscious needs, like Mrs. A.'s maternal and protective feelings toward her son, we might address this productively at the level of direct work with the parent.

However, this is only half of the story:

Mr. A. has his own concerns; he is a son in a family that is quite patriarchically organized. His father, an eminent physician, has for a long time been the authority and benefactor for the extended family, and Mr. A. feels much respect for his father's position. It is also important for him to assume a patriarchal position in his own nuclear family, since this is the particular family configuration with which he is most familiar and comfortable. What complicates the situation and creates conflictual experiences for Jonathan is that Mr. A.'s authoritarianism frequently comes into conflict with Mrs. A.'s protectiveness. A common episode in the family is Jonathan's refusal to obey a command, his transgression of some rule, or his distress over some parental restraint. Mr. A. admits to becoming frustrated and feeling the impulse to hit Jonathan, partly to reestablish the familiar hierarchy. When this occurs, Mrs. A. insinuates herself into the argument in order to rescue her son from any potential violence or reprimand.

This information leads the therapeutic interventions in a particular direction. The therapist works for several sessions on what appears to be a central dilemma for this child. What seems necessary here is to shift the balance of the projections: mother feels protective and father feels angry; they have constructed a situation in which the more protective mother becomes, the more anxious father is that Jonathan will be weak and unmanly. Yet the more frustrated father becomes and the more punitive, the more empathic and therefore protective is mother. This then becomes the therapeutic goal: the therapist must deconstruct this dynamic pattern and help the parents to recognize their previously unconscious fantasies about themselves and their child, potentially to transform some of the child's internalized self-images and to expand his repertoire of self-referents.

The therapist works with cross-identifications. She increases the couple's awareness of their unconscious fears; for mother, the suggestion is made that she believes that Jonathan will be frightened and insecure, and for father, that Jonathan will be weak and infantile. They are encouraged to try other modes of relating, even to exchange roles so that father assumes the job of soothing and comforting when Jonathan is distressed and mother sets the limits and enforces rules. This strategy proves to be quite fruitful;

after a few weeks Mrs. A. begins to feel relieved of the burden of protecting Jonathan against father's reprimands; and Mr. A. is astonished at how much warmth he feels for Jonathan.

To return to the symptom:

Mr. A. reveals a long-held secret anxiety about an incident that occurred when Jonathan was 3 years old: Jonathan was in the care of an unscrupulous baby-sitter who, the parents later discovered, had exposed himself to the young child. For years, Mr. A. has been distressed about the fact that Jonathan might have been traumatized by this incident. This distress has escalated into a generalized anxiety that his son will be sexually insecure and frightened. In light of this, the therapist offers an interpretation. Perhaps the symptom, the bedwetting, is not a random occurrence or merely an expression of anxiety. Perhaps it is Jonathan's unconscious way of demonstrating to his father that his penis is in working order while demonstrating to his mother that he is, indeed, still her "little boy." If we look at the symptom thus, as a clue to the relational configuration that the child must maintain, we can approach the treatment in more productive ways. In this case, the therapist was markedly impressed with the creativity of the boy's unconscious process. Her apparent admiration for such a clever solution to his relational dilemma allowed the parents to take some pride in the very symptom that had, beforehand, felt so problematic. Even more important than whether this interpretation was indeed correct was the fact that it served as an effective intervention thatnsformed shameful feelings about their son's vulnerabilities, and enhanced their sense of his positive attributes. They were each able to convert their fears about him into an appreciation of him as stronger than they had previously believed.

This illustrative sequence extracted from an ongoing consultation emphasizes that the symptom itself is not the primary object of consideration. Rather, the symptom represents, in a lived" way, the interface between a mother's need for an enduring maternal preoccupation and a father's need to surmount his own ambivalent investment in masculine power, along with the boy's own struggle in defining his role in the family and in the world.

We have briefly touched on some of the disadvantages of treating this child in individual psychotherapy. It might appear that family systems theory is especially well suited to address the issues the child confronts. Let us reexamine this consultation from this alternative perspective. Family therapy tends to replicate the hierarchical structure thatitions and privileges the therapist as the authority, and implicitly suggests that the child may be acting out unresolved marital conflicts. While it may be extremely beneficial to release the child from this burden, both parents and child may suffer from the perception of the parents as the root cause of the symptom. The tacit agreement among all parties is to depathologize the child while, unintentionally, pathologizing the parents' behavior, interactions, and internal representations. But in the above case, Mr. A. is unlikely to respond favorably to interventions that threaten his position of authority. The consultation with the parents alone allowed for change to occur without destabilizing either parent. Mr. A. was able to maintain his authority because he entered the consulting room as the expert on his own child, an expertise that remained unchallenged by the therapist. Mrs. A. adhered to her role as Jonathan's protector. However, both parents were able to move fluidly into the other's position as their curiosity and collaboration were encouraged, and defensive competition between parents and therapist was minimized.

Another case, in which the need for psychotherapy was entirely obviated, occurred when an alarmed couple sought treatment for their 8-year-old son:

When Alex was 5 years old, he was taken to a psychologist for an intellectual assessment with the intention of placing him in a program for gifted students. He was a charming, mature, and intellectually gifted youngster who, as a result of the evaluation, was recommended for an enriched educational program. Three years later his parents once again solicited the therapist's advice, stating, rather urgently, that he was in need of therapy. When the therapist met with the parents they enumerated various symptoms, some of which were quite alarming to them, particularly to his mother. Alex had become more aggressive; for example, he had recently destroyed the notebook of a fellow classmate. When the psychologist inquired about his educational program, she was informed that he had remained at the local school in a regular mainstream class. His mother's political and civic values had finally precluded his placement in a gifted program; she was determined to have him attend a neighborhood school and be in an integrated setting with "regular" kids. In the last year he had become more argumentative with his mother, provoking her to extreme levels of distress.

Most alarming of all to his parents was the following incident, which had recently occurred, and was reported to the therapist thus: Alex had been playing at his friend's home and on his return had informed his mother that they had watched *Cinderella*; at a later date, during a particularly intimate moment, Alex confessed to his mother that he and his friend had actually watched *In Cold Blood*. Alex's parents were overwhelmed with distress and went to the extreme of renting the movie, pushing themselves further into alarm and agitation about the meaning and emotional repercussions of this event. After some time and painful soul searching, they were informed by Alex that he had fabricated the *In Cold Blood* story and had actually watched *Cinderella*. It was at this point that they contacted the therapist with the intention of placing their son into therapy.

Further discussion with these parents revealed a subtle disequilibrium in their approaches to parenting; they seemed to have developed a particular dynamic relationship in which Alex harassed his mother until his father exerted a more authoritative and powerful intervention. This usually cleared the air and solved the conflict between mother and son. Something in this relational matrix, though not an uncommon one, appeared to warrant further exploration. The therapist speculated that there was some conflict and anxiety that Alex was struggling with through his apparently provocative behavior.

Results of a psychological evaluation, prior to intervention, indicated that Alex was struggling with his sense that he had to do the impossible and that he was unable to live up to parental expectations; he seemed to have, unconsciously, perceived his father's concern that he might not be sufficiently competent. However, his powerful identification with his mother prevented him from approaching tasks and relationships with greater assertion and vigor.

The evaluation indicated that Alex was a lively, empathic, and relatively well adjusted child who was struggling with internal and dynamic concerns which clearly needed to be addressed. What was the appropriate approach for the problems he was facing? He seemed to be grappling with conflicting projections and shifting identifications: a mother whose goal was to raise a socially conscientious, civic-minded, sensitive person, and a father whose covert, but very real, desire was to raise a strong, confident, male, who could defend himself on the tough city streets.

The model of parent therapy seems highly pertinent here. It is important to note that the traditional mode of placing the child into individual treatment implies the possibility of creating a new set of problems for the child; it may tax the child to a greater extent than he is already taxed by burdening him with the feeling that the struggles that confront him are fundamentally self-generated, resulting from his own badness, so to speak. Many children do experience concerns about themselves if they are considered sufficiently problem-ridden to warrant therapy, and it is sometimes difficult to overcome the self-derogation or the sense of fragility that may then ensue.

More important, perhaps, is the underlying concern that the parents are unable to cope with their child's experience—a concern that may have other numerous consequences: the child may be led to feel that he is incorrigible, ill, or vulnerable, or that his parents are inept and undependable. Moreover, the parents, largely unaware of the intersubjective and constructed nature of their child's problem, may experience a sense of incompetence and therefore believe themselves to be at the mercy of a derogating therapist. If one considers, in contrast, a parent therapy approach, the following possibilities emerge.

The consultation with Alex's parents developed along these lines. They were advised by the therapist that their child was a reflective, lively, and empathic youngster who was having difficulty in satisfying two equally compelling and vitally important forces in his life. The parents were comforted by the reassurance and also persuaded by the idea that their child was experiencing conflict. This made them amenable to thinking about ways in which they could become more aware of the unconscious pulls and demands to which they were subjecting him.

Through relatively brief parent therapy, the parents revealed many of their anxieties regarding their son; although they had great respect for each other, and valued each other's devotion to Alex, each had a personal set of concerns, generated by their own characters and backgrounds. The father was quite candid and spoke extensively about his desire to imbue his son with a sense of power in what he perceived as a threatening world. The mother stated that she was committed to the idea of developing a sensitive, socially conscientious, and humane child, unburdened by conventional standards of masculinity.

The therapist, while empathizing with each parent's concern, spoke about Alex's behavior as his particular way of attempting to respond to both sets of unspoken demands: being aggressive for father but denying it for mother, and being meek for mother but denying it for father. The therapist further explained that the continual shifting between these states was what constituted the symptom, the underlying causes of which were not previously uncovered but were rooted in the multiple and competing projections and introjections.

The burgeoning research in infant and child development has done much to support the object relational view of development; it has demonstrated how much of relational patterning is instrumental in the structuring of individual experience. The theory rests on the assumption that character structure is at least partially created by the internalization of interactions between the child and the caregiver. Since Melanie Klein's (1948, 1957, 1975) theoretical innovations, there has been a continual refining of the idea that the developing child introjects the interactive experience with the object, and this interaction is bidirectional and mutually regulatory.

When a child is referred for therapy, a complex set of interactional events can occur that are analogous to the projective and introjective processes that have occurred earlier in development. A third object enters the relational matrix and complicates it in various ways. What can happen, in this context, to the self representations of the parents and child?

Let us examine the course of treatment in a traditional, once-a-week therapy with a child supplemented with collateral sessions with the parent(s):

Many children are brought to therapy as a result of distressing levels of depression. This was the case with Jennifer, whose development was complicated by the protracted illness and ultimate death of her father. She was referred for treatment by her mother, Ms. M., because she was not functioning optimally in school and was clearly depressed. She also seemed to have regressive symptoms at times and often wanted to "lie around" sucking her thumb.

Jennifer's father had died when she was 6 years old and, due to his illness, her mother had been overwhelmed, preoccupied, and depressed, and ultimately felt intolerable guilt about her unavailability to her children. In consequence, she felt pity for her daughter and also felt inadequate, herself, to many of the more demanding tasks of parenting. She often projected her sense of defeat onto Jennifer, and felt that many ordinary tasks were too great and too difficult for Jennifer.

The causes of Jennifer's academic difficulties were somewhat unclear; there was a question about whether they were largely a result of depression and infantilization, or of actual learning problems. When reading problems persisted, Jennifer continued in therapy but was also referred for tutoring. However, the tutor was far from home, and Ms. M.'s heavy work schedule was so exhausting that Jennifer was often late for therapy and tutoring sessions. What ensued is an example of some of the unfortunate pitfalls of the traditional child treatment paradigm.

Ms. M., left alone with three children and with pressing work demands, often had difficulty in negotiating her busy schedule. On several occasions she was unduly late in collecting Jennifer from the tutor's office. Despite the parent's apologies, the tutor was irritated by this imposition on her time, and maintained the belief that Ms. M. was an irresponsible and neglectful parent. The therapist also felt, at times, concerned about Ms. M.'s own feelings of inadequacy and her difficulties in providing sufficient structure for her children. What is salient here is the fact that the availability, reliability, and stability of the therapist can often be counterproductive to the treatment and psychic growth of the child. In this case it frequently served to re-inforce Jennifer's internal experience that her mother could not al-ways adequately care for her emotional needs in ways that the thera-pist, in fact, could. The therapist's office became a safe and comfortable place for Jennifer, but her attachment to and identification with her mother remained the primary force and influence on her internal life.

On some level, Jennifer identified with her mother's own sense of inadequacy, and, as she lived out her mother's projected failures, she unconsciously knew that academic drive and mastery could disunite mother and daughter. On mother's part, Jennifer's failure, depression, and infantile neediness allowed her to alleviate her guilt over past failures by providing her with the opportunity to offer the nurturant care and soothing that was perhaps more appropriate for a younger child. In this way Jennifer's immaturity and depression were maintained, partly because she craved closeness with her mother, and partly because the mother's collateral visits with the therapist were not sufficiently ameliorative in a situation where self and object representations were created and maintained in the relational environ-ment that constituted the majority of the child's experience.

In this case the therapist's competence served as an unfortunate counterpoint to Jennifer's life experience. Were we to view this treatment situation from a parent therapy paradigm, we would see the therapist and the parent as collaborators, in a matrix where the parent is considered an expert on the child, and the therapist as an expert on child development in general. Ms. M. was a sensitive and intelligent parent and primarily needed assistance in developing a sense of competence and overcoming her guilt. That she "gave over" the care of her child to an expert "parent" pushed her further into self-doubt and feelings of helplessness. Her difficulty in seeing herself as a strong and inspiring parent was, precisely, the thing that contributed to the emotional problems of her daughter for which she sought help. But this difficulty could not be sufficiently dissipated through traditional once-a-week treatment of the child.

The therapeutic intervention here would appear to be at least benign, and both mother and daughter perceived the psychotherapist as a benevolent figure. Yet, significant problems arose, iatrogenically, through this traditional model. The benevolent but powerful and authoritative professional is counterposed to an inadequate parent as well as an inadequate child. Thus, despite the benefits of individual and family treatment models, it may be useful to consider alternative approaches that may be more ameliorative and less problematic for some families. To evaluate the merits of particular therapeutic approaches, it may be useful to consider the current thinking about child development.

3

Current Research

*R*esearch in infant development over the past several decades has emphasized the centrality of relational influences on character and cognition. A relational theory of development suggests that self-regulation develops through the internalization of mutual interactions; thus, it is the emotional attunement of caregivers and the interactive experiences between parent and child that become the prototypes for attachment experience in general, and for interactions in the world. Current trends in neuroscience also emphasize the impact of relational experience on the developing brain of the infant and young child. With clinically depressed mothers, for example, the misattunement between mother and infant may lead to a negative affective core; there is greater agitation on the part of the baby, fewer vocalizations, and greater gaze aversion (Field 1988, 1995; Sameroff and Emde 1989, Weinberg and Tronick 1997). These manifest reactions potentially can lead to both behavioral and learning difficulties that ultimately bring children into the therapeutic milieu. The failure to achieve a secure attachment and a stable representation of a positive object is reflected in such behavioral difficulties as the tendency to enter into aggressive relationships, difficulties in regulating emotions, failures in the capacity for empathy, the tendency to shift from dependent to oppositional behavior, and separation difficulties. Winnicott (1965) suggests that the capacity for constant relationships depends, developmentally, on the existence of a good object in the psychic reality of the child. Interpersonal relatedness is based on the child's experience of being alone in the presence of the mother, and eventually this supportive environment is internalized so that the mother's presence is no longer needed to maintain relatedness. Winnicott is referring here to the child's capacity to evoke good internal objects, and this ability is facilitated by a reliable, benign, peopled environment in childhood. The failure of this benign cycle leads to childhood problems that are often manifested in separation anxieties.

Many theorists in the field of infant research have made significant contributions to clinical work with adults as well as with infants and children. Tronick's work (1989, Cohn and Tronick 1983, 1984, 1987,1989, Weinberg and Tronick 1997) with infants and their regulation of interpersonal exchanges, and the disruption and repair in parent–infant relationships, and Field's (1977, 1987, 1995) work on depressed mother–infant dyads have fostered a shift in clinical thinking about environmental influence on the infant's psychology to an earlier period of development. Significant researchers such as Beebe and Lachmann (1988, 1998), (Beebe et al. 1992), and others have also turned our attention to the clinical implications of intervening in the relational environment of the child. Many theorists have helped to pave the way for relational theory to influence clinical practice through an emphasis on mutuality and intersubjectivity (Mitchell, 1998, 1999, 2000, Mitchell and Greenberg 1990).

One researcher's work in exploring the internal world of infants has great implication for clinical intervention with parents through the relational patterns that develop in families. Daniel Stern (Stern et al, 1985) focuses on the sense of being with an other as a core experience for the infant. He supports the theoretical work of Winnicott and agrees that the absence of a loved other does not imply psychic absence; rather, even in her absence, the mother is experienced as a "living, palpable presence" (p. 100). Stern thus sees the developing infant as deeply embedded in an interactional matrix, and he furthermore sees attachment as a mutually created experience. We learn from his work that being with an other, is an act of active integration rather than of passive differentiation of self and other. What is most salient, however, is the idea that primary objects play an essential role in developing basic security. The security promoted through cuddling, molding, and gazing into another's eyes, according to Stern, cannot exist as part of a self experience without the experience of an other. In this schema the caregiver also regulates the child's attention, curiosity, degree of engagement, and capacity for exploration. Stern emphasizes that the experience of a core regulatory other is not simply a cognitive association; nor is it a memory, like the recollection of a thought or an event. Rather, it is part of a "common unit of subjective experience that includes the self and the other" (p. 110), and preserves the specificity of their relationship.

According to Stern, when an infant has a certain feeling, that feeling will call to mind a deeply embedded experience of the self with a regulatory other. He refers to this internalized interaction as a representation of an interaction that is *generalized* (RIG). The RIG, established through meaningful interactions with the mother (parent), becomes part of the child's subjectivity and subjective experience of others. When the RIG is activated it will bring into consciousness, and therefore reactivate, the original interaction that created the feeling. We can see from this paradigm that what is evoked for the child in these interactions are components of the original relationship with a primary other. It is the internal representation of a loved caregiver or attachment figure that thus forms the most powerful influence in the behavioral life of the child and, more importantly, is not easily abolished. Stern further suggests that the more past experience there is, the less potential for change any single event in the child's life will have. In other words, the most potent internalized representations of self and other are created by primary attachment figures and are relatively resistant to change. In addition, when a child's primary relational world is peopled by those same attachment figures, representations of self-other interactions clearly remain active and meaningful in that child's emotional life. This is the paradigm that best captures a relational theory of development.

With this in mind we can see that a therapeutic relationship that recognizes the potency of the parent-child interaction and sees that interaction as the locus of treatment is not simply better equipped to modify internal and external events for the child, but is more consistent with the theoretical underpinnings of object relations. As researchers like Carol Gilligan (1982) have taught us, the paradigms with which we organize our thinking, and from which we create working models, should represent a successful coalescence of ideas. If, for example, one predicate of relationally informed psychotherapy is that we are able, through transference interpretations, to expand and reorganize our patient's representations of self and other, how do we translate this to child therapy? For the child's relational world is, in some ways, more complex. In the transference relationship the adult patient can experience the therapist as both an old and a new object. For the child, however, this is no easy matter, owing in part to the fact that the child lives, daily, with the old object. In other words, the old object is still new, and the representations of self and other are continuing to become integrated as the child develops.

Family systems theory has made notable contributions to therapeutic work with children by placing adequate emphasis on the interpersonal origins of children's manifest behavior. However, relational theory is concerned with the interplay between the intrapsychic and interpersonal worlds of the child. Thus, one advantage of the parent therapy model is that it overcomes the conceptual problem that is inherent in the child therapist's attempt to make structural changes in a child who is seen for 45 minutes a week and who returns to an environment in which primary attachments and interactions remain determining developmental influences. The position here is that, instead of becoming a conduit through which the child can reorganize the internal representations of interpersonal life, it is more fruitful for the therapist to provide enabling support and guidance to the parents so that they can develop the capacity to provide more ameliorative care for their children.

II
A Comparative View

4

The Classical Model

$\mathcal{W}$e now explore some of the distinguishing features of the parent therapy model in relation to other models of therapy for children. This chapter looks at a classical approach to individual, analytically oriented child therapy and a family systems approach, delineates how this new paradigm differs in basic conception and in clinical method, and considers aspects of contemporary relationally oriented child treatment to demonstrate how parent-focused treatment is a natural outgrowth of relational theory.

Two factors significantly differentiate the classical approach. The first is theoretical: for the most part, classical conceptions of development maintain the idea that there are universal, biologically driven developmental occurrences in human experience, resulting in a view of character that is heavily weighted on predetermined intrapsychic and instinctual forces. Pathological developments are more generally attributed to the unfolding of oral, anal, and oedipal conflicts and the fixations that develop around them. Thus, symptomatology is understood as having its roots in the physiology and instinctual life of the individual. The second factor involves clinical technique. The aim of treatment—symptom relief—is perceived as being accomplished through the careful deconstruction of the conflicts and fixations that have emerged in specific psychosexual phases. Symptomatology is seen as phase-specific rather than relationally based. There seems to have emerged, in this model, a fairly myopic perspective on child development that has restricted its view to the child's interior experience almost entirely without reference to actual life events. Context (in the form of familial and other interpersonal relationships), temperament (of both child and primary objects), and cognitive and physical endowments tend to be neglected as significant factors in the child's experience.

Let us consider several clinical examples from one of the major works on analytical child therapy (Pick and Segal 1992). In one case, a child analyst discusses the penis envy and oedipal competition of an 8-year-old boy, in three-time-a-week analysis, entirely without reference to the child's actual relationship with his father. It is assumed, by the analyst, that the child's drawing of a whale with big teeth and big tail represents his rageful and aggressive feelings toward the more powerful phallic force represented by the father, and that bringing this into the boy's consciousness will be generally ameliorative for his emotional life. This child, it is reported, was temporarily taken away from his mother at birth because of his early medical difficulties. Although the child's separation anxiety and abandonment feelings are seen by his therapist as significant factors in the treatment, there is at least an equal emphasis placed on oral, anal, and oedipal conflicts. In this regard the tone and content of the analysis differs markedly from interpersonally oriented and family therapies and relationally informed child therapy, all of which are more concerned with the actual relationship between parent and child, regardless of whether interpretation is seen as central to the treatment process.

We are told that this child, the creator of the whale, experienced particular and prolonged expressions of dependency and separation anxiety, and kept his bottle until the age of 7. In the analytic treatment he has a strong reaction to the anticipation of his therapist's vacation. It is during this phase in the treatment that the drawing of the whale becomes pertinent and is interpreted as a reflection of the child's erupting anger, devouring greed, and the "projection of anal feelings into the father's penis" (p. 438). Another drawing of whales, sharks, "a blood forest, a volcano, and a plethora of poisonous objects" is interpreted as "representing dangerous fecal and urinary excrement" (p. 438). The child's sense of object loss is thus linked to his fantasied attacks on the loved object. In addition, there is some reference to the boy's oedipal fantasies about the therapist, whom he thinks will be "sleeping with a man and going to a restaurant" (p. 437). In this therapeutic case we might wonder how we could best make use of such interpretations and how they could be transformed into something usable for a child in anxious distress. We might see the child's drawings, for example, as a grandiose defense against the feelings of vulnerability that are reactivated by the therapist's impending vacation. There are a range of views about how to seize the opportunity to help the child resolve some of his profound fears and concerns. In our own estimation, however, the parents themselves are potentially and optimally in the best position to help this child resolve such conflicts. The transferential issues with the analyst notwithstanding, we might consider the idea that the upcoming hiatus in the treatment also represents a rupture in an ongoing relationship. That is, the very sense of connectedness, the instability or insecurity that pervaded his early attachment experience, and his resulting vulnerability and distrust in the face of object loss would all be primary concerns in a parent-focused intervention. Rather than interpret the child's oedipal competition and the anal expulsive reactions, the parent therapist would intervene in ways that could potentially enhance the child's relationship with primary objects and mitigate his painful experience of object loss without injuring or further injuring his primary relationships.

The therapeutic method that follows from more classical child treatment emphasizes the interpretation of infantile and transference neuroses. There is some concession made to the idea that a true transference neurosis does not develop, or develop fully, in the child, precisely because the primary objects continue to play such essential roles in the child's life. Nonetheless, the aim, which derives primarily from the analysis of adult patients, is to bring unconscious psychic material into conscious awareness, and psychoanalytic technique implies the interpretation of the pathological ways in which the individual wards off instinctual impulses. This defense analysis takes place in the context of abstinence and optimal degrees of frustration. For child analysis there are minor modifications of the adult analytic method based on the idea that sustained free association is more difficult for the latency-age child to achieve, so that the analyst's task is to use the child's affects as a substitute for verbal free association. This is encouraged by establishing a particular frame in which affective expression can occur in what is thought to be its most unadulterated form, free of intrusion from others. In this classical model the concept of neutrality is synonymous with the abstinent position, that is, the nongratifying position of the therapist. Whatever effect this position has on the development of a particular type of transference in the treatment of adult patients, who presumably have the ability to consent to this methodology, children may find it quite disconcerting.

Furthermore, many classically oriented analysts and therapists maintain that parents should be avoided and seen only in the event that their exclusion will cause them to sabotage the treatment (1992). It is interesting to note, in this context, that early in the history of child psychoanalytic therapy, the treatments were conducted in the child's home. This situation was later rejected on the grounds that a proper transference could not be established unless the analyst was something significantly distinct from ordinary life (Pick & Segal, 1992). Thus, the special and private relationship was quite purposefully cultivated, and the parent was deliberately excluded from the treatment situation. In fact, in classical analytic work the parent is encouraged to refrain from particular behaviors with their children during the course of treatment, especially gratifying ones, with the express purpose of having the child act out fantasies in the therapeutic encounter. Moreover, advice to parents, which might otherwise be helpful, is kept at a minimum and is considered necessary only to ensure that the analysis can proceed without undue parental interference. In this way the analysis itself becomes more crucial and pivotal than the relational life it is presumably designed to enhance.

A very dramatic example of this is elaborated by Paul Kay (1992) in his paper, "Gifts, Gratification, and Frustration in Child Analysis." Kay is especially cautious about things that may appear gratifying or pleasing to the child. In some respects his paper is designed to clarify how child analysts have recognized in recent years that children are able to tolerate greater deprivation than had previously been thought. Certain forms of frustration are delineated as specific tools that enhance the analytic process.

In a curious paradox, Kay refers to the treatment experience as one of the ways to enhance the child's relationship with a parent. The attention derived from the parent's accompaniment to the sessions, the child's feeling of being considered important for the first time, or the child's receiving candy or toys on the trip to the therapist's office is considered a fortuitous by-product of the child's analysis. It seems remarkable that the primary relationship with the parent takes a secondary role, and parental attention is diminished in relation to the analytic relationship. In this way, classically oriented child therapy has been divested of its original intention of assisting the child in life, and the therapeutic encounter has been reified and exaggerated in importance so that it supersedes the child's actual experience. We believe that it is not only more parsimonious but also more reasonable to directly enhance the parent-child relationship rather than make it a by-product of the analytic encounter. What also seems relevant here is the fact that earlier incarnations of child analysis were of relatively brief duration and were therefore far less disruptive to the child's everyday life. Contemporary analysts plan for longer treatments than they did in Freud's day. Freud met with little Hans' father only a handful of times. The joke that not making life decisions when in analysis made sense at one time because historically analyses lasted six months and marriages lasted a lifetime, but today marriages last for six months and analysis lasts a lifetime is certainly fitting here. One analyst recounts approaching the parents of a child patient in an attempt to discuss the intense marital fighting that had become deeply troubling to his patient. After managing to defuse the parents' fighting, he remarks, "This not only had a beneficial effect on the parents, it also helped [Jimmy's] analysis" (Glenn, et al. 1992, p. 419). We see here, once again, the overvaluation of the treatment experience in which life events are seen to be in the service of the analysis rather than vice versa.

In his discussion regarding the giving of gifts in the therapeutic encounter, Kay (1992) explores a case that focuses on a child's wish to give the analyst a gift:

> The patient, Bobby, was reared by an indulgent mother during his early childhood. After several years and following the birth of a second son, his mother became intermittently withdrawing and withholding because of personal preoccupations and because of concerns that she might have been spoiling Bobby. It was at this point that Bobby's temper tantrums and defiant behavior began. Kay refers to this experience as a "psychological loss of his gratifying mother" (p. 324), a loss that was followed by her actual loss when she died when Bobby

was only 8 years old. In contrast to his generous and affectionate mother, Bobby's father is described as conscientious but anxious and grim. In the analysis Bobby is described as a "fun addict," moving about ceaselessly and seeking continual supplies of food, toys, and free time. The analyst emphasizes his point about not gratifying the child and purposefully frustrating him, to which the child reacts with anger or defensive fantasies and jokes.

Eventually Bobby talks about the loss of his mother; he reveals to the therapist that he has kept quite a few of her possessions, and the therapist, we think wisely, understands that this is Bobby's way of keeping her alive. The therapist states that "giving himself good feelings through . . . gratification also seemed important in helping him bear the pain of her absence" (p. 325). The therapist, on the other hand, is equated with the more withholding and sober father who refused to play with Bobby. As Bobby is about to leave therapy for summer vacation, he brings the therapist the gift of a pipe. Bobby states about this going-away and "Father's Day" present that he had first thought of getting the therapist a fish for his fish tank but had "decided that 'a pipe doesn't die'" (p. 326).

The therapist perceives this as Bobby's way of asking the therapist to take him inside of him so that he would not feel that they were separated and, of course, it is a painful and poignant comment on the child's profound experience of actual loss. However, the technical position here is that the therapist cannot and should not accept the gift and smoke the pipe. The rationale for this lies in the therapist's interpretation of the gift as a transference resistance, designed to "protect [Bobby] from facing the loss of his mother in the transference" (p. 329). The idea that the boy's neediness and desire for the therapist's love is merely transferential seems to beg the question of the child's actual need and the therapist's personal resistance to this need. In this way the neediness is, to some degree, iatrogenically created by this therapist's unwillingness to engage in any provision—to "hold" the child and to soothe his painful sense of loss in any way other than through interpretation and his own abstinence.

For many relationally oriented therapists, and particularly for parent-focused therapists, abstinence and frustration are not the technical tools that are seen as the most effective. Rather, the provision of a holding environment and a containing presence and, above all, the recognition of the child's subjective experience are the tools that are conceived as most effective in the amelioration of symptoms. However, the reinforcement of these qualities in the parent-child relationship can, we believe, ultimately be the most transformative. The relational therapist would be more likely to focus on the attachment issues: Bobby's profound fears of loss and abandonment, which have presumably been transferred from his mother to the therapist. Freud tells us that the ego gains mastery of the traumatic situation of being overwhelmed through active anticipation and preparedness. Like the child who throws a toy down in order to have it retrieved or plays peekaboo to master the anxiety of disappearance, Bobby's desire to leave something with the therapist served many psychically comforting functions. For the relational therapist, the pipe not only would have allowed Bobby to make reparations to his lost mother, but also would have served the purpose of satisfying his wish to remain in the psychic reality of the loved mother/therapist. It could be understood as mitigating the original loss, as in the transitional arena, when the child holds on to the mother through a cherished symbolic object. The gift here could represent Bobby's wish not only to hold onto the relationship with the therapist, but to make certain that the therapist would hold onto him.

The parent-focused therapist would go even further in considering Bobby's father's inability to provide the warmth, nurturance, and exuberance that Bobby's mother once did, and would be likely to approach the situation with a different goal in mind. In the parent therapy model the goal might be to encourage the father to provide the warmth and nurturance that this boy so obviously craves, in order to alleviate some of the child's symptoms. Of course, this would entail the exploration and resolution of the father's emotional distance. Whether his distance resulted from a lack of information about his child's capacities and needs, or a complicated combination of his own mourning and his early history, the work would address the impact of these on his relationship with his son. In parent therapy it is precisely this exploration that is seen as the primary aim of the therapeutic work.

Another case in which theoretical commitments held sway over an exploration of the interpersonal life of the child is presented by Bernstein and Sax (1992).

Dolores, a 9-year-old girl, is a beautiful child whose mother was anxious about her from birth, especially about her eating habits and her aversion to certain foods. Despite the fact that there was no evidence of malnutrition and she was reported to be in excellent health, her parents sometimes attempted to force certain foods on her. Her mother also feared that Dolores would be shunned by other children and would be generally dysfunctional. Yet Dolores was reported to be generally well adjusted. At age 4 she became more demanding, was quite interested in nudity, her father's in particular, and began to ignore her mother and idealize her father. At this time, conflicts around food escalated and the mother sought psychiatric advice. Therapy was recommended for the child, although the parents did not pursue it at that time. Curiously, three years later, the mother, in another consultation for therapy for Dolores, reveals that she herself has entered analysis and in consequence had "loosened my hold" on her daughter. In the discussion of this case the child therapist focuses on Dolores's latency issues, stating that during this period drive pressures are diminished in order to allow for greater ego development and mastery. Dolores is described as asymptomatic except for a slightly limited diet, which has, however, been greatly expanded from previous years. The child's notable derogation of her mother is interpreted by the therapist as defensive, while the mother's own anxieties are not given central importance in the relational scheme or in Dolores's character development. Rather, conflicts around phallic wishes, orality, and castration anxiety are emphasized. Dolores's need to have her mother assist her on a daily basis with her homework is interpreted as a symbolic rejection of feeding from her mother, with a displacement to the symbolic academic feeding.

Despite the fact that Dolores is reported, through diagnostic assessment, to have ego functions that are intact and adaptive, psychotherapy is definitely recommended for this child. The brief reference to Dolores's anger at her mother's intrusiveness is given less weight in comparison to other more instinct driven interpretations. For example, her participation in activities such as theater and ballet are highlighted as "neutralized gratification of phallic wishes" (p. 81). Bernstein and Sax, in their analysis of this case, are primarily interested in the girl's food refusal as an expression of a negative oedipal wish expressed through oral aversions.

In marked contrast to this approach, the parent therapist would be most interested in the parent-child relationship, which seems fraught with problems, and with the girl's relatively successful attempts to resolve her apparent conflicts over attachment and autonomy. Although it would be understood that the child has her own reactive and subjective experience, the emphasis would most likely shift to the impact of her mother's anxiety, and her resulting intrusions on her daughter's body integrity. It seems that the mother had a profound concern about her ability to satiate the child's needs in general, and her nutritional needs in particular. This persistent anxiety apparently caused overvigilance about food intake; in other words, the anxiety about nourishment served as a symbolic representation of the emotional insecurity with regard to her nurturing capacity as a parent. The child, in turn, may have attempted symbolically to ward off her mother's invasions, and responded to the mother's projective identification by withdrawing from and rejecting her, particularly through the symbolically charged process of food intake. The treatment objectives for the parent therapist would therefore be quite different, and would focus directly on the mother's conflicts around her maternal capacities. By bolstering the mother's sense of her own sufficiency and nurturant care, we might very likely decrease the child's anxiety about "taking in" supplies from the outside.

We must question the value of placing this child in treatment, thereby creating conditions for the mother that might only serve to exacerbate her sense of inadequacy. Presumably, many of the problems between this parent and child will be resolved through the mother's own treatment. In addition, however, we might wonder about the deeper implications, for

Dolores, of being placed into treatment prior to which she had been a relatively well-adjusted child. Reviewing this case left us wondering whether psychoanalysis would be recommended for every child whose parents sought consultation since every child does indeed have intrapsychic dynamics that could be explored.

In a 1950 paper in *The Psychoanalytic Study of the Child*, Hedy Schwarz discussed the advantages of working with the parent in the child's therapy sessions: "The intimate relationship between mother and young child makes advisory work with mothers of prelatency age children so successful and preferable to the treatment situation which interferes so radically with the bond between mother and child"(p. 344). Although she does not make the leap into thinking about working entirely with the parent, Schwarz does favor transferring her analytic knowledge to the mother so that the mother herself can effect changes in her parenting and thus transform some of the significant aspects of the child's world. Schwarz further commented, "It is one of the great advantages of mother and child being together in the treatment that in the child's mind there is no clash of loyalty towards analyst and mother and that the child patient does not . . . need to feel guilty for trusting the analyst or confiding his secrets to her. Neither can the child have the impression that there are two sets of standards, one which the mother approves, one which the analyst approves" (p. 346). We find here an immensely persuasive argument in the early literature, and one that considers the ambivalence that is created for the child by the treatment process. The point appears to have been lost or obscured by the predominant view, which loses sight of this potential conflict for the child, and through which the analytic encounter and the transference experience supersede the child's primary relationships and actual experience.

Other psychoanalytic child therapists have attempted to bridge the gap by incorporating the child's relationships into an understanding of the development of symptoms. For example, Doris Gilpin (1994) recounts her therapeutic relationship with an oppositional child. At the outset, she suggests that the oppositional child is often one who has been bossed around by an authoritarian or insensitive parent and anticipates the same treatment from the therapist. The defensive reaction of the child is thus one of resistance and defiance. The author describes the initial establishment of a therapeutic alliance through the careful attention to the child's subjective experience and through a deliberate support of the child's own choices and decisions in his play activities. While the symptom itself is understood in terms of its interpersonal context, there seems to be virtually no attention paid to altering the relationship with the parents. In consequence, we believe that some vitally important aspects of the child's experience tend to be overlooked.

Let us explore this particular case:

The boy, who was first seen at the age of 6, was expelled from three different schools for being uncontrollable. He engaged in the therapy, initially through drawings, and it is through this process that the therapist invites him to exercise his own decisions and choices. The goal appears to be to alleviate this boy's experience of having to submit to another person's control. Gilpin informs us that later in the treatment the patient draws a picture of his mother but does not allow the therapist to see it. The therapist interprets this as the boy's wish to keep separate his feelings for his mother and his feelings for the therapist. When he eventually displays the mother's drawing, it is a flower with the words "I love you." The therapist then talks about the nice feelings the boy has for his mother, at which point he makes another drawing of a ferocious dinosaur. The interpretation then is that the ferocity is a reaction to his tender feelings for his mother. Gilpin remarks that when the boy doesn't let the therapist know things and doesn't let her have things, it makes him feel big and strong. We are also told that the boy's father has been unfaithful, that his mother is enraged, and that the father has developed ulcers.

Let us pause here for a moment. All of these interpretations seem apt; we too might understand that the opposition and defiant stance served the defensive function of masking the child's fear and vulnerability, perhaps organized through a primary identification with a passive and distant father and an angry and domineering mother. We are told that the father has been unfaithful and that the mother is enraged. There is significant quarreling and loss of control in the family. We might think, on the other hand, that intervention at another level would be more efficacious. If, for example, this family were to develop more harmonious interactions, the boy might feel less anxious about the hated, rejected, and sick father, and less fearful and angry at an angry mother. In the more traditional Kleinian-informed approach presented by Gilpin, the therapist engages the child in interpretive exploration of his feelings about significant others, about "how they handled, mess, and rage, and self-control" (p. 92). According to this model, the move toward resolution had to take place in the therapeutic relationship. Here, the working-through is done in the transference through which the patient is presumably helped to face his own feelings about his enraged mother and his impotent father. When this sort of transferential work is done with adults, there is an analysis of the residual implications of internalized old objects and the ways in which these contribute to current self representations. Yet the child continues to develop, in daily life, in the context of his object world—a world that is in the process of being formulated and reformulated. It does not then make sense to apply the technique of residual transferential analysis to current relationships, when those relationships are still active and available.

Gilpin goes on to discuss the middle stage of treatment and her focus on the boy's masculine identity. She states that as he talked about his father he began to make "long pointed structures" out of clay. She talks about his desire to feel tall and important, that boys like to feel tall powerful and important , and that "one thing that made them feel that way was the penis" (p. 92). Throughout the discussion of this case, the implication is that the child is able, through his transferential encounters, to proceed to a more confident masculine identity and to a recognition that establishing a masculine identity does not have to imply danger and rejection. The therapist tells the boy that he can have a long, pointed, and proud thing (the penis and masculine identity) without being rejected and abandoned. The critical point here is that this model links the boy's problems, in part, to his unstable and insecure phallic identity. This is somewhat of a shift from a completely intrapsychic focus; the boy's issues are understood to be rooted, in part, in family dynamics. The therapist tries to help him resolve his conflicts around the drive for masculine power and the fear of domination. However, we must ask what happens to a boy who is accepted by the therapist and allowed to make independent choices in the treatment room, but continues to have conflicts with his angry mother and continues to experience daily life with a weak and rejected father. We are told that in the play therapy the patient acts out the feeling that the therapist is not helping with the real things that are occurring in his life. Although the therapist accurately identifies the child's anger, his life situation remains unchanged, and he remains "vaguely unhappy." The therapist seems to miss the point of the child's commentary on this unfortunate situation, when the boy refers to her as a "vampire trying to suck words out of me" (p. 93).

During the termination phase of the treatment, the boy talks about his wishes to go home with the therapist; he is struggling with his distress about the termination, and rather curiously the therapist talks to him about anal conflicts and the rewards of self-control. She tells him that one part of him wants to "make a mess with your shit instead of putting it in the toilet and the more grown up part is in charge of your shit and is in control" (p. 94). A critical point here is that many of this child's symptoms were linked to anal fixations. Although the ultimate goal was to liberate the child from symptoms, the symptoms became highly decontextualized in order to fit a preconstrued theoretically driven idea. The decontextualization further distances the patient from many important concerns and relationships. It fails to address, as the child himself identifies for the therapist, some of the real difficulties in his object world and his real though problematic attempts to mask his insecurity and vulnerability by internalizing aggressive aspects of the maternal object.

This case suggests some of the ways in which child psychotherapy has become divorced from its original goals of alleviating the symptoms of children. There are many instances cited in the psychotherapy literature that allude to the fact that children do not feel assisted with the real problems they confront. We are reminded here of some of Freud's more unfortunate cases such as his work with Dora, in which the real occurrences in her life were overlooked in favor of presumed internal conflicts. One case cited in the classical child analytic literature (Scharfman 1992) is that of a 5-year-old girl who developed extreme fears of leaving or being left by her parents. Analysis is recommended, and in the first several months of the treatment the child prevails upon the therapist to help her by telling her parents to limit their social life. When the analyst tells her that he is unable to do that, she becomes quite distressed and further confesses that she is afraid that some harm will come to the parents as she frequently hears them fighting in their bedroom at night.

As the analysis proceeds, the child also talks about her jealousy of her younger brother, her conviction that her parents, especially her father, prefer boys, and that little girls are "no good because they have nothing up there or down there." In addition she states that if the therapist "liked me he would give me a baby and then I would be a grown-up woman" (p. 292). The therapist interprets all of the girl's oedipal wishes, which he states began first in the transference, and focuses much of his discussion on the child's unconscious fantasies of oral impregnation, her wishes to seduce the father, and her penis envy and sense of inferiority. The treatment primarily centers around the idea that the therapist is used "as an object of displacement (. . . curiosity about the parents' sexual activities), as a transference object (wishes to have daddy's baby), as well as a new object (therapist and helper)" (p. 294).

There is much to be said about this case; however, what remains prominent is the fact that penis envy and oedipal conflicts form a central focus of the treatment. What seems to be obscured in this theory-driven work is the actual marital discord that apparently contributed to the child's original anxiety and wish to keep her parents in her presence. Thus, despite the real-life concerns that the child offers to explain the development of her symptom, the analyst has a predetermined agenda and interprets the data with this already in mind. Methodologically, the work begins with psychosexual conflicts in place, and the therapeutic process, which seems exclusively interpretive, follows from there. When the girl is curious about where the analyst lives and with whom, for example, the therapist interprets the inquiry as a displacement of her curiosity about her parents' sex life. We see here the overvaluation and reification of theory and the classical idea that development is rooted in psychosexual stages and fixations. In this scheme the obvious is often missed and the child's perhaps simple interest in her therapist as a person is entirely lost.

5
Family Systems Therapy

$\mathcal{T}$o some degree, the family therapy movement developed in reaction to the overvaluation of the treatment process and the obfuscation of the treatment *purpose*. The move toward the interpersonal world of the child emerged in various ways, depending on the particular school, with varying degrees of emphasis on the structural issues within the family, the communication styles, and the strategic shifts in familial alignments, as well as the transgenerational transmission of conflict or trauma. All of these trends appear to have arrived from a similar goal, and implicitly, a common critique of the emphasis on drive theory and on the intrapsychic life of the child.

In general, family therapists focus on modifying the relationship system in a family. In this paradigm there is a tendency to avoid focusing on intrapsychic forces and rather to maintain the idea that by altering the roles played in the interpersonal system, the entire system will be altered, thereby changing each participant's experience. Therefore, the goals and the therapeutic process differ from individual models in that the family as a whole, as a system and a structure, is the target of intervention. Family therapists have shifted treatment from the individual to the processes between people, and tend to define psychopathology exclusively as problems in relationships (Haley, 1971). Relationships are no longer seen as a product or projection of intrapsychic life; rather, intrapsychic process is viewed as a product of the interpersonal situation. The focus of intervention lies in changing the roles that the family has assigned to each member, and therefore is largely an interactional focus. This focus, we believe, errs in the opposite direction from the classical model and, in consequence, directs too little attention to the internal, subjectively felt experience of the individual.

The systems concept of triangulation in which two powerful people, the parents, reduce their own anxiety or conflict by focusing on a defect in their child obscures the part played by internally generated, temperamentally driven aspects of each individual child. The family therapist in effect asks the parent to "assume the working premise that the problem is in the parents and not the child" (Bowen 1978, p. 435). Bowen states that the child is never seen as the patient since "in the act of seeing the child, there is some automatic confirmation that the child is 'sick'" (p. 435). We would concur that it is not useful to pathologize the child; however the pathologizing of the parent seems equally problematic.

The centrality of the social, interpersonal field was established with family therapy. The emphasis for most family therapists lies in the reorganization of some aspect of the basic family structure. Bowen, with his background in psychoanalysis, focuses on several ideas that are somewhat closer to psychoanalytic language; he hypothesizes that what is pathogenic in the individual is a lack of self differentiation vis-à-vis the "undifferentiated family ego mass." Many others, including Minuchin (1974), also see pathogenic families as unable to establish appropriate boundaries and alliances. However, in this systems model, the individual is not seen as subjectively motivated or temperamentally motivated; rather, the individual is lost in a set of systemic contingencies and is largely a conduit for the disavowed needs and conflicts of the collective family ego. To some degree, the therapeutic technique that follows from this paradigm also loses sight of the individual; with the primary goal being to destabilize the existing family structure, the affective life of particular individuals may become casualties in the therapeutic action.

Let us look at Minuchin's work with one family, in which the adolescent daughter is deteriorating emotionally and is at risk for psychiatric hospitalization. The family is treated by one of Minuchin's trainees while Minuchin observes from behind a one-way mirror, sometimes phoning in suggestions. At certain points he enters the consultation room with the family and their therapist. The following is a summary of part of the session:

The husband, Mr. Braun, complains that his wife is always screaming, that he cannot take it any longer. The wife, in tears, responds that the husband leaves everything to her. In the observation room Minuchin, after listening to this, says, "I'm going to attack the mother again." He enters the treatment room and says to the mother, "I am concerned about what you are saying. I am concerned that when you leave here today your daughter will go crazy again. And I think the reason she will do it is to save your marriage. Children sometimes act in very weird ways to save their parent's marriage." He then turns to the daughter and says, "Yvonne, I suggest that you go quite crazy today so that your parents can become concerned about you. Then things will be O.K. between them." Minuchin continues in this way, explaining to the parents that Yvonne will sacrifice herself in order to unite the parents. He ends by saying to Yvonne, "You are a good daughter, and if you see a danger, go crazy" (Sander 1979, p. 191). The explicit idea here is that bringing the family for treatment, rather than designating an identified patient, already creates the possibility of ameliorating what is an organismic or systemic process.

Minuchin's understanding of the child's symptom, like some of the psychoanalytic conceptualizations, may have a large measure of validity. However, we must question how the treatment intervention affects each of the family members, particularly the child herself. The idea that the problem is exclusively reactive neglects the importance of individual, internal experience, and, indeed, this is not the target of intervention. But what happens, in this case, to the girl's object world? She is placed in a position of enormous power in her family: they are seen together for treatment because of her. Minuchin grants her this or reinforces it in numerous ways. Our concern is not only with this issue, and whether or not it fuels a malignant grandiosity. We are concerned with the parents' experience of themselves as parental authorities. They are in the presence of their child (or perhaps children) who is defined as commandeering the family stage, alongside a therapist who is more of an authority about their family dynamics and their own children than they are. This scene is then interrupted when the *real* authority arrives in order to better intervene with their child. In this way both the parents and their therapist are reduced in status and superseded by Minuchin's authority and superior insight. The point here is that it does not much matter whether his interpretation is correct—its implementation may nonetheless be damaging.

Another implication of this work, with its exclusive focus on the interpersonal field, is that, paradoxically, the child's own proclivities are not sufficiently factored into the interpersonal matrix. The parents' problematic marriage is perceived as influencing the girl's behavior, with unidirectional impact. There is no attention given to who the child is as an individual, why she is the one in the family to play this particular role, and what she herself contributes to the interpersonal dynamics. At what point, we might ask, is the child assumed to become an active participant in the interpersonal dynamics? Her own temperament and capacities are given short shrift aside from the behavior itself. Yet, even looking exclusively at the family system, we might want to consider that each child is born into a somewhat different family culture as family life changes with the parents' ages, with changes in professional or economic status, and with different sibling constellations. These changes are accompanied by changes in parental projections for each child, and these, too, shift with other changes. Parent therapy focuses more intensively on deconstructing these issues and the concomitant implications for child and parents, in a way that family therapy cannot. It furthermore focuses attention on the impact of the treatment process on all individuals.

Whitaker also attempts to disengage the family from the triangulations in which children are enlisted to maintain the homeostasis in an unstable marriage. In their book *The Family Crucible*, Napier and Whitaker (1978) describe their work in resolving problematic oedipal issues. They state: "Don [the son] was indeed the victim of a family process which created in him the fantasy that he was older, smarter, and stronger than he actually was. Without meaning to, his parents had trained him in a kind of subtle delusional thinking about himself, one that implied that he could beat his father in a contest of strength and that he could be his mother's substitute mate"(p. 179).

In the treatment situation Don's fantasy is punctured by a "therapeutic moment" in a spontaneous but "unconsciously" enacted wrestling match with Whitaker. In their therapeutic philosophy and method, Whitaker and Napier engage in the therapeutic encounter with a conscious assumption of the role of surrogate, "symbolic" parents. They purport to be a "professional marriage" and aim to present "maybe a superior model" of parenting (p. 91).

When Whitaker then asks the family to turn to the therapists for help rather than to each other, the father justifiably asks, "Where does that leave us when you guys aren't around?" (p. 121). This vignette illustrates, once again, the problem of "showing up" or outsmarting the parents, particularly in the presence of the child, and the father astutely points this out to Whitaker with his question. His challenge thinly masks the ineptness he feels, which has been highlighted by the therapist's masterful intervention. Now both father and son have been overpowered by the family therapist and are, ironically, inappropriately equal in status again.

Despite the enormous contributions that the family therapy movement has made in shifting clinical work away from a narrowly intrapsychic focus and turning its attention to the family system, there are, we believe, numerous problems embedded in this clinical model. The theoretical emphasis on systemic problems in the family may often obscure the internally motivated, subjective experience of the individual. In addition, the impact of the therapist on the family system can often serve to undermine parental authority and confidence, thereby creating reverberations throughout the system.

6
Relationally Informed Child Therapy

$\mathcal{R}$elationally informed child therapists predicate their work on yet a different set of assumptions about the nature of psychopathology, and therefore have different ideas about what constitutes the therapeutic action that will be most ameliorative. The issues that dominate relational child treatment are grounded in the interface between the child's intrapsychic and interpersonal worlds, and the ways in which each influences the other in the child's life. In some sense, then, we can conceptualize relational child therapy as emphasizing and even embodying the transitional space between the intrapsychic focus of the classically oriented child therapist and the interpersonal sphere that comprises much of family therapy.

Influenced by various theoretical perspectives, ranging from the American interpersonalists (e.g., Sullivan, Fromm, Wolstein), the British Middle School (e.g., Winnicott, Bowlby, Balint) to Freudians and neo-Freudians (e.g., Anna Freud, Sandler) and in conjunction with empirical work in the areas of infant and attachment research, relational clinicians have placed context in bold relief when locating what is central to their clinical work. Yet, with very few exceptions, these theoretical and empirical shifts have not resulted in a paradigm shift in the therapeutic process of child therapy. A notable exception may be found in the work of Pantone (2000) and his discussion of his own metamorphosis from child therapist to parent-focused therapist. In his paper, Pantone discusses how and why he has become more conservative in his recommendations to parents about placing children in therapy; he seems to have become aware that child psychotherapy is a treatment that, like all others, is not simply innocuous and may indeed have side effects.

Clinicians working with infants prove to be the notable exception; infant research, with its focus on the relationship between the infant and the primary caregivers, lends itself more obviously to dyadic work. This work, while it does have the dyadic relationship as a central focus, is not exactly dyadic from the perspective of the parent therapist. It is the presence of the therapist that, we believe, must be included in evaluating the treatment experience of the parent and child. The concern, then, relates to the implications of the paradigm itself on the relational life and interactions of all family members, particularly in the realm of unconscious experience.

A 1997 symposium on child analysis in *Psychoanalytic Dialogues* explored some of the issues and tensions embedded in the relational approaches to contemporary child treatment. In these clinical and theoretical discussions, prominent relational therapists addressed issues related to attachment theory, the uses and functions of play in the treatment setting, and the efficacy of child treatment. These discussions thoughtfully evoke the relational nature of the child's internal conflicts and elucidate the ways in which these issues are enacted on the psychotherapeutic stage. However, what we believe can be more fully explored are the ways in which the therapeutic setting itself influences the child's relational world.

At the symposium, Neil Altman (1997) described his work in once-a-week play therapy with Ronald, a 7-year-old suffering from numerous social, academic, and familial problems. Ronald had difficulty in managing affective arousal, and transitions, both affective and behavioral, were problematic for him. The case study specifically highlights oedipal issues in the treatment setting, and the continued usefulness of the oedipal construct in general. It is an extraordinary case, combining the many elements that bring the therapeutic work and the child himself alive for the reader. Altman's humor, compassion, ability to maintain treatment boundaries, and clinical flexibility promote an empathic and complex view of Ronald. This therapist allows himself to be "used" by the patient, in the Winnicottian sense, for multiple purposes. The two engage in their weekly drama fully and enthusiastically. Meanwhile, Altman keeps his eye on more than simply promoting and maintaining the relationship; he is primarily concerned with Ronald's progressive development of internal controls, particularly those in the service of managing his feelings of humiliation and vulnerability concerning his developmental delays.

Altman limits his discussion of his ancillary work with Ronald's parents to the following: "I believe that we faced similar tasks: to help Ronald contain his impulses and challenge him to risk using and stretching his capacities without crushing his grandiosity. Their job, of course, was far more difficult than mine, given that they had to do theirs under the stress and strain of real-life conditions from which there is no break after forty-five minutes" (p. 739). From our perspective, the tasks faced by the therapist and the parent are quite different, and it may not actually benefit the family to have so much perceived overlap in function. The difficulties encountered by the parents involve many domains that never affect the therapist, such as decisions about schooling and the concomitant negotiations with school personnel and other children and families. A more extensive exploration of such real-life conditions would have been useful in the discussion of this case, since we believe that they become significant aspects of the child's relational world. The ways in which Ronald's parents have to struggle with these issues on a daily basis will, to some degree, permeate the familial atmosphere, both consciously and unconsciously, and will, in turn, affect Ronald's self representations.

Altman's treatment of Ronald seems simultaneously containing and expansive. He explicitly characterizes the work as analogous to an aspect of parenting: "I tried to take a position with Ronald that corresponds to my conception of what an oedipal parent does. . . . I wanted to engage Ronald's competition with me in a way that would empower him without abdicating the power I had in my position as an adult in relation to a child" (p. 738). He goes on to depict the work in very much the way we might depict an optimal parent-child relationship: mutually engaged, yet containing, reflecting, and admiring. This is precisely the kind of interaction we might encourage in a parent-focused treatment. As the focus of Altman's discussion concentrated on the multiple functions of oedipal dynamics in Ronald's world, we might ask how the therapist could help the parents expand *their* appreciation of the oedipal themes that were relevant in Ronald's experience. In a very important sense, this would entail an expansion of the parents' insights into their son's struggles, his shame, and his difficulty in conveying his needs in socially appropriate ways. Altman is aware that 45 minutes per week is minimal in the life of this child, compared with the intense demands for the parents' involvement. This suggests, for us, that the 45 minutes perhaps might be better spent in engaging the *parents* in this kind of therapeutic process. In lieu of having the therapist take the position of the oedipal parent, the child might benefit from the expansion of the father's capacities as an oedipal father. Altman's keen observations of Ronald's behavior and his empathic guidance, in the sessions, of that behavior into psychically manageable interactions seem clearly to be skills he would be able to help the parents develop in greater abundance. The difficulties in raising a child who is so impulse-ridden is burdensome, and it is possible that the child-focused therapy might, in some respects, actually exacerbate the strain. For example, we might consider the idea that Ronald could use an idealization of the therapist as an implicit denigration of his father or feel that Altman's play skills highlighted his father's deficiencies, creating for him a painful ambivalence and guilt around this recognition.

Altman's presentation of the case stands in rather sharp contrast to some of the more rigidly organized adherents of oedipal theory reviewed earlier. His analysis of Ronald's conflicts never interfered with his relationship with the child; instead, he uses his understanding *in the service of* that relationship. We suggest, however, that he could go even further in expanding Ronald's relationships by using his analysis in the service of Ronald's relationship within his family.

Another discussion from a relational perspective highlights some of the most complex aspects of direct therapy with children. In his paper, "The Play's the Thing," Jay Frankel (1998) presents a discourse on play and its specific meaning in child therapy. This is a thoughtful presentation of ideas by an obviously talented therapist. Yet, it places into bold relief the insular nature of much of the thinking about child treatment. From Frankel's perspective, play, that is to say, metaphor, is an essential, perhaps *the* essential, ingredient in the psychotherapeutic endeavor. He has gone far beyond the use of interpretation as the sole or even central therapeutic action. Drawing heavily on Bromberg's (1994, 1996) work on multiple self states, Frankel describes how play serves to bridge the gap between discordant self representations, and how this, in turn, helps to achieve greater integration and self-cohesion. He uses the analogy of play acting to illustrate how pretending integrates the imaginary and the real. Using Winnicott's idea of transitional space, he concurs with Winnicott's (1971) definition of psychoanalysis as "a highly specialized form of playing in the service of communication with oneself and others" (p. 41). In this regard Altman was able to help Ronald "play" with ideas about himself as the two acted their roles variously as victor and vanquished. He too used the activity of play in favor of explicit interpretive statements. From the perspective of the parent therapist, however, two thoughts emerge about Frankel's approach to child treatment. We believe that his concept of play in the therapeutic setting can be fruitfully applied to the consultative model in working directly with parents. It is the parents, after all, who most need to appreciate the value of play in their children's experience.

Frankel (1998) discusses therapy as an ideal setting for play because it "offers a world for the patient to construct and reconstruct . . . the therapist . . . as someone the patient can *use*" (p. 153). Yet Winnicott's concept of object use refers, originally, to the ways in which children use parents. Frankel goes on to suggest that "the pleasure we take in playing with our child patients communicates our sense of connection to the child and our *personal* knowing and acceptance of the child" (p. 156). We must ask here, Why our child *patients* and not our children? Would it not be greatly beneficial to the child if we could expand the parents' capacities for and enjoyment of play?

The parent therapy model is predicated on the realization that there are often significant obstacles that inhibit parent-child play. Frankel discusses some of the obstacles that exist for therapists in the treatment of children, and the therapeutic action that is designed to overcome them. He is particularly interested in "recognition," which he defines as accepting the other's difference from ourselves. Clinical work with children thus rests on the appreciation of the child's difference. This may be understood in terms of Fonagy's reflective function, which, if developed more abundantly in the parent, can significantly enhance the child's sense of being recognized.

Bromberg's (1994, 1996) concept of integrating the dissociated and disavowed aspects of self "through the ongoing intersubjective field" (p. 69) is pertinent here. Frankel draws largely on Bromberg's work with adults who, presumably, were insufficiently recognized as children, and for whom the therapeutic encounter can then provide a space in which "an act of recognition can take place" (p. 69). It is our contention that this reintegration might be more effectively accomplished in the most meaningful intersubjective field: the parent-child relationship. There is much for the relational child therapist to draw on in Ferenczi's work (1931) with adults, as Frankel illustrates. Yet, in all of the examples cited from his therapeutic endeavors to help patients engage and reintegrate dissociated aspects of self experience, Ferenczi is attempting to rework, transferentially, something that was never fully achieved in childhood. Aron's (1996) work on mutuality in the adult treatment setting furthers this point with the suggestion that, "mutual regulation is a given, mutual recognition is a goal" (p. 70). This is an idea that can be meaningfully directed back to the parent-child relationship, as infant research has taught us. Thus, enhancing the parents' own abilities to more fully recognize their children can then help to expand and integrate the child's self experience. The irony here is that relational child theorists are borrowing from psychoanalysts in their treatment of adults, who are themselves leaning on ideas from infant and child development— in other words, from the implications of the parent-child relationship. We believe that the natural extension of current developmental theory is to refocus the locus of child treatment on that relationship directly rather than through the intermediary of the treatment transference.

Frankel's clinical examples suggest that he is simultaneously both a keen observer and an active participant who is fully engaged in the therapeutic process. This ability to be in both states simultaneously is the very capacity that we might hope to develop and expand in parents. Frankel's work fails to address how parents are included in the therapeutic process and what, in fact, the implications of this exclusion are for the child. Let us consider the following clinical vignette:

> Lisa was 6 years old when she began psychotherapy with Frankel. She is described as anxious and depressed, which may have been related to the difficulties in her attachment experience with her mother. Her anxiety created social difficulties and problems in interacting with

others. In his analysis Frankel (1998) sees this in terms of conflicts associated with her relational world and furthermore sees her wish to terminate the therapy as related to her growing attachment to him. While this interpretation is plausible and empathically generated, it seems equally plausible to consider the increased strain and ambivalence that the therapy may have created for Lisa. In her sessions Lisa herself devised a creative solution in the form of the following compromise: she continued to attend the sessions but played alone in the privacy of a tent. Frankel lets her play in her tent undisturbed because this "felt right," and it is at this point in the therapy that Lisa's anxiety abates. We might suggest that this was Lisa's way of managing the conflicts created by the therapy itself—a way of maintaining her loyalty to her family by means of her separateness and refusal to interact, and of maintaining her compliance by continuing to attend the sessions.

Of course, the primary objective of therapy, particularly with children, should be the enhancement of children's overall lives. It is for this reason that the questions about child analysis posed by Fonagy and Target (1998) are so crucial to consider. Their discussion focuses on several core questions: For whom is child therapy most effective? Which treatment approaches are most useful for children who don't fall under the rubric of "analyzability"? What is the therapeutic action of child psychotherapy? What role does interpretation play? Which issues are useful to interpret? Does child treatment have cost-effective benefit for children and their families?

Altman and Frankel both address elements of these issues. However, Fonagy and Target, and Coates, in her commentary on their paper, pursue the matter further and remain receptive to the outcomes of their empirically based research. Openness to new ideas has pervaded psychoanalytic history from its earliest inception, but a rigid adherence to a core set of principles has often followed these periods of creativity. Ultimately, this results in an ossification of ideas, and treatments that adhere to fixed principles, without reference to what is most salient in people's lives. Fonagy and Target (1998) review treatment outcomes for child therapies of a range of intensity conducted at the Hamstead Center, considering their results with reference to *Diagnostic Statistical Manual* (*DSM-IV*) diagnostic criteria. Their discussion, and Coates's subsequent response, focus largely on the "capacity to mentalize." What is most germane for the parent-focused clinician is the emphasis these theorists place on the parent's reflective function in the development, not only of a secure attachment, but of the child's own ability to mentalize. To a large degree, the parents' lack of such an ability is linked to the development of psychopathology in the child. According to Fonagy and Target, the capacity to mentalize not only permits the possibility of coping with adversity, but also provides for the transgenerational transmission of this protective capacity. Coates (1998) also sees this issue as essential to our understanding of child development and the relational structures in which children are embedded. She discusses the ways in which the reflective function can be developed in the therapeutic setting. However, many of these ideas seem to lead naturally to the idea of intervention potentially being most effective in direct work with parents. With regard to the nominally effective and even negative treatment results reported in the outcome research, Coates states, "We might well consider the development of reflective function from what might be called a public health perspective. That is to say we would want to encourage those child-rearing practices that fostered this capacity in the child. . . . We could significantly raise the proportion of children who would benefit from less intensive forms of treatment when and if they became symptomatic" (p. 126). She goes on to question "how we conceptualize analytic intervention in relation to the ordinary processes of parenting."

The capacity to mentalize relates to the mirroring, holding, and containing functions parents perform in their children's lives. Coates, and Fonagy and Target offer many references from quotidian family life of the ways in which parents keep their children's "mind in mind," from earliest infancy throughout the course of family life. Much of this discourse leads us to the thought that it is through intervention with parents that this reflective function can be most ameliorative for children. Coates describes how, in her own clinical work, the work with parents "can create surprisingly rapid changes in both the mother (and/or father) and the child" (p. 143). She concludes:

Potentially we can also begin to generate technical interventions with parents that can be thought about more selectively and fruitfully than before. This is a major challenge to our field, but it is a challenge in the very best sense; it opens up the possibility for theoretical and technical creativity as we try to find out under what circumstances and with which cases and at what ages such interventions will prove most efficacious. [p. 144]

Parent therapy, in its attempt to utilize both the internal and interpersonal worlds of the child, represents an effort to meet the challenge noted by Coates. In this paradigm the access to the child is achieved through contact with the parents in order to expand the parents' containing functions and enhance their capacities to think empathically about their children. Simultaneously, the goal is to intervene in ways that are the least intrusive in the child's life. The direction of relational child work, in emphasizing the most salient aspects of the psychoanalytic attention to intrapsychic life, along with the interpersonal contributions from family therapy lead, naturally, to the theoretically integrative paradigm of parent therapy.

III
Parenting Issues

7

Enhancing Parental Capacities

A seminal influence on the work of John Bowlby was Melanie Klein, with whom he trained. During his treatment of a young, anxious, and hyperactive boy, who suffered from what Bowlby would later come to see as an attachment disorder, the child's mother was hospitalized for a psychotic episode. Bowlby's experience with this case solidified his idea that real-life events have a profound impact on children's development. He had been concerned, from the beginning of this treatment, about the mother's emotional state but, despite his strong inclination to meet with the child's parents, Klein counseled strictly against it. Klein expressed her position that only the child's internalized experience was of any importance, and further-more challenged the notion that a therapist could have any ameliorative influence on the child's relational environment. When the child's mother was hospitalized for anxiety and depression, Klein was concerned only about Bowlby's having to find a new case for supervision, since the child's therapy would have to be interrupted. That the mother's breakdown was of no clinical interest to Klein proved to be transformative for Bowlby, who, in disagreement with her, refined his focus to reflect what was, in his opinion, most critical in children's development.

In obvious contrast to Klein's emphasis on the intrapsychic experience of the child and the primacy of individual treatment, Bowlby's attention to attachment and separation issues expanded our understanding of object relations, which, unfolding in the real world, have great impact on intrapsychic experience. Hence, the rupture in his patient's attachment experience, actually taking place in the child's life, became, for Bowlby, the most meaningful occurrence for the child, rather than the disruption of the treatment. Bowlby and Klein concurred that simply providing parents with advice would be of little or no utility, and could in fact serve to intensify their anxiety and self-doubt. Yet Bowlby, in contrast to Klein, believed that it was possible to have an impact on the child's internal experience through modifications in object relations, and furthermore, that therapeutic intervention with parents could affect those object relations (Karen 1994).

Klein's innovative thinking about the intrapsychic experience of infants and children, Bowlby's attachment theory, Winnicott's now axiomatic conception that there is no child without a mother, and his emphasis on contextualizing our understanding of the child's inner experience—all of these have shifted our thinking and have paved the way for a bidirectional, interpsychic model of development. Current clinical work, which reflects much of this thinking, along with new developments in infant research and neurobiology, suggests an exquisite understanding of the relationship between context and temperament in the development of character and its concomitant unfolding in the treatment setting. The parent therapy model amplifies this understanding with the concept that the bird's-eye view and the view from within the nest together yield a more incisive and encompassing perspective than either one alone. With this model, an assessment of the child's problem is conducted both contextually and collaboratively. The combination of the consultant's outside perspective, which has the advantage of distance, with the parent's more experiential and intimate vantage point becomes the mode of effecting change. As in the supervisory experience, in which the patient's specific problems are less pertinent than assisting the therapist in working more effectively with the patient, it is the parents' needs, perceptions, and propensities on which the therapy focuses.

This therapy, from the outset, at the initial interview with the parent, is a process that is simultaneously an assessment and an intervention. Thus the introduction of a treatment format is part of the treatment process itself. Just as the process of conducting a diagnostic evaluation can itself have therapeutic value, the parents' collaborative engagement with a clinician, around gathering information, becomes an effective treatment intervention. It emphasizes the value of information in guiding behavior, and assumes that knowledge is not the exclusive domain of one individual but, rather, the result of a mutually pursued enterprise.

Several authors have highlighted the growing awareness among clinicians of the necessity for parent involvement in the treatment process (Aronson 2000, Pantone 2000, Warshaw 2000). However, despite the attempt to increase their interactions with parents, many therapists continue to rely on the traditional paradigm of seeing the child individually, in play therapy, and later meeting with the parents to convey ideas about the child and provide guidance and advice. One therapist (Aronson 2000) discussed his determination to engage the parents of his child patient, and, after gathering a good deal of data about the family, ultimately advised the father to spend more actual and intimate time with his 4-year-old son. There is not much difference here between this type of intervention and the kind of collateral work that has characterized child treatment models heretofore. Another therapist, following his meeting with a child, asked the parents what things in particular they would like to know about their child. This approach, unfortunately, denigrates and disqualifies a great deal of information, accrued over time, from the ongoing and emotionally informed relationship that parents have with their children. In the consultative parent therapy model, the knowledge of the trained professional is valuable insofar as it is based on skilled listening in the context of developmental knowledge. However, the clinician is clearly not in a position to know what it is like to live each day with a particular child. It is the parents' knowledge, from more intimate and sustained experience, that can be integrated with the therapist's for a more complete assessment . It is thus the collaborative nature of the work that distinguishes the therapy approach. Moreover, it is its relational character that determines that each therapy will depend on the specific nature of the problem, combined with the specific needs and capacities of the people involved. The interventions of the consultative model can never be predetermined precisely because they are generated by the inherent attributes and issues of a collaborative dyad or triad and are cocreated by them.

There are many instances in which parents are helped to reflect on their own experience with their child, and the reflection generates new ideas and new approaches to their parenting.

One parent came to a therapist because she felt unable to manage the tantrums and demands of her 8-year-old son. She felt emotionally overwhelmed by the child's rage and aggression and claimed to be in continual distress because her son would often attempt to hit her. Through a brief but intensive therapy, she arrived at the realization that she had often restrained her own impulses to hit her son; it was through a process of projective identification that the mother, who felt both angry and helpless in the face of her own aggression, had engaged in a dynamic in which her child became the aggressor. In consequence of the fear of her own rage she became unduly timid, and was unable to set reasonable limits for her child. The son, on his part, was struggling to achieve a firmer, more secure grounding from his mother. His aggressive behavior was, in part, an expression of his frustration, and, in part an attempt to achieve greater guidance.

What needs to be stressed here is that parent therapy is a way of entering a relationship in which the family's specific relational aspects and demands are addressed through a collaborative deconstruction of events and feelings; interventions, therefore, are tailored to the specific, individual needs and capacities of the parents and the children involved. In this case, advice about how to manage a child's aggression would most likely have been of little avail; it could not have been a compelling intervention because the heart of the matter involved unconsciously organized feelings and motivations that were lived out behaviorally in both mother and child. It allowed the parent to avoid an awareness of her own aggressive feelings and yet maintain a justification for her anger.

Consultation or parent therapy involves the deconstruction of relational issues, which is designed to contextualize symptoms and problems. Owing to the individual nature of these problems, each intervention will be responsive to the specific needs and capacities of the consultees. In the above case, the therapist, by inquiring in a detailed way about the episodes between mother and child, paved the way for the mother to arrive at many of her own answers. The consultant questioned the mother about her own affective experience during each stage of her son's tantrums, and this inquiry into her anger uncovered two interwoven themes: that she could, indeed, think about herself and her own feelings, and that the tantrums had levels of affective intensity that varied from beginning to end. The discussions allowed the mother to pursue aspects of the interactions that she had previously been unable to consider. The consultation focused on *her* experience of rage at her son and connected it temporally to the hitting episodes. Previous to the therapist's references to the mother's anger, the mother had been unable to verbalize her more rageful feelings. The function of parent therapy, in part, is to provide a forum for the expression of previously prohibited feelings, whether consciously suppressed from a sense of shame, or dissociated from conscious awareness because they create too much anxiety. In this case the consultant was able to suggest to the parent that some of her anger was simply a natural part of parent-child interactions.

This case highlights two other important uses of the parent therapy model: first, it diffuses the sense of shame that many parents have about the rageful or anxious feelings they have toward their children, creating an atmosphere in which these feelings are normalized; second, it provides the parent the opportunity to absorb new understanding from someone who stands outside of the emotionally charged orbit of the relationship. In this case, it had not occurred to the mother that her son's tantrums and hitting behavior had a range of affective intensity that correlated with her own aggressive feeling.

Some parents are highly adept in their capacities to conceptualize their children's development and are able to use the consultative experience to effectively reflect on their own parenting behavior.

A mother who went back to school when her daughter was 5 years old, stated, "This has really been a difficult year for Sarah; we're a family in transition and it was very hard on her when I went back to school." When her child was having problems separating from her mother at school, this parent recognized the child's need for greater contact, and proceeded to offer more intensive support. When she discussed the morning routine with the consultant, she indicated that, after breakfast, she sent Sarah to her room to finish dressing while she finished getting ready herself. What occurred repeatedly was that the child would resume her play in the privacy of her room and would then have difficulty in leaving her playtime at home in order to get to school in time. The consultant suggested that this might simply be a logistical problem and the parent, sensitive to her daughter's need for the comfort of home and familiar things, decided that the solution would be to wait until the child was fully dressed before finishing her own chores.

This is what the work looks like with a particularly thoughtful and resourceful parent. Other parents have different capacities and need different kinds of interventions. Some parents benefit from more educative approaches in order to amplify their understanding of children's developmental capacities. This can aid them in modifying their expectations, which, in some cases, may be unrealistic and may create tension for the child around the sense of inadequacy. This was the case cited in Chapter 2, in which a young mother brought her toddler to a busy medical clinic without sufficient play things or snacks. She was subsequently angry at the child's incapacity to tolerate the prolonged wait, and was unable to recognize that her 2-year-old had not yet developed the sustained composure for such a situation.

We can offer other examples:

A father took his 12-year-old daughter to a serious and complex movie and, in a discussion following the viewing, became irritated and disappointed when she was unable to grasp the abstract and metaphorical meaning behind the concrete details in the film. He argued with her insistently, driving home the more sophisticated meanings that she was unable to understand because of the obvious cognitive and social limitations of her age. What was extremely problematic here was the father's failure to understand the developmental capacities of his child, and the unfortunate expectations of her that therefore ensued. Had he had greater awareness of, or sensitivity to, her age-determined abilities, he would not have been so disappointed in her predictable reactions, and he might have picked a more suitable movie so that he could have enjoyed the evening in the company of his 12-year-old daughter.

In contrast to the above case, another parent was challenged by her 6-year-old daughter, who was disturbed by the fact that the female heroes in fairy tales were consistently referred to as "beautiful." Since the child was raised to abstain from judging people by physical appearance, she was concerned about the injustice and superficiality that seemed to characterize the tales. Her mother, because of her keen understanding of the child's intellectual capacities, explained the concept of metaphor, and the shorthand use of "beauty" as a stand-in for the inner beauty of the fairy-tale figures or, in other words, for more abiding virtues.

There is a complex interrelationship between the failure of theoretical knowledge and the particular narcissistic needs and projections of parents, such as the father in the first case. It is understandable that parents want to be gratified by their children's assets and strengths. However, the extent to which the parents' narcissistic needs interfere with normative perceptions of their children and more prudent approaches to their children's needs becomes a matter for exploration. In the first case the father's need to see his daughter in a particular light, and his difficulty in maintaining adequate boundaries between them, which would have allowed him to perceive the ways in which she naturally differed from him and from his expectations, led to his unfortunate anger and misplaced denigration. In contrast, the mother in the second case, who was called upon to respond to her daughter's criticism of fairy tales, was clearly in a very different position. She could be narcissistically gratified by her child's incorporation of the family values and worldview. She was pleased by the child's support of internal virtue over physical attributes, and thereby had the equanimity with which to offer tolerant explanations of literary devices, her knowledge of which she was also gratified to be able to share with her daughter. The important point is that both knowledge of childhood capacities and personal self representations and projections underscore and form the basis of much parenting behavior. In these situations the parent who was prepared with developmental knowledge and was not narcissistically injured by the age-specific concreteness of her child's thinking was better equipped to accommodate the child's needs. She was also able to see her child's challenge more benignly because it was consonant with her view of herself as a good parent. In contrast, it was in precisely the same way that in the first case, the 12-year-old's views disrupted or were dissonant with her father's sense of himself as a parent.

> Another parent was working vigorously to prepare his 3-year-old son and himself for the imminent arrival of a new baby into their family. This father had been conscientiously reading about the emotional implications of this event on family life. He had judiciously spent time speaking with his son about the imminent changes that were to occur, and had even obtained an instructional video for the child about life as an older sibling. They watched the video together. In one scene, several children were having milk and cookies and talking about being big sisters and brothers. The boy immediately asked his father for a cookie and seemed to lose interest altogether in the video.

The father had wanted to help his child achieve a successful transition at a heightened emotional moment, and was committed to his role as a sensitive and wise parent. Yet, at the same time, he grasped immediately that he and his son had divergent agendas: the father wanted to prepare his son for a momentous life event and to protect him from emotional distress; the child wanted a cookie. This father understood at that moment that attuning himself to the experience of his 3-year-old required less projection and more observation. His capacity to recognize his own overidentification was considerable, and he was therefore able to make the transition to respond to the child's real need.

In assessing parental and child needs in a consultation, and in formulating a treatment plan, as in any other therapeutic endeavor, one must give the greatest attention to the capacities and emotional responsivity of the people involved. Understanding the emotional terrain on which a person functions allows the parent therapist to make informed interventions that can be effectively used by the parent. If we ask as therapists, as we must, what use a patient can make of an intervention, then we must ask as supervisors what use the supervisee can make of the intervention, and, analogously, what benefit the parent can derive from a particular therapeutic approach. There is an extremely broad range of approaches that can work and be effective in any given therapeutic process with parents. Where one family or parent may benefit from concrete parenting and developmental advice, others may prefer to use the consultation for an investigation of their perceptions of their children. Still others may use the consultation regarding a child's problem as a preliminary entry into individual treatment of their own, or as a transition into exploring marital issues or interpersonal conflicts more directly.

In some cases, the segue from parent therapy to individual treatment is easily made because of the issues raised in the initial consultative meetings.

One couple, for example, presented concerns about their children and their conflicting perceptions of their children's behaviors. The father was troubled by the mother's harshness and negativity and the mother was distressed because she felt that both the father and the baby-sitter were careless and remiss in their disciplining of the children; she resented the playful nature of these relationships and felt burdened by the need to be the sole disciplinarian and naysayer. In therapy she described her feelings of jealousy over her children's apparent preference for the baby-sitter. The distress she felt about her children's attachment to other people suggested that her envious and jealous feelings were critical, enduring preoccupations for her. The therapy created an awareness of this, which the patient then became intent upon exploring. It also became clear after a relatively short time that she did not actually have profound concerns about her children, who appeared to be developing within normal ranges of behavior. Thus, this mother used the therapy about her children to begin a course of individual treatment.

What became apparent in the consultative discourse was that the dynamic with her children was a recapitulation of an earlier self state and familial experience in which she was the less preferred child of her own parents. The patient's feeling that she was her children's second choice—second to her husband, and second to the babysitter—was easily pursued by the consultant, who asked if there was anything familiar about this feeling. The patient embarked on a prolonged recollection of her feelings as a child, of having always been the "third," feeling herself to be the gratuitous extra in every interpersonal dyad. This theme was subsequently elaborated and explored more deeply in her individual psychotherapy with frequent reference to the ways in which the same issues emerged for her, repeatedly, with her children.

In this case, developmental information and the interpretation of the children's behavior would have been insufficient in effecting change, largely because it was the mother's distress, not the children's, that needed to be addressed. What was noteworthy was that the mother herself recognized this, and understood that the therapy was a way for her to embark safely upon a journey toward greater personal exploration.

In contrast, some parents enter the consultative relationship with acute concerns about behavior management, and solicit guidance with practical issues as well as information about normative development. Nonetheless, they may become further intrigued by particular ideas that emerge in the therapy and may subsequently move into a personal treatment experience. In any given parent therapy, there is an array of possible interventions; the specific content determines which intervention emerges in the therapeutic work.

Because of the relational character of parent therapy, we attempt to ascertain specific types of information about parenting styles, capacities, and emotional needs. The capacity to maintain adequate boundaries or to exert parental authority without undue internal conflict are important functions that are often implicated in harmonious or problematic family situations. Perhaps even more important is the parents' capacity to reflect on these functions, to have a level of self-awareness that allows them to make their own assessments of their children's capacities and developmental needs, as well as to recognize their children's separate identities. Thus it is often vital for the parent therapist to develop a thorough understanding of the parents' perceptions about their own temperaments as well as those of their children.

The level of developmental awareness that parents have is a significant factor that implies a variety of issues. How parents understand phase-specific developments is a matter of great importance. Many parents have difficulty recognizing that many of their child's struggles and behaviors are developmentally induced, are characteristic of specific ages, and are therefore both normative and temporary. Because developmental achievements are accompanied by the ambivalence of simultaneously losing or relinquishing something while gaining something, children often manifest irritability or regressive behaviors that may appear pathologically symptomatic. These apparent symptoms, however, are representations of the internal conflicts generated by the child's sense of what is lost as growth ensues. Thus it is important for parents to be able to keep in mind that what may look pathological is actually normative, even when their child's behaviors are especially trying, as they are during the "terrible twos" or during adolescence.

One extremely loving and attentive parent was propelled into a parenting crisis in part because she was not sufficiently aware of some normal developmental phases and conflicts. She reported that she needed to take her 2-year-old twin boys to a play therapist because of their behavior problems. Questioned about her understanding of these issues, the mother noted that her sons seemed easily frustrated by limitations in their communicative abilities, that they often competed ferociously over toys or for her attention, and at times could be willful in ways that felt quite overwhelming for her. She worried that they might be asked to leave their preschool class despite the fact that the school personnel assured her that they were able to cope easily with the children's behavior. She was convinced that it was she herself who was inadequate to deal with the children and felt, hopelessly, that she was a bad mother. More significantly, she felt that a child expert was needed to repair the damage that she had likely already caused, which was evidenced by her sons' behavior.

Although this mother was a highly intelligent, well-educated scientist, she had had no education in child development, and this both propelled her into, and was compounded by, her deep insecurity. While she was understandably overwhelmed by caring for two active alert toddlers during this heightened developmental moment, what became most deleterious was her inability to conceptualize her children's behaviors in a developmental context. After she described her children as unruly, obstreperous, and aggressive, she was advised by a child therapist that therapy was called for to ensure that the problems would not seriously intensify. Thus, the therapist tacitly colluded with the mother in corroborating her own sense of inadequacy in regarding herself as a parent. The therapist seemed to have responded to this woman's anxieties in ways that exactly mirrored her already vulnerable sense of her parental self. This self representation might have been supportively transformed and strengthened, for the benefit of the entire family, had the therapist empowered the parent by meeting with her alone. She might have explored the boys' behavior in the light of the particular developmental struggles they were experiencing and cast it in more normative terms. She might have explained the difficult nature of language acquisition, self-assertion, and self-definition, in terms of the internal experience of toddlerhood. This might have helped the parent to understand something about the ferocity with which toddlers appear to rigidly adhere to one self state, and therefore lessen her concerns that the children were developing pathological conditions. In fact, other qualified adults, such as the educators at the boys' school, perceived their behavior as typical for their age.

One of the difficulties in these situations is that child therapists tend to treat, largely because the common presumption is that psychotherapeutic treatment does not cause harm and that the absence of it can. Unlike other medical treatments, in which a risk-benefit analysis of treatment is always factored into the decision about whether or not to treat, child psychotherapy treatment models traditionally have not considered the possible negative repercussions of treatment. However, in some cases, harm may result from the denigration of parental authority and the intensification of parents' insecurities.

There are periods in childhood and adolescent development that are especially troublesome and are often felt by parents to be personal rejections. This is so because there are developmental accomplishments that by their very nature require the renunciation of parental engagement. As Margaret Mahler (1968, 1975, 1979) and Winnicott (1975) have taught us, it is of vital importance for parents to survive or tolerate these periods during which children experience ambivalent attachments and are striving for greater separation. Parents who bask in the dependency of infancy but feel rejected when their babies become mobile, for example, may be especially vulnerable at these times, particularly if they have not anticipated their children's ambivalent attachments and intermittent strivings for distance and independence.

Adolescents struggle toward a more separate identity and are likely at times to use a more contemptuous attitude toward their parents in order to achieve this.

One parent became deeply concerned when she was informed that her 16-year-old daughter had engaged in casual sexual activity. She was a liberal-minded parent who simply wanted to discuss crucial issues about sexuality with her daughter. The daughter, however, was extremely offended and rageful, and engaged in a vituperative argument with her mother. She refused to discuss her behavior and, in an insulting manner, insisted that her mother was ignorant of current sexual mores, was out of touch with generational differences, and was in no position to provide any sound advice for her, and furthermore was invading her privacy. The mother, however, understood in a deeply empathic and prudent way that her daughter's rebuke reflected a normal adolescent rejection designed to protect the daughter from the humiliating awareness that she did not have access to the full range of sexual knowledge that is the purview of adulthood. Ultimately, this propels teenagers into greater maturity, and it is this push toward greater maturity that initially feels conflictual and frightening for the child. The mother, because of her awareness of this, did not feel the narcissistic sting of the insults, and was able to persist in her attempt to engage her daughter. The ensuing talk about sexual matters was extremely soothing and reassuring for this adolescent.

Compare the following vignette about a family that engaged a therapist for a child's problems with an earlier vignette.

In one family, the baby woke with great frequency during the night, in order to nurse. In the consultation the parents discussed the difficulties and seemed to agree that their baby, Sophie, used nursing to soothe herself to sleep, both at bedtime and during all other awakenings, and that the awakenings were not initially related to hunger. They also had an aversion to having their baby develop a dependency on a pacifier or a nighttime bottle, yet both parents were suffering exhaustion from chronic sleep deprivation. There was a developing irritability in each of them and in the marriage as a consequence of this problem. These parents were in complete accord with each other in their assessment of the problem, and were able to use the parent therapy to establish a plan for nighttime weaning. Following their plan, they reported that their baby had been manifesting far greater flexibility at bedtime than they had anticipated, and there had already been a decrease in nighttime waking. The parents poignantly described the first night that the father had put 15-month-old Sophie to sleep, with stories and a bedtime bottle. This represented an emotionally charged shift for both parents. Mother celebrated the baby's progress and the potential for her own freedom at Sophie's bedtime, but she also mourned the loss of her exclusive role as caregiver and her exclusive intimacy with Sophie at bedtime. Each parent felt both the exuberance over the child's growth and the sense of nostalgia as their baby moved out of the cocoon-like sphere with mother toward greater maturity and independence.

This is a prevalent experience for many parents: the ambivalence of watching their children move toward greater autonomy. Inherent in this ambivalence is both pride in their child's accomplishments and sadness or longing at the anticipation of greater and greater independence and, ultimately, separation. What is not as common is the capacity for self-reflection demonstrated by these parents, who used the framework of the parent therapy to refine and reinforce their own thinking and required little "holding" or information from the therapist.

In a subsequent meeting with the therapist, the parents indicated that there had been relatively little improvement in the baby's sleep cycle since the initial progress. Mother was feeling especially discouraged, since she had recently returned to work after a year of maternity leave. She was feeling not only the stress of continual exhaustion, but concern about her daughter's ability to tolerate the new separation. Although she had hoped to begin the weaning process at this time, she believed that this would now be too stressful for her baby. This seemed to be reflected in Sophie's behavior: she greeted her mother on her return from work with excited smiles and cooing, but this was accompanied by insistent demands for nursing, which seemed especially urgent. The parents felt that this was her way of reconnecting and repairing the trauma of the day's separation. However, Sophie did not otherwise appear to be distressed at the morning departures, or during the course of the day with her caregiver. At this point, the therapist asked if there were any other indications of distress. The parents both suggested that Sophie seemed frustrated at her attempts to stabilize and perfect her walking, and to say the numerous words that she knew but could not yet clearly articulate.

In the context of the therapist's question and the parents' response, the three of them began to formulate another idea. The child's forceful insistence that her mother nurse on demand might be temporally associated with the current developmental moment in the child's life. On further reflection, Sophie's parents recollected that these more demanding behaviors had actually preceded mother's return to work. They reached the conclusion that Sophie's demands might be a way of exerting some control over an environment in which she felt, momentarily, on shaky ground. This idea was easily assimilated by the parents who were able subsequently to formulate a new perspective. Where previously they had been able to see her crying only as an expression of suffering and protestation, they were now able to focus on it as an expression of frustration around mastery and transitional developmental moments. What is particularly noteworthy here is that these parents had the capacity to establish sufficient distance from their own affectively laden developmental transition in order to evaluate what was actually occurring for their child. They could now experience simultaneously an empathic responsiveness to their child's needs and a willingness to explore their own projected sense of loss. It is this loss, which is a developmental achievement for parents, that is necessary for the advancement of children's mastery and autonomous functioning.

This loss is experienced by parents in a variety of ways; whether it is accompanied by understanding will determine much of the relational implications that follow. For the parent therapist, there must be a focus not only on how to conceptualize what the problem is, but also on where to enter the system, both intrapsychically and interpersonally. The most fruitful course of action will depend on the array of emotional resources available in a given family. To be truly relational, the parent therapy is structured in multidirectional ways, ways that respond to the unique character, temperament, and degree of defensiveness of each individual.

Some parents are needier than others and will require a great deal more holding and soothing support. The receptivity to this support also varies with the level of defensiveness.

One teenage mother brought her two children to a mental health clinic for evaluation. She expressed concern that there was something wrong with her 2¹/₂-year-old daughter. She stated that the girl had become a "monster child" and furthermore that the same thing was beginning to occur with her 1¹/₂-year-old daughter. This mother, Frances, was pregnant at the time and was eagerly awaiting the arrival of a new "good" baby into her home. At the interview, Frances spoke affectionately of her younger daughter, Keisha, noting how sweet she had been until the past few months, during which time she had become increasingly difficult to handle, particularly since she had become more mobile and tended to run away from her mother at every opportunity. The older child, Angela, had become extremely "wild" and unresponsive to maternal authority, and, in Frances's view, most likely had a severe mental disorder.

During the initial phase of the consultation Frances was asked to describe Angela and their relationship, from conception until the current time. She was asked about what her fantasies of the child had been, what she imagined the father's role would be, who had been there to help her with the baby, and how she had learned to care for her. The interview continued in this way and was designed primarily to encourage Frances to focus on her internal experience of her daughter in the context of her social and familial life. It seemed important to attend to the social, academic, and economic impact of such a life-altering experience as the birth of a child, particularly at Frances's young age. Many of the questions focused on highlighting the distinction between Frances's fantasies of motherhood and the more strenuous reality.

Despite the fact that many of the adolescents in her community were also having babies, Frances was nonetheless quite socially isolated. Curiously, although Frances had anticipated that the clinician would be evaluating her children, she seemed immensely pleased by the opportunity to discuss her loneliness, her sense of being overwhelmed by the demands of two young children, and her disappointment over the unavailability of Angela's father.

Like many parents, Frances became deeply interested in reflecting on her experience as a mother. It shifted the focus from the demands of the children to her own thinking about herself. The therapist's empathic listening to Frances's thoughts about her life also mitigated to some degree the pervasive loneliness that marked her life with her children, and in this regard it provided the most valuable aspect of the consultation.

We can contrast this with the earlier vignette of Sophie's parents; they too used the consultational therapy to explore themselves as parents. However, for Frances, the structure of the consultative interview created a means through which she could actually "collect her thoughts." Her previously chaotic and inchoate experience was held, through the structured engagement with the therapist, in a more coherent collection. She had rarely had the advantage of reflecting on her life, and her experiences had remained largely in the realm of the "unthought known" (Bollas 1987). For Sophie's parents, a great deal of thinking had already taken place; they had been able to hold each other and could then use the therapy simply to reorganize some of their thinking. It was the therapist's holding of Frances, who did not have this intrinsic self-reflective capacity, that allowed her to "know" what she was actually thinking.

A father came for a consultation to discuss stress management for his 9-year-old daughter who was suffering from chronic abdominal pain. This parent's concern exceeded the usual parameters of the request for child therapy, insofar as one of his preoccupying concerns was the conflicting views that he and his wife had about the etiology of the stomach pain, and the consequently differing approaches each had toward its management. The consultant had requested that both parents attend the next meeting. However, the father was apprehensive about revealing that he had had a consultative session with the psychologist and worried that his wife would be defensive and contentious. The therapist, in meeting alone with the father, offered suggestions about how to engage the mother in the process. This was effective because it reduced his anxieties about raising the issue with his wife, and the following meeting was attended by both parents. The differences in their attitudes and approaches to parenting were immediately apparent, and it seemed that their controversy around their child's symptom was the only conscious manifestation of the conflict and tension between them. Mother believed that the girl's stomachaches were not real but rather functioned to manipulate the father into providing the daughter with more solicitous attention. Alternatively, the father was disturbed by his wife's "callous attitude" toward their daughter's obvious pain and discomfort, and furthermore contended that the stomachaches were most likely exacerbated by the mother's dismissive and often angry manner. Overall, he believed that his wife's conservative attitudes toward child rearing derived from her own

austere European childhood, and were out of step with, and deleterious to, the needs of their three daughters.

In conveying this to the consultant he offered, as an example,
a common occurrence in the family. During the previous weekend,
their 15-year-old daughter, a stellar student in all of her academic
pursuits, approached her parents to review her plans for the day. She
planned to have a bath for purposes of relaxation, and would follow
this with math homework and a history report. She also had plans to
meet with a friend after dinner. The father felt sufficiently comfortable
with this plan and saw no need to intervene with any adjustments.
Mother, on the other hand, suggested that she postpone the bath and
directly attack her homework and, in addition, advised her to cancel
the social plan, which she believed would be too fatiguing after the
stress of doing homework. She further explained to her daughter that
this is what she herself would do in the daughter's situation. At this
point in the therapy session, the mother felt compelled to justify her
advice, maintaining that her plan for her daughter was more reasonable and more efficient. She further revealed that she was disgruntled
at her husband's lack of support and felt disappointed that he was not
more of a parenting partner.

The therapist followed this exchange by referring to the
presenting problem of the girl's stomach pain, recalling that the referring physician had diagnosed it as stress related. He had explained
that emotional tension can convert, rapidly, into an excess of gastric
acidity. Despite this, the mother rejected the idea that her daughter
was experiencing tension and anxiety, and maintained her conviction
that the chronic illness was attention seeking. She continued to chastise
her husband, believing that his sympathy for the daughter's discomfort
reinforced the symptom and, moreover, served to undermine her own
authority with her children.

We can understand this mother's attitude as a function of her
pressing need to exert her authority, and the permeable psychic boundaries
that contributed to her difficulties. Thus, underlying her intrusive control

of her daughter was her difficulty in reflecting on her own thinking, and the concomitant difficulty in imagining what her daughter's internal experience might be, as distinct from her own. The capacity to "mentalize," Fonagy's (1991, 2000) idea of thinking about thinking, creates the environment in which empathy can occur as a result of the awareness of separateness, rather than through identificatory processes. In other words, this mother would have to have recognized, and reflected on, her own temperamental propensities in order to identify the temperamental differences between herself and her daughters. Parents who are better equipped for self-reflection are often able to consider which parent may be better prepared temperamentally to manage particular cognitive and affective transitions, and to best tolerate the emotional atmosphere evoked by particular stages that their children undergo.

These ideas are linked to an array of reflective activities in which parents may participate. Often, parents reflect on their children's temperamental and characterological attributes, contemplating, for example, the ways in which a child may resemble one or the other parent. Statements such as "Johnny is like me in this regard, but more like his father when it comes to that . . ." require a certain degree of self-reflective, though not entirely self-referential, thinking. Knowing one's particular parental talents and proclivities is also a part of this reflective capacity. For example, some parents feel most engaged during infancy when children require the most nurturant care, while other parents are drawn to the greater liveliness and independence of toddlerhood, when there is more developed language, motor skill, and social relatedness. Knowing this about oneself, that is, knowing which developmental phases one is more drawn to, requires both a considerable degree of self-awareness and a significant capacity to differentiate oneself from others. The ability to think about oneself in relation to others and about others in relation to oneself enhances one's ability to hold in awareness the subjective experience of one's child, which is a reasonable approximation of the child's actual experience. Moreover, it is this awareness of the child's subjectivity that mitigates cruder forms of projection and prevents the foreclosure of possible approaches to the child's behavior that were not previously envisioned. With this idea in mind, we can see that, to some degree, the mother who attempted to organize her daughter's homework and recreation schedule, despite the fact that the girl had already exhibited a high degree of self-discipline and organizational skill, demonstrated a reflective insufficiency and boundary diffusion that contributed to an unfortunate authoritarianism.

This does not mean that parents' self-representations and the representations they have of their children attain perfect consistency or synchronicity with a consensual reality. Rather, it is useful in parent therapy to be able to work with some articulable ideas about familial and interpersonal relations. When we think about the mother and daughter in conflict over the child's weekend homework, we must consider that one of the features of this relationship was the mother's inability to think explicitly about her relationship with her daughters and how this inability interacted with her perceptions of their problems. Because the mother had not yet developed a sufficient capacity to mentalize, this anticipated the direction that the parent therapy would take. The therapist gently focused on what the parents had found most effective for their daughter thus far, with questions such as, "What kinds of activities seem to be most relaxing for her?" and "When she is becoming tense and worried, what signs does she demonstrate?" When they had difficulty in responding, the therapist made more explicit inquiries such as, "What do you notice about your daughter's behavior when she has a stomachache?" "What immediately precedes the episodes? Are there specific things that relieve them? Does she calm down more easily if she is left alone or if she is distracted by something?" These concrete questions were designed to assist the parents in increasing their observational awareness and to suggest that different people exhibit and respond to stress with a range of manifest behaviors. Although the mother was tenacious in her insistence on what *should* be effective, the therapist judiciously redirected the discussion. The parent was not directly challenged during the meeting; rather, there was some degree of commiseration over the fact that what might have been effective for some people was not working adequately for her daughter.

What must be highlighted here is that the therapist was in a precarious interpersonal configuration; had the meeting taken place with one parent only, an alliance between the therapist and the parent might have been used to expand the empathic resources of that parent. When parents' overt conflicts with each other predominate, the consultative terrain is somewhat more difficult to navigate. The therapist suggested that, in general, parents are not equally versatile in all realms of parenting. She invited them to reflect on which domains each of them was best suited to, enjoyed most, and felt most effective. Although this was concrete advice for this couple, it also moved their interaction in a different direction; the mutual engagement in thinking about themselves as parents extricated them from the impasse of their mutual recriminations. Subsequent to the consultation, these parents returned to the therapist for couples therapy, and the mother began individual treatment as well. The child's symptom had functioned as a lightening rod for the submerged conflicts in the marriage, which, sufficiently accentuated in the consultation, could then be addressed directly.

Another parent engaged in a consultative moment in the context of his own therapy.

He came to his session in considerable distress when his daughter returned home for a visit during her first semester at an out-of-town college. This semester was her first separation from her family, which consisted of her parents, a teenage sister only slightly younger, and a young brother. After the girl's departure from home and return to school, her sister discovered that she had gone off with numerous possessions from her wardrobe and was intensely distressed at the loss of a particular dress that she had planned to wear to a party. The parents, who were active in their church and were deeply committed to their children's moral education, were very disturbed by their older daughter's transgression. Although they were not inclined to be excessively punitive, and were sensitive to their younger daughter's material deprivations, as they functioned on an extremely limited budget, they were also concerned about the message that would be conveyed if they did not punish the older daughter. In discussing the situation, the psychologist asked the father to think about what feelings might have underscored the girl's behavior. The father was receptive to the therapist's exploration of the possibility that the daughter was anxious about the separation from her family. In this new light the "theft" could be seen as her way of denying that separation, and maintaining a symbolic closeness by keeping something of her sister's with her while she was away at school. When the father realized that it was the separation that had been painful and difficult, he felt a deep empathy for his daughter; he was able to feel her anxiety and sense of loss, and this significantly mitigated any more punitive or retributive feelings he had previously experienced.

What we wish to highlight here is this father's capacity to "mentalize," or to think about his daughter's thinking and subjective emotional state. It is through this mentalizing that he was able not only to empathize with her experience of loss and depression, but also to transform his formerly more authoritarian and punitive attitude.

This mentalizing function begins in toddlerhood, when the child develops the capacity to hold one state in mind while in another state. It is at this time when thinking becomes self-referential, and it is possible for the child to be in one state and simultaneously observe the particular affective experience of a different state. The development of this reflective capacity is fostered by the relational experience of having someone observe and respond to one's affective state. For example, the 3-year-old child in the throes of distress, and in the arms of a soothing parent, may catch a glimpse in a mirror of himself crying. The child will often resist altering his state because what fascinates him is the view of himself being soothed while crying. As this function becomes internalized, the child experiences and observes at the same time, creating a bridge between multiple self states, leading to a more coherent sense of self. We see that this model is prominent in the therapeutic process itself, where a patient experiences a particular state of affective distress, and can, with a supportive, holding presence, observe that state, and the awareness becomes ameliorative. Supervision draws on the same mental process by assisting the supervisee in thinking about something from within and from outside simultaneously. In the same way, parent therapy cultivates this same function in parents so that they can help their children with the development of a reflective faculty.

It is through this mutual reflection that affective life may be not only understood but also modulated.

In parent therapy, the assessment of parents' capacities to foster the ongoing growth in their children is based largely on how the parents respond in the consultative process. The parent therapy model is useful, not only to ameliorate developmental or dynamic derailments, but sometimes, simply to help families to better manage the ongoing vicissitudes of raising their children. As with psychotherapeutic processes, there are inevitably moments in a child's development when families get "stuck." There are unexpected problems that through under- or overidentification can feel overwhelming or insurmountable. Levenson (1995) describes the process through which a therapist can become entangled in a relational knot with a patient. In this situation, the therapy progresses when the therapist can begin to achieve a perspective on how this may have occurred. Only then can the therapist extricate himself or herself from a rigidly constructed relational configuration. Similarly, parent therapy offers parents the means by which to shift from a fixed interpersonal state to a more fluid one, in much the same way that supervision is helpful when therapists cannot achieve this analogous disentanglement. The consultation generates new ideas and thereby draws the parent into more flexible thinking. Although Fonagy and Target's (1998) work on mentalizing focuses on developing this capacity in children, the concept is useful in work with adults as well. This is so because, despite the fact that most adults have achieved this capacity, under the stress of difficult interactions with their children it can periodically be temporarily lost or dissipated. The consultant, by encouraging dialogue about internal conflicts and concerns, can help parents restore the mentalizing function and reestablish an empathic attitude. For someone who stands outside the fixed or rigidified relational pattern, it is sometimes easier to see the ways in which parents and children are acting to maintain the existing dynamic configuration that has persisted between them.

Dynamic configurations are at play on many levels and time frames here. As Stern (1971) has emphasized, it is the generalization of particular, repeated interactions that become internalized as self and object representations. Thus, it is the persistence of particular configurations that becomes instrumental in the development of character structure by way of internalized interpersonal experience. When difficult exchanges occur, as they do frequently with children, the existence of channels through which a parent can diffuse the frictional moments will be immensely helpful. Children are inherently labile and emotionally vulnerable because they have not yet perfected the regulatory capacities with which to control their moods. A slight failure in the environment can engender a sense of catastrophic disappointment, and when parents are unable to distance themselves from the child's rage or pain, they can be locked in a power struggle from which it is difficult to disengage. It is only through a flexibility in modulating one's reactions that discrete events are prevented from eventuating into fixed patterns.

> A father and his 2-year-old daughter engaged in an intensely negative affective moment. This father, in state of chronic sleep deprivation as a result of caring for a 9-month-old as well, had awakened early with his daughter in order to allow his wife an extra hour of sleep. The child was irritable that morning and was behaving in an especially needy and demanding manner. The father had been attempting to meet his daughter's demands but ultimately became irritated himself and in exasperation admonished her for being a "crybaby." He further remarked that he "could not put up with her any longer." At that moment the mother emerged from her bedroom to take the crying child into another room. She spoke to her child with the purpose of soothing her, and in this new relational interaction the child was able to reestablish a calmer mood and demeanor. When she and her mother reemerged and returned to the father's presence, he and his daughter were able to engage in a calm and affectionate reunion.

This incident illustrates an aspect of a common occurrence in family life. The momentary disruption in a usually harmonious relationship was easily repaired, in part because an outsider, that is, someone outside the event and the affective intensity of the moment, was able to assist the father and daughter in restoring some emotional composure. In this case a second parent was more advantageously positioned to disentangle parent and child from the momentary lapse that threatened to overwhelm them. Under different circumstances, such as a single-parent home, sustained marital conflict, chronic illness, or other major stressors, these moments may become more difficult to modify. Being called a crybaby in this instance was unlikely to be a significant event for this child, because of the anomalous nature of the event. Had the exchange typified the nature of the relationship between father and daughter we might speculate the child's relational world would to some degree develop around it. The experience of anger at a critical father, shame around her own neediness, and the sense of deprivation at not having needs met might be installed as part of her internal self and object representations and, later in her life, could reverberate in her relationships with others. In this instance, the mother's presence facilitated a transition to a different affective and relational state for both parties. What is important to note is that both the fundamental capacity to shift states and the facilitation of this capacity in any given moment are what prevent conflictual moments from becoming more enduring interpersonal and intrapsychic states. Conflicts are recurrent in relationships, and what alleviates conflict and restores equilibrium is the capacity to distance oneself from narcissistic injury and rage or relinquish a rigid sense of authority. When parents have the advantage of sharing the responsibilities of child rearing with a partner, it may be easier to restore fluidity in familial dynamics involving the children. Often, however, the multidirectional nature of the interpersonal arena, with intricate and overlapping dynamic struggles, precludes this, and outside intervention is then useful.

The father who was concerned that his daughter had, in effect, stolen from her sister needed only a gentle encouragement to see additional elements in her motivation in order to think differently about her behavior. He had, for a variety of reasons, become "stuck" or limited to seeing the situation from one angle only. Because he had sufficient flexibility to shift sets in general, it required only a minor reframing for him to see other possible meanings in her manifest behavior. He was able then to see her act not so much as a shameful moral lapse but as a function of a complex psychological response. Flexibility here implies the capacity to see multiplicity in the motivations that underscore behavior and to hold in mind multiple meanings simultaneously. For example, the act might have suggested an attempt to garnish more attention from the family when she was separating to return to college, or it might have been an angry expression of envy and competition in relation to the sister who remained comfortably in the family fold. It was this father's own predisposition that allowed him to see his daughter in a sympathetic light, and the thought that she was motivated by a desire for closeness was most concordant with his values and his optimal view of her. In consequence, when he did approach his daughter, she was able to respond openly to his more benign attitude.

We have explored a variety of situations in which parents develop conflicts with their children. Some parents lack developmental knowledge but easily incorporate new information into their representations of their children; other parents experience too great a narcissistic injury around some of their children's behavior; still others seem to have difficulty in their capacity to make transitions or shift easily between interpretive frames in order to see multiple meanings and dimensions in the same behavior. In assessing parents' capacities, there are many aspects of affective and cognitive processes that we have highlighted as salient for the development of a useful consultative plan. Many of the clinical illustrations here have focused on the ways in which parents' narcissistic concerns are activated in relation to various aspects of their children's development. But it is not the narcissism per se that is most relevant in formulating an effective treatment plan. Rather, it is the degree of flexibility in the thought processes of the parents. Thus, a crucial distinction has to be made between narcissism and rigidity. The capacity to shift cognitive and/or affective sets in the service of broadening one's perspective can be understood as the relational salve that prevents interpersonal conflict or trauma from becoming fixed aspects of the child's internal world. If we look at the father who engaged in vituperative argument with his daughter at the movies, we can see that it was not simply the narcissistic shame that activated his criticism, but his difficulty at that time in calling into consciousness other feelings toward his daughter. Had he been able to access the more prideful feelings that sometimes existed, he might have avoided the distress of experiencing her only as a disappointment. The mother who felt compelled to engage her daughter around sexual issues was helped in her parental relationship because she had an array of emotional responses around her daughter's behavior; she was able to maintain sufficient distance from her child's assault in order to move them both into a more advantageous relational configuration.

It hardly needs to be said that narcissistic pride in a child's accomplishments is an essential ingredient in the parenting process. The important point, however, is that parents' narcissism must be used in the service of the child's growth and self-esteem. Enhancing a parent's knowledge about development, for example, can transform narcissistic injury into narcissistic pleasure only if the parent's overidentification or insufficient identification can be repositioned. This was the case with the father whose daughter left home with her sister's dress. The therapist was able to identify with the father's subjective experience of disappointment, because she had an appreciation of his values. Through this appreciation, which diminishes defensiveness and the need to rigidify one's thinking, she was able to engage him in exploring alternate perspectives. This, in turn, created the possibility for an affective shift. Furthermore, his experience of himself as a recipient of empathy allowed him to turn his empathic resources toward his daughter and to see her act in a different light. This is in part the advantage of the parent therapy paradigm; had the girl been seen in individual treatment, such a case might have taken on a different configuration, and the parent-child relationship might have remained unaltered. In this case, the father, while maintaining his parental position, was also able to assume a therapeutic role with his daughter and help her through a difficult life transition.

The idea of emotional distance is important here; our culture has in many ways been forced to surrender many of the benefits of the extended family model or the tribal experience. With the prominence of the nuclear family there is little opportunity to use extended relatives as consultants. However, we should note that a grandparent or friend is often in a position to act in a consultative capacity, precisely because they are not as vulnerable to the projections and identifications that are so pervasive for parents.

8

Dealing with Discipline

*P*arents frequently solicit therapeutic assistance about discipline issues. In many cases, the need for intervention implies relatively pronounced and long-standing difficulties in the structure of the parent-child relationship. Underscoring many of these problems are parents' deeply embedded ambivalence about authority and power as well as conflicts between parents regarding these issues. Because people are raised with a variety of discipline styles themselves, they tend to approach their own children in ways that attempt either to repair their relationships with or to sustain their loyalty to their own parents. Concomitantly, children tend to behave in ways that reflect their own needs for autonomy and that simultaneously gratify their parents' unconscious desires. In this way, discipline becomes a complex and often unconsciously conflictual sphere of parent-child interaction.

Many parents are faced with the genuine dilemma of maintaining their authority while trying to encourage their child's capacity for self-expression and exploration of the environment. The integration of these goals, combined with unconsciously motivated needs and projections, makes discipline a difficult terrain to negotiate.

We conceptualize the function of discipline in a child's life as a means of maintaining the safety of the child and simultaneously assisting the child in regulating affect states in order to make fluent transitions from one state to another. In addition, the function of discipline is to develop children's capacity to tolerate the day-to-day frustrations of living in a world in which they must respond to external demands such as waiting in line, taking turns, or sharing toys with others. In adult life these daily and routine necessities become critical in meeting the demands of both social and professional activities; we are, to some degree, successful at negotiating our lives if we are able to wait for a return call, fall asleep after a frustrating or arduous day, and get to work and appointments on time. The central meaning of discipline in the child's life is the development of the lifelong capacity for self-discipline and the internalization of behavioral control.

Perhaps the most meaningful implication of early childhood discipline is that it provides a foundation for the tolerance of frustration and the prevention of disorganizing levels of rage. When there are gross failures in the developmental processes that lead to self-control, the means that are used to cope with rage and frustration are deeply deleterious to both the individual and to the culture. These failures can lead to such consequences as substance abuse, eating disorders, and violence, because of the impaired capacity to regulate painful affect states and the need to dispel intolerable affect. These impulse disorders can thus be seen as attempts to achieve affective equilibrium and to curb inchoate affect states through some means of self-soothing. Similarly, bulimia and anorexia can be viewed as an effort to negate and discharge unacceptable feelings and impulses felt to be dangerous or toxic. In some ways, the tantrum of the preverbal child, which requires containment from a reliably helpful caregiver, translates later in life into the frustration and rage that require self-discipline for affective control. With children who have not yet acquired the mitigating force of language, the mother's capacity to make meaning of the inchoate and overwhelming feelings aids the child in developing reflective capacities. It is through introjection of this function and identification with the caregiver's soothing that children learn to "hold" their experience. Later in life, this internalized caregiving function translates into self-discipline and leads, during moments of stress and disorganization, to remedies with which to assuage painful feelings. The adult who has internalized this function not only anticipates these moments, but also has developed a repertoire of activities through which relief and control are achieved. The capacity for self-control is contingent on the past experience of soothing care that has established the trust and conviction that control can be achieved. The adult who can endure distress and relieve it by reading a book, lying down to rest, or taking a bath has been able to convert early experiences of nurturance into mature processes of self-containment.

When parents are able to reconsider the drive for authority and the sense of power through command, they will use discipline in the service of the child's development of regulatory abilities. If the child's compliance is seen as a means toward a reliable sense of autonomy and self-control, and not a means to bolster the parent's domination, then discipline can become a positive, mutually enhancing experience in the parent-child relationship. When this occurs, discipline appears to be an almost seamless negotiation, and, in this context, does not look like a coercive imposition of authority. Instead, it takes on the appearance of collaborative work. What is crucial in establishing this type of discipline is a basic trust in the motives and wisdom of the parent. What the parent is suggesting is accepted and acquiesced to by the child because it is supported by the assumption that parental requests are derived from the wish to nurture and protect rather than the wish to control.

Let us look at two quite different approaches to the idea of "time-out," each arising from different relational matrices that can be usefully explored through parent therapy. In one approach time-out is equivalent to punishment; the child is banished to his room at home, isolated from others. If the child misbehaves, for example he teases his younger brother, is hit by the brother, and retaliates by hitting back, then he is sent to his room for a time-out. He protests the injustice, insisting that his parent recognize that his brother hit first. However, he is told that he is older and therefore should know better. An extension of the time-out is then meted out as a punishment for the youngster's protest, which is perceived as a defiance of parental judgment. The child angrily complies and subsequently experiences the time-out in a submissive but rageful and victimized affect state. What has transpired in this episode emanates from the particular ways in which family relationships are configured. Age assumes asymmetrical value; for adults it carries with it status, power, and authority, but for children it demands greater responsibility and more mature control. One might deconstruct this configuration by exploring the particular intrapsychic experience of the rule-making parent. Perhaps he himself felt compliant and victimized as a child or as an adult. He must therefore assume much authority over his own child, both in an identification with and support of his own parents, and also to assuage his anxieties about his own weaknesses. In this parent's internal life there is a tie both to authoritarianism and to the connection between age and responsibility. He projects his sense of responsibility onto the older child along with his repressed anger, thus perceiving his son as both recalcitrant and uncontrollable. He may simultaneously identify with and sympathize with his younger son as the victim of oppression. What is salient here is how the parent's behavior is a function of internally shifting self experiences and the projections of those experiences onto his children, the understanding of which can create more ameliorative solutions for his children's discipline.

In another example, a child is playing while her parents and her parents' guests are dining. Because there are guests, she is permitted to stay awake past her usual bedtime. But as a result of her fatigue and excitement, she becomes overly aggressive in her play and is instructed by her parents to control herself. When she is unable to accomplish this self-control, she is given a time-out. She and her mother retreat to her bedroom so that she can be helped to reregulate her affective arousal and to calm down. She reemerges from her room smiling at her accomplishment: she has been helped to shift states so that she can reengage in the social scene in a more acceptable manner. The relational experience here is one in which the parent functions as an auxiliary container, enabling the child to begin the developmental process of internalizing the parental capacity for greater control. In this case, the parent understands that the child's behavior, however disruptive, arises from her social excitement; the mother does not defensively feel that her position is threatened and therefore is not compelled to intensify her maternal authority.

In both of these situations the parents' authority prevails when they are displeased with their child's behavior. However, in the first case, the time-out is most likely a way for the parent to calm himself and to ward off anxieties around his own negative self-perceptions. Although it reduces the threat of any further aggression from the older child, it also provides a calming period for the father. The exertion of power is one aspect that assists the parent in shifting states; it allows him to experience greater control over the external environment while his internal conflicts are at their fullest intensity and threaten to undermine his sense of control. He emerges from the child's time-out more able to focus on ensuing activities and feeling that things are more manageable than they were during his more rageful state. He feels more effective as a parent, owing, in part, to managing the older child's aggression, and protecting the more "vulnerable" younger child. What is obscured, in this solution, are the potentially injurious effects for everyone that are created by the negative attributions directed toward the older child. When the older child is vilified in order to maintain the parent's sense of control, when this child is seen as out of control in order to preserve the father's own affective composure, there is the risk of creating an intolerable, toxic self experience for the child. In this way, the parent is protected from the knowledge of his own ineptness, and the child is also protected from this knowledge of the parent; what is sacrificed is the child's perception of the parent as a soothing, containing force and himself as sufficiently competent to comfortably exert control over his own impulses.

In the second situation the mother emerges from the time-out in a more tranquil state because she and her daughter have reregulated their arousal states together. Several things make this possible: first, this mother does not need to exert her authority over the perceived ruthlessness of her child; she has the capacity to see her child's excitement as a natural consequence of the social experience and is not unduly angry. More importantly, perhaps, is the difference in relational patterning. In other words, this parent is not afraid of either her own powerlessness or her child's unruliness, and does not therefore imbue herself or her daughter with threateningly negative qualities that must be disavowed or banished. In this time-out the child need not be separated from the parent and the parent can become a reliable presence who assists the child in calming herself and establishing a prototypical way of producing shifts in her own affect states.

What is apparent in these two episodes are the differential capacities or self representations of the parents involved. Let's explore what it is that contributes so critically to what we conceptualize as integral in the parental capacity to discipline reasonably, in the service of the child's growth. This capacity derives in part from the ability to distance oneself from one's fantasied or projected representations of the child. For most parents emotional experience is intimately intertwined with that of their children's; problems arise, in part, when parents are unable to adequately differentiate their own reactions, impulses, and self experience from their children's. What they disparage in their children they may feel identified with, and what they must disavow in themselves they are likely, through projective processes, to perceive and condemn in their children. What differentiates the mother in the second instance is her ready awareness of the porousness of emotional boundaries; the father in the first instance would not be likely to initially reflect on the reciprocity between his and his son's psychic experience. Were these parents to solicit a consultation about discipline issues, the process would clearly unfold in significantly different ways. The father, invested in his own position of authority, may have unrealistic expectations of his son that lead to perceptions of his child as oppositional, defiant, and demanding. The second parent might engage in the consultative relationship in order to obtain suggestions about coping with difficult behaviors and exploring her own responses to and provocation of her daughter's conduct.

Underscoring many of the discipline problems parents encounter is their degree of parental confidence and their related feelings about their own authoritative competence; it is the parent with the greatest confidence who least needs to demonstrate overt influence over the child. When parents' projections reach extreme proportions and significantly distort the perception of the other, the child may be seen in a variety of deeply problematic ways; the parent who feels too weak to exert authority may see the child as a monstrous and insolent rebel, while the parent who projects his own fears into his child may then see him as a timid and ineffectual weakling. In these extreme cases, the adult's need to externalize bad self states may lead to tragic abuses and have permanently deleterious effects. What should be understood in the consultation, however, are the ways in which mistreatment and punitive approaches stem largely from the unresolved conflicts and self-deprecation experienced by adults.

It is our contention that when parents can be assisted in understanding some of the complicated but highly influential dynamic forces unconsciously played out in parent-child relationships, they will be able to see their children's behavior not as simply defiant or inadequate but as attempts to preserve a measure of identification with an admired parent and also maintain a sense of self-worth. They may be able to see aggression as a failed plea for acceptance from a disapproving parent or a realization of some unconscious wish of the parent.

A youngster who had recently emigrated from South America was having significant adjustment problems in his kindergarten class. Jose's lack of English proficiency and his relocation to a new and vastly different cultural milieu had understandably predisposed him to emotional distress. His teacher, who had a relatively unstructured teaching style, tended to allow him to wander, somewhat aimlessly, around the classroom where, unable to integrate himself into the group activities, he often resorted to physical aggression.

His mother engaged a psychologist because she was distressed about and ashamed of her son's behavior. She had been repeatedly contacted by his teacher, and she had been diligent in punishing her son. She revealed to the psychologist that she had him sit in a corner facing the wall for prolonged periods of time. She was bewildered by the fact that the negative behaviors persisted and that her punishment seemed ineffective. In consultation, she reported that she had come to this country in the hopes of improving her life, and had obtained a good job. She left her young son in the care of her elderly mother. But she had recently decided that her mother had been too permissive with him. Her understanding of his behavior resulted in the idea that he had been spoiled by his grandmother, and the mother was now faced with the job of disciplining him.

After consulting with the mother, the psychologist considered the fact that, coupled with her desire to achieve a higher social status and her self-consciousness about this, and her guilt about having abandoned her son to questionable caregiving, she had been left with feelings of considerable shame and guilt around her own life choices. It seemed possible that the projected representations of her child carried with them the disavowed self-criticisms and led to the conviction that her son was a bad, unruly, and recalcitrant child. Two goals were crucial in the consultation: to relieve the mother's sense of her own badness, as reflected in her son's misbehavior, and to mobilize both her understanding of her child's developmental capacities and her empathy for his transitional experience. In her drive to repudiate her own guilt and escape from self-recrimination, she was unable to focus on the emotional trauma her son was experiencing. His behavior created a painful rupture in her own need to see herself and her son as embarking on a new and better life and therefore had to be summarily stamped out. First, the psychologist supported her self-image as a mother who was making vigorous efforts to provide a more enriched life for her son. When she subsequently felt less vulnerable to criticism, she was able to consider the suggestion that her son's unruliness was largely a reflection of his fear and isolation in a new culture in which he could not yet communicate. His anxiety, created by unfamiliarity and the lack of structured containment from his teacher, was markedly disorganizing, and left him feeling painfully inadequate. When Jose's mother, through consultation about these issues, was able to appreciate and ally herself with her son's more fragile and vulnerable self, she was able to establish a more empathic understanding of his experience; she could now see the frightened, inadequate child, not merely the irascible, aggressive child, and could therefore generate more protective feelings toward him.

The psychologist accomplished this attitudinal shift in part by asking the mother to describe her own early immigration experience. She questioned her about what had been most frightening, what it felt like to come from a small village to such a large city. She pursued questions about language difficulties and the foreignness of the newly adopted culture. When Jose's mother was given this opportunity to reflect on these vulnerable times she was able to do so, and it was at this point in the therapy that the parent and the psychologist were able to consider new strategies for improving Jose's situation.

The psychologist also explained that the particular punishment that the mother had been using was ineffective, largely because children are unable to tolerate and make positive use of techniques that heighten a sense of badness and self-hatred. She explained that what might be occurring for Jose during his periods of banishment was a sense of isolation and rejection, which only served to replicate and compound his experience in the classroom. The isolating nature of the punishment also served most likely to induce both anxiety and rage reactions and an envy of the good children, on whom he then released his aggression. This interpretation invited the mother to consider her child's behavior as a reflection of several psychological processes rather than a resistance to discipline. She welcomed the psychologist's suggestions and was able to make use of them because the support in the consultative relationship had established a sense of collaboration. She subsequently became more protective of her child, and when she was no longer ashamed of his behavior she was able to solicit the help of the school administrators. After considering the situation, they arranged a class change so that Jose could have greater guidance from a more organized and emotionally available teacher. These interventions were enormously effective; Jose's behavior greatly improved and he began to interact with other students in a more congenial way.

It was not necessary in this consultation to explore other ambivalent feelings that Jose's mother may have had about having given over her son's care to her mother while she worked to establish a new life in New York City. Jose's attachment to his grandmother, and the possible unconscious competitive feelings that his mother experienced not only about his affections but also about her own mother's affections for a child other than herself may have been complicating factors in the mother–son relationship. However, the mother's responsiveness to the consultation and her easily mobilized empathy obviated the necessity for greater, more intensive exploration of her psychodynamic experience. Some people welcome the transition from this type of parent therapy to the deeper self-exploration of psychotherapy. But the consultation itself may result, as it did here, in a sufficiently significant realignment in the relational matrix so that greater emotional comfort ensues for both parent and child.

Perhaps of singular importance in the integral and pervasive relational character of the parent-child dyad is the self experience of the parent, which is often challenged during the experience of parenting. The intense narcississtic vulnerability, unearthed in the process of parenting, may be unparalleled in other realms of ordinary human experience. In this regard, discipline, which affects how parents view their own capacities to shape and influence their children's development and how effective they are in the world, is thrown into the boldest relief in its impact on individual esteem. The world views children's behavior as a direct reflection of parental capacities; when children are courteous, their behavior is attributed to their parents' competence and capacity for responsible care, as well as to their authority and mature judgment. Children's disciplined or undisciplined behavior is the most obvious conduit for feelings either of pride or of anger, shame, frustration, and anxiety. Other attributes, such as beauty and achievement, may be narcissistically gratifying or disappointing; however, they are not often approached with the same moral scrutiny and judgment as children's attitudes and behavior.

The attribution of parental responsibility for behavioral manifestations is easily noted in comments that children are "well raised" or "well brought up." As early as infancy, babies are considered good if they cry only infrequently and require little soothing. Comparisons with babies who never cry are not only deleterious to parental composure, but also speak to the pervasive and profound moral accountability to which parents are held. Implicit in the cultural attitude toward unruly or difficult-to-soothe babies is the idea of parents' lack of discipline, disorganization, or timidity. The mental health community has historically contributed to this idea with advice to parents ranging from early twentieth century prohibitions against kissing babies lest they become spoiled, to Bruno Bettelheim's (1967) contemptuous labeling of the mothers of autistic children as "refrigerator mothers." The implication here is that these mothers actually caused their children's condition by providing insufficient love.

That we now understand autism to involve neurological deficits has none-theless not entirely mitigated the tendency to confound temperamental or inborn proclivities with the moral failures of parents. The shame and hu-miliation of the parent whose child, in a particular developmental transi-tion, has had difficulty in regulating behavior, can be intense. This shame often drives parents to seek treatment for their children, partly in an effort to externalize the experience of moral condemnation. We can see this dynamic at play in the relief that some parents feel when their difficult child has been diagnosed with an attentional disorder, because what is problem-atic can then be seen as something within the child that is medically rooted and that can be medically remediated. The child's behavior then becomes a source of sympathetic commiseration rather than an implicit reproach of the parent.

The self-images that parents construct and attempt to preserve in their reflexive vision of their children tend to result in dualities of benevo-lence and authority. The powerful needs for approval and the self-percep-tions of kindliness or strength often mitigate parents' capacity to maintain a clear and distanced perspective on their children's behavior. When their own expectations and disappointments come into play, they may interpret normative behaviors as negative and project their own sense of inadequacy onto their child. Because the child's behavior is so deeply bound up with the parent's self-esteem, transgressions, even minor ones, may be perceived as disruptive simply because they threaten the narcissistic experience of the parent. The anger that a parent feels toward a child when the parent's benign self-image is undermined often leads to miscarriages of parental guidance. Thus, when a child's behavior must not only please but also support the parent's self-esteem, momentary failures or disappointments may become intolerable and lead to problems that are not easily repaired.

Here is an example of how an ordinary interaction that is momen-tarily ruptured can deeply threaten parental pride.

A mother, recently separated from her husband, is at home with her children on a winter evening. She has made a fire in the fireplace and is roasting marshmallows. The older child is thrilled at this departure from the daily routine: turning a cold weekday night into the delight of a summer campfire. He announces to his mother that she is the "coolest" mom in the world. She is pleased, even excited by her son's approval and admiration but timid about this idealization, and thus alludes to "other cool moms." Nonetheless, he prevails and affirms that she is the "coolest." Unfortunately, the adventure is disrupted by a couple of accidents: one marshmallow falls and stains the rug, and another burns the child's fingers. The moment of mutual pleasure and admiration has been shattered. The child screams and the mother, crushed by her disappointment in herself and distressed by her loss of status as a "cool" mom, becomes angry. Her frustration is sufficiently palpable that the younger son asks her if this is the worst day of her life. His naive but empathic intervention has an immediate and ameliorative effect. She is able to regain her composure, her sense of humor, and her usual skill in maintaining affective equilibrium for herself and her children.

It is important to note here that this parent's emotional flexibility was reestablished, in part, because she felt comforted by her younger son's concern and his capacity to direct her attention to her emotional reaction. It is equally important to note that her sense of parental competence and her vulnerability were heightened because she was parenting alone for the first time. Her son's observation helped her to focus on the feelings that had been activated by the failed event, and she was able to see the connection between the occurrence and her own internal concerns. In her own psychotherapy she had been exploring her guilt about divorce, its implications for her children, and her anxiety about her ability to cope with the rupture in her children's lives and to parent them without assistance from their father. She realized that the rupture of the moment reactivated these concerns and exacerbated her feelings of ineptness. In this case, the parent's understanding was underscored and aided by the expertise and support of her therapist; her alertness to her internal processes allowed her to recover, mitigated her anger toward her son, and permitted a more flexible interaction. Moreover, the capacity for reflection depathologized much of her reaction and made it vastly less threatening for her.

In contrast, here is a far less successful interaction that also aroused anxiety and disappointment in a parent. In this case the projection of a bad, inadequate, and guilty self representation contributed to the perception of a child's malevolence.

A single mother, in her first year of financial stability, became greatly excited by the anticipation of providing Christmas gifts for her 5-year-old son. As they had had only meager gifts in previous years, she was planning to lavish many gifts on him and spoke repeatedly to him about the many presents he would be receiving. One week before Christmas the child found a closet filled with his gifts and, in the intense exhilaration of the moment, he opened all of them. When his mother returned from work she was overcome with rage; she was overwhelmed by the sense of deprivation of her anticipated Christmas pleasure, and felt her son to be the agent of her disappointment. The child was severely punished for his transgression. He was beaten and was not permitted to keep any of his presents. Nothing was forgiven him, not even on Christmas day. His mother's dismay continued for weeks and her own sense of deprivation, which her fantasy of a lavish Christmas was unconsciously designed to repair vicariously, remained intense and unmitigated. She engaged friends in discussions of her son's misbehavior, his impulsivity, and his disregard of her feelings. Her friends, in their efforts to empathize with her disappointment, reinforced her feelings of victimization. As her anger persisted, she began to worry about her child's judgment and capacities for self-control. Thus, the support that she received for her distress and for the inappropriateness of her son's behavior further provoked her anxiety about him.

Had the mother been able to reflect on the internal motivations of both herself and her son, she might have reached significantly different conclusions. She might have considered, for example, that in some important ways her son's behavior was much like her own. In some parallel or identificatory way, then, he was overly excited about the holiday and was easily overstimulated. Like his mother, he became easily overwhelmed and impulsively sought gratification. Hadn't she been both impulsive and overzealous in her punishment, and perhaps in the fervency with which she approached the holiday at the outset? Might she have considered the fact that her sense of deprivation and the subsequent overinvestment in the holiday were related to the fact that she was a single parent, and that unconsciously she might have harbored feelings that her son had made her life more difficult? Did she perhaps feel guilty about any resentment over this and about her child's deprivation? With these considerations in mind, it is possible that the emotional insult of the boy's transgression might have been so intense because it represented, symbolically, all that she had felt deprived of in her life as a single parent and all that she had deprived her child of. Unlike the previous example, however, in which the parent was able to explore and therefore detoxify her reactions, this parent had no assistance in this endeavor. There was no one to help her engage in a process of self-exploration to examine her own motivations or her son's unconscious attachment and wish to bond with her through similar and consonant behavior. There was no one to help her to understand and therefore to tolerate the developmental capacities of a 5-year-old, and that his impulsivity was not atypical for his age.

When a parent's benign self-image is injured, repair and restoration derive from the same kind of emotional regrouping that the supervisory experience provides when a psychotherapist becomes disproportionately discouraged about a patient. Often, the supervisor is able to identify the positive features of the treatment and help to clarify the reasons for the rupture or derailment in the therapeutic alliance. What is ameliorative for the therapist is the supervisor's understanding that interpersonal derailments are inevitable and remediable. The supervisor's capacity to empathize with the therapist's disappointment becomes a corrective experience in the same way that it is helpful for parents to appreciate that children become frustrated and distressed over their own perceived failures. The supervisor, the parent, and the parent therapist all have the potential for detoxifying an injurious relational moment. It is the capacity to maintain perspective, more easily achieved by someone who can stand outside of the affective intensity of the moment, that facilitates the metabolizing of the painful experience. In this way, parents who are helped to achieve distance from their own affective reactions can offer a distressed child some suggestions for relief, or can help the youngster to achieve the transition to a more tolerable self state. Thus, under the influence of supervisory composure, the therapist is able to return to the therapeutic encounter with greater perspective, and the parent, through consultative work, can return to the child with greater patience, tolerance, and wisdom.

The following illustration from a long-term parent therapy reflects the complexity of factors that contribute to parents' individual styles of discipline.

Louisa was referred for a consultation by her physician, who suggested that her chronic somatic complaints seemed linked to psychological factors. What emerged as the consultation proceeded was Louisa's deeply felt anxiety about her capacities to raise her child on her own. This generalized anxiety at times overwhelmed her with specific fears, and as a result she had obsessional concerns about dying of a heart attack or from unspecified cancers. She was exhibiting, in addition, mild obsessive-compulsive symptoms that frequently impaired her daily functioning.

Noteworthy in Louisa's childhood experience was her own sense of deprivation and her pervasive fears, deriving from the fact that her mother had been unable to provide sustained maternal care and had frequently placed her daughter in foster care. Ultimately, when Louisa was 11 years old, her mother died of a drug overdose, and she was sent to live with an aunt and uncle, her mother's sister and brother-in-law. Louisa's care in her aunt's home was harsh and punitive, particularly in adolescence, when Louisa's normal, developmentally driven exploration around sexual behavior was negatively viewed and rigidly forbidden. She was reproached for any adolescent striving for individuation, such as wearing makeup, and was forbidden to date. Indeed, any such transgression was associated by her aunt with Louisa's own mother and was accompanied by the predictive attribution that she was " just like your mother" and would "turn out just as she had." During her adolescent years she was sexually abused by her older cousin, but never revealed this to her aunt for fear that she would be assaulted with blame for her perceived wantonness. Through this experience, Louisa continued to internalize the negative self representation, begun earlier in childhood, through both the identification with and the abandonment of her mother. Owing in part to her aunt's persistent recriminations, she developed an image of herself as bad and sexually provocative and deviant, despite the fact that she was predominantly a shy, studious, and fearful girl.

When she was 18 years old, Louisa married. She had a child one year later. She was abandoned by her husband a year after this brief marriage in which he was an unfaithful and neglectful partner, just as her mother had been previously. Once again, the abuses that she suffered in her marriage were attributed by her aunt to Louisa herself, and her own self-doubt and insecurity became further entrenched in her psychic life. Nonetheless, in her forbearance, Louisa managed to obtain an associate's degree and she began work in a hospital-based child social work department. Over a period of several years she significantly altered her attitudes toward child rearing and, in particular, discipline techniques, having learned much about child development through her work situation. She was proud of her accomplishment in learning how to substitute verbal engagement and reasoning in place of hitting and punishment. However, one day she returned from work and entered her 10-year-old son's room to find him engaged in sex play with a friend. Her sense of panic and outrage overwhelmed her and, overcome with rage, she beat him severely.

Louisa immediately phoned the consultant, explaining in great distress that something terrible had occurred. Despite her experience of the episode as catastrophic, when she met with the psychologist, her initial anxieties were surprisingly amenable to relief through the consultation. Her conscious concerns centered around her fear that her son might become sexually perverse: a sexual abuser or victim, or a homosexual. She expressed her anxiety that through his sexual acting out she would lose her influence over him and he would be "lost to the streets."

As we have repeatedly suggested, we understand Louisa's behavior to be the result of a complex configuration of self and object representations; what was apparently reactivated for her by her child's behavior were all of the internalized interactions through which her bad self had emerged— the bad maternal self and the bad sexual self, both of which were identified with perverse sexuality and promiscuity. This was clearly compounded by her past experience of sexual abuse, superimposed on her son's act, made his behavior a frightening representation of indecency. He became an incarnation of her damaged, victimized self, and also of her abuser. She could only see her son as bad, owing in part to her confusions about childhood sexuality and in part to her perception of him as following a familial line of damage and debauchery. It was essential for the therapist to tease out all of the strands of these self and object representations, to explore and understand the interpersonal structures, in order to decode what the child's behavior meant to her symbolically. Without this understanding, Louisa had little alternative to considering his act troublesome at best, and despicable at worst. She would have solicited a therapist for her son, in order to address his emotional problems.

The therapist informed Louisa that boys commonly inspect each other's genitals at this age. More importantly, however, she was able to empathize with Louisa's anxiety and the self-recrimination that generated the assault on her son. What is important to note about the parent therapy model is that it offers the clinician the opportunity to establish an expanded array of transferential and countertranferential experiences. Thus, had Louisa's son been the focus of the treatment process, it is highly likely that an intense negative transference would have developed toward this mother, plunging her deeper into a negative maternal self representation and self-hatred. This, in turn, would likely have been projected onto her son with obviously deleterious consequences. The empathically colored countertransference, mobilized by the therapist's understanding of the salience of Louisa's own family history, made possible an atmosphere of mutual emotional openness.

In this context, the traditional approach diverges from the parent therapy model. This consultative relationship was presented to a group of child psychologists, and the response from the group seems typical of what can occur when a therapist treats a child. For many child therapists, their attempts to engage the parent do not sufficiently mitigate their identification with the child patient, and this inevitably colors the nature of the meetings between therapist and parents. Thus, in the case of Louisa and her son, the child psychologists focused their empathic experience on the child, and perceived the mother as abusive. Had the child been in treatment, this attitude could conceivably have reified Louisa's already deeply felt insecurity and self-doubt, and reinforced her guilt and remorse over the incident, for not only had she experienced a cascade of fears about her son's behavior, she had also felt deep remorse over further frightening him by the severity of her reaction. More painful for her, however, was her perceived regression to a previous and now repudiated disciplinary mode. This was an important and painful reality that could be, and was, discussed with her in the parent therapy, but was given less attention and empathy by the group of child therapists. It is a monumental task, for most of us, to maintain a stance that is equidistant between parent and child while working primarily with the child. Noteworthy here is that when Louisa's own tragic childhood was discussed with the therapists, they were able to turn their attention to the other abused and traumatized child in the family—Louisa herself.

In the parent therapy, Louisa was able to deconstruct her own and her son's behavior in an atmosphere in which her shame and her motivations were appreciated and could therefore be deactivated. She was able to re-establish her equilibrium in lieu of intensifying her multiply determined anxieties. Thus, her capacity to tolerate her overreaction could be contextualized into the fabric of her continuing efforts to raise her child in empathic and supportive ways. What was mitigated through the therapy was her own horror at her son and herself, both of which, unchecked, might have led to a spiraling of cruder forms of admonishment. For both Louisa and her son, the consultation served to maintain generally positive views of each other and their relationship and deterred them from inflating the significance of this single episode in their lives together.

9

Responding to Aggression

*O*ne of the cultural myths from which our society has not fully detached is the idea that children are archetypes of innocence and do not harbor any malevolent thoughts and feelings. The old dictum that children should be seen and not heard reflects the perception of children as existing not only outside of the orbit of adult privilege, but also outside of the adult expressions of emotional experience. Despite conflicting mythologies that sometimes characterize children as unsocialized and savage, there is a persistent drive to idealize them as innocents playing harmoniously in an idyllic world. In this scheme, emotional rage and aggression are seen as the exclusive purview of adult experience. Thus, we live with jarring contradictions that characterize children as virtuous, on the one hand, and recalcitrant, on the other. When we confront the realities of childhood aggression, our cultural confusions come actively into play, and it becomes difficult to recognize and to tolerate what constitutes acceptable aggressive thought and behavior. Although aggressive behavior directed toward peers may be tolerated, and is actually often encouraged in order to support the parent's need to see a child as strong and competent, it may be fiercely condemned when directed toward an adult. This reflects the adult ambivalence about childhood initiative and agency. Adults encourage a child's sense of power, but at the same time do not want themselves to feel diminished or weakened by children's unruliness. Some parents, on the other hand, have difficulty tolerating any deviation from entirely benign images of themselves and their children. Their children's expressions of frustration and rage are then met with grave concern and repudiation.

Parents brought their 7-year-old son for therapy. They were reasonable and gentle parents whose son was well adjusted, academically and socially, and with whom they seemed to have a warm relationship. One day he was working with his mother at the computer and became very engaged and excited by the activity. When his mother realized that they did not have sufficient time to complete their project, she gently urged him to end his activity. The boy was unable to curtail his enthusiasm and continued working as his mother persisted in her attempts to achieve closure and move on to the next activity. This constraint on his excitement proved to be too much for him to tolerate, and in his frustration and difficulty in shifting sets he typed onto the computer screen "I hate you." The boy's behavior was horrifying to his mother, who felt that his assault was sufficiently disturbing to warrant therapy.

What seemed difficult for this mother was the idea that her child had even transient violent thoughts, and had difficulty in integrating them into her overall view of him as a reasonable, gracious, and well-adjusted child. This often occurs with aggressive behavior: it becomes, for many parents, a defining moment in their experience of their child. The mother here, for example, extrapolated from this single expression of intense but probably fleeting hostility, a characterization of her child as a frighteningly angry person.

Winnicott (1975), among others, considered hate and aggression to be expectable experiences in a child's early development. However, the unmitigated expression of hate and aggression is clearly precluded by the demands of living in a social world. What transforms the earliest expressions of aggressive affect into more functional forms is the interaction between the external environment and the child's own temperamental propensities. The ways in which children modulate their arousal levels and temper the aggressive fantasies that sometimes accompany them, depend on the relational context in which child and parent are embedded. Many theorists tie the ability to manage impulses to an environment that is sufficiently tolerant of, yet simultaneously capable of containing, the child's expressions of aggression, whether they derive from anger and frustration or simple overexcitement. Thus, what may begin as excited play may at times reach extreme intensity and consequently require containment and transformation by an adult. The parent who is able to titrate excitement and aggressive fantasy is able to help the child internalize capacities for control and modulation.

In an environment that can tolerate aggressive thoughts and feelings, this tolerance can be internalized; it can be accepted as part of the self and can therefore be integrated into the personality as a whole. It is productive insofar as it can be converted into energetic work and play. When aggression in thought is not tolerated but is met with retaliation, it can turn into violence and destructiveness. The child's inhibition and suppression of impulses develops gradually, in accordance with emerging cognitive capacities as well as with relational dynamics. It is the dissociation of aggressive impulses that can lead to the behavioral leakage that we see when consciously expressed feelings are not tolerated and instead must be repressed into the realm of the unconscious.

Winnicott (1975) conceptualized aggression in the infant as originally a part of appetite, or "instinctual love." Underlying such a theory of child development is the idea that infantile relatedness is initially "ruthless," and that ruthless love necessarily precedes the capacity for concern: "The normal child enjoys a ruthless relation to his mother, mostly showing in play, and he needs his mother because only she can be expected to tolerate his ruthless relation to her even in play, because this really hurts her and wears her out. Without this play with her he can only hide a ruthless self and give it life in a state of dissociation" (p. 154).

Several mothers playing with their toddlers at the playground illustrate some of the relational and social contexts of early childhood aggression. The group of children is feeling the elation over expanding skills and the developmental shifts that provide new opportunities for play. One mother–child dyad plays a game of chase in which there is as much emphasis placed on the reunion as on the chase itself. This child has recently acquired proficiency in running and, in the moment of reunion, bites her mother, apparently out of the thrill of running and the simultaneous pleasure in being caught. The mother is more than simply surprised; she feels the sting of the bite and momentarily interrupts their play. The child is startled also, and anxiously scans her mother's face. The mother, who appreciates that her child's "ruthlessness" occurred in the context of play, is nonetheless taken aback, and this momentary lapse in play creates a sufficient interlude to slightly reduce the child's arousal level. The mother, by resuming their play, is then able to reassure her child that she is not injured and to mitigate any sense of guilt and anxiety. In this situation the mother perceives the aggressive behavior as part of the child's overall appetitive enthusiasm, rather than an intentional injury, and so she is able to regain her own emotional equilibrium and to facilitate a comfortable transition back to harmonious play.

A second mother plays with her child, but her interaction is more predominantly supervisory. Several children convene on the jungle gym to practice climbing skills; some verbally reinforce the activity by chanting, "Up and down." This mother's child approaches the jungle gym steps and, in his efforts to engage in the play, pushes a perceived obstacle, another child, out of the way. The child/obstacle falls and cries out, and the boy's mother, appalled at his behavior, quickly and angrily removes him from the playground, admonishing him repeatedly. This mother seems to have some difficulty in facilitating her child's explorations and interactions, owing in part to her own anxiety and in part to her insufficient grasp of his developmental limitations. She has perceived the child's aggressive act as purposeful and malevolent. However, we need to be mindful of the fact that the toddler does not yet have the verbal proficiency to express thoughts, and may lack the cognitive capacity to fully process the consequences of his actions. The mother who can recognize these limitations can also provide new frameworks for her child to cognitively assimilate. She may verbalize for him the urgency of his needs, and facilitate his awareness of the obstacles that need to be navigated. In this way she may expand his repertoire of behaviors so that, with encouragement, he can develop greater empathic awareness. In other words, parents who are not overly identified with their children's behavior and do not themselves become humiliated by it may intervene in ways that promote the children's capacities to negotiate new and more mature social interactions.

A third parent alternately played with her child and chatted with other parents in the playground. When her daughter possessively refused to share her toys with other children, the mother gently spoke to her about the possibility of allowing others access to some of her things, but at the same time accepted the child's prerogative to refuse. This mother did not intervene further, but spoke affably with another parent about the pervasiveness of envy and competitiveness, and its escalations into adulthood. She was not unduly disturbed by her child's behavior and assumed it to be part of a toddler's natural possessiveness. Her capacity to perceive her daughter as a separate person, whose behavior was not a reflection of her own, allowed her to maintain an empathic responsiveness and to circumvent a condemnation of her child that might have been internalized as self-denigration.

In each of these instances, aggression or ruthless interaction is integrally linked to the developmental phase and particular capacities of the children. Children's experience of their own aggressive behaviors will vary with their ability to connect behavior with immediate consequences for others, and with the responses from their caregivers. The ensuing complex of self and object representations will also depend on the meaning of the aggressive acts in the context of cultural and familial expectations. However, the "ruthlessness" of early childhood, whether originating from excitement, envy and competition, or social ineptness, is rooted in a developmental stage in which aggressive behaviors occur continually. Optimally, children in this stage can be assisted in emerging into more civilized life stages in which they can establish greater inhibitory control over their more unruly impulses.

What we are emphasizing here in each of these dynamic interchanges is the idea of an optimal balance between the breakdown and the restoration of control. The parent who is able to provide a way for the child to de-escalate arousal or repair the breakdown in his self-regulation and the parent who feels neither personally injured nor unduly anxious about the child's decorum or compliance will most likely be more effective in helping

the child develop regulatory control. Where there is an inhibition of impulses before the child has developed the cognitive and emotional capacity
for this, there is likely to be a problem with impulse control.

Consider the following exchange between a mother and her 4-year-
old daughter.

The daughter had begun to have difficulty controlling her angry
impulses, particularly around maternal authority. This difficulty emerged
unexpectedly in a relationship that previously had been especially
affectionate and harmonious. The angry outbursts were confusing and
disturbing for both mother and child. This situation, from the vantage
point of the developmentalist, may be seen as a normally expected,
phase-specific turning away from the mother, supported by a recently
occurring, more intense engagement with the father. In this family, the
father, who was at work for long hours while his wife assumed most
of the child care, was intensely gratified by his daughter's increasing
interest in him and thus unconsciously supported the growing competition with her mother for her father's attention. After several weeks
of uncomfortable and escalating dissension, the mother consulted a
psychologist and met to discuss her concerns. The psychologist listened carefully to the particulars of this family's situation and to the
mother's unique perspective on her child's developmental history.

In the consultation the mother reported that the child had
been weaned from the breast easily, had surrendered her bottle vol-
untarily, and had been toilet trained without incident. Interestingly,
she could not recall her own involvement in these events and had the
recollection that her daughter had simply accomplished them on her
own initiative. This parent had no awareness that negotiations around
such events could be conflictual, or that parent and child might have
different and therefore conflicting agendas. It was in this environment
that the child's anger and aggressive outbursts were occurring.

Ultimately, the mother was advised on several points: one,
that the child's behavior seemed developmentally driven, since she was
at an age when there typically is escalating interest in and affection
for the father; and two, that the previously harmonious relationship

was rather unusual in its extreme lack of conflict. This allowed the mother to gain some distance from feelings of personal rejection and to maintain some curiosity about her daughter's internal state. The therapist encouraged this, and furthermore suggested that she remain as receptive as possible to any of her child's unvoiced thoughts and feelings. The psychologist stressed the fact that the daughter also had had little opportunity to explore and therefore cope with her own conflictual and unsettling feelings.

Shortly after this session, the daughter approached the mother and suggested that she move out of their home. The mother, though startled, was able to feel simultaneously intrigued, and, supported by the parent therapy, became interested in pursuing her child's thinking. She questioned the daughter about what would happen if she were to miss her mother, maintaining an exclusive focus on the child's thought processes and subjectivity. The child responded, "Well, Dad and I can visit you on vacations and sometimes on weekends, but during the week we'll stay here." "And what will you do if you get hungry and need a sandwich?" the mother asked. They continued their conversation in this vein, an approach that was designed to remind the child that relationships are fluid and have multiple configurations. The child was thus invited to contemplate the idea that she could need her mother yet simultaneously envy and compete with her.

The child's wishes to "do away" with mother, annihilate her in fantasy, could be understood in the context of this family's dynamics, coupled with developmental issues, and were met with a benign containment. The child paused to consider this message and, after some time, did appear to process the idea that she and her mother had a relationship that encompassed much more than a rivalry for her father's affection. In this way the mother had encouraged the child to experience her as both a good and bad object. She thereby facilitated for herself and her child the capacity to experience two relational configurations and affect states at the same time. Subsequently, the child's aggressive behavior diminished, as a result of this exchange, as her heretofore inchoate and unacceptable conflict was understood and absorbed. Such an intervention is predicated on the parent's capacity to tolerate a child's hostile feelings without fear of consequent damage, and also to remain curious about the child's interior life of unconscious thoughts and feelings.

This parent had had to survive, in Winnicott's sense, considerable assault, and with little previous preparation. The relational experience of both parent and child develops contextually, and this particular dyad had had very little prior opportunity to rehearse their own form of conflict resolution with each other. As children develop, their desire for increased independence creates a continual interpersonal tension with parents. The developmental milestones that they face enable parents and children to navigate this terrain from earliest infancy and to create the relational patterns that are continually shaped and reconfigured. In this case, mother and daughter had functioned so much as a unified dyad, with relatively little involvement from father, and the child had such unusual capacities for self-regulation, that the negotiation of transitional events was rather seamless. The repair of the mother–child relationship, therefore, had to address both the capacities of this particular pair and the dynamic style that they had themselves created. In parent therapy, we derive our understanding of the child's behavior and developmental capacities from the relational matrix within each family. Parenting books may offer some useful guidelines about the chronology of developmental phases and behavioral problems, but they cannot make use of the parent's own expert knowledge of the interface between their child's development and their unique family life.

The intolerance of normally occurring aggressive feelings and the expression of these feelings, as we have suggested, lead to repressed or dissociated forms of aggression that may then have to be discharged in cruder or more explosive ways. Thus, behavior problems and more uncontrollable forms of aggression may actually be the result of parents' fundamental aversion or disavowed attraction to manifest forms of aggression. Such conflicts usually lead to parental attitudes that are based in an undercontrol or an overcontrol of their children's behaviors.

There are aggressive behaviors that are deeply problematic and arise not from natural exuberance or ruthlessness but from disorganizing levels of anxiety, depression, and rage. It should be recognized, also, that there may be a complex or coalescence of factors that contribute to the development of pathological aggression. These include a range of physiological, genetic, and constitutional processes such as pre- and peri-natal trauma and congenital anomalies. What the parent therapy paradigm addresses, however, is the confluence of familial factors and the relational environments in which milder forms of problematic aggression may develop.

The following account presents a situation that developed as a consequence of parental *overcontrol* of a child's behavior and the child's particular responses to this:

> Susan began individual therapy after having been recently married, and she had her first child during the course of the treatment. Marriage and motherhood were predominantly satisfying experiences despite the emotional exertion of these life passages. Her relationship with her son Aiden was extremely precious to her and she guarded it closely, maintaining the fantasy that outside glimpses of their mutual affection would endanger the relationship through destructive assault. Susan herself had been raised in a socially reclusive family; her parents were modest and reticent people who cultivated in their children the sense that the world outside of the family was dangerous and needed to be avoided. She was unable to recall a single instance when her family socialized with outsiders, and even gatherings with extended family members were extremely rare. She was raised to be courteous, but guarded and vigilant of the potential onslaught of negative outside influence. In her own treatment, Susan recollected an anxiety-filled childhood in which she was in continual fear of being humiliated for possible bad behaviors. Specifically, she was concerned about the manifest expressions of her frustration, and the management of her anger. She had always had difficulty in soothing herself and managing affective transitions. Her parents had been authoritarian in their approach and had provided little guidance in helping her to manage stressful experience. By the age of 5, she was unduly intolerant of her own difficulty in accomplishing the tasks at which her older brother was already proficient. When she became frustrated and overtly expressed anger, her parents would banish her to her room for hours

until she was able to calm herself on her own. They provided no soothing through verbal, physical, or emotional engagement, leaving Susan feeling abandoned and rageful. In her therapy sessions she associated these episodes with a deep sense of personal shame, an intense drive to control herself, and a need to limit her contact with others lest she have humiliating outbursts of emotion. The family's emotional range was highly constricted, and effusiveness of any kind, even joyousness, was discouraged as unseemly.

Eventually, during her high school years, Susan suffered a serious depression that required psychiatric intervention. Subsequent to this, the treatment was never referred to in the family and her condition never discussed. However, Susan harbored persistent fears that she would relapse into her previous depressive state. She perceived the depression as another reflection of how emotions can become overwhelming and impede functioning. She was only occasionally able to see the episode as a desperate and valiant protest against her own inhibition and emotional deadening.

Susan had begun psychotherapy for severe anxiety attacks. After three years of intensive treatment the anxiety significantly abated and the therapy was concluded. She returned to the therapist after the birth of her second child, and began parent therapy. She felt deep concerns that her own emotional experience might impede a smooth transition to her expanding family. Specifically, despite the fact that she and her husband were educated and ostensibly prepared for parenting, she worried that she had unrealistic expectations of maturity from her 3-year-old Aiden. This was not only an apparent replication of her childhood concerns about herself, but it seemed to predispose Susan to perceiving her son's behavior as literally dangerous, and attempting to control the perceived destructive affect. The therapist, in deference to Susan's tentativeness, offered gentle invitations to reveal her concerns, and eventually Susan reported having great apprehension about her son's aggressive behaviors. She proceeded to describe a variety of aggressive acts, ranging in degree from fantasy play to verbal attacks and physical assaults on the younger sibling. For Susan, all of these behaviors were equally disturbing because of their aggressive content. She was as alarmed by Aiden's aggressive fantasy play as she was by his actual violence. Almost as disturbing to her was her own limited repertoire in handling her son, with whom she had always shared such tender affection. Although she did not subject Aiden to the hitting that she had herself experienced as a child, she did exile him to his room for protracted periods of time. At these moments she would also become identified with her son's sense of abandonment and rage, and consequently would enter his room to offer soothing embraces. The child invariably responded with great relief, and she would then explain why he had been banished.

This scenario was played out over a period of months, with no apparent change in Aiden's behavior, before Susan sought assistance from her former psychotherapist. She had been considering other measures to curb his aggression, including the extreme recourse of medication. Both parents were becoming increasingly alarmed and began to consider his behavior highly pathological. They were particularly disturbed, for example, that when his father left for work in the morning, Aiden pretended to shoot him. They admonished him and tried vigorously to instruct him about the malevolence of guns. At this point in the consultation the therapist inquired about what might occur if Aiden's father "played along," pretending to be shot, thereby engaging the son's fantasy. Susan was shocked, never having considered indulging, or "playing with" the aggressiveness. Aiden's father, also shocked, was nonetheless curious, and tentatively engaged the child in this play. He and Aiden, to their mutual surprise, began to enjoy the rough and tumble play and mock displays of aggression. The therapist's suggestion was designed to transform some of the unvoiced anger and aggressive affect into the safer expression of contained play. In this way, play served the function of detoxifying confusing and unmetabolized aggression. Aiden was able to voice his anger toward his father through fantasy, seeing his father tolerate, "survive," and even enjoy, the adversarial interaction. As in play therapy, internal aggression, ambivalence, and anger could be safely expressed, yet, unlike play therapy, it was relationship building within the family, and further served to fortify positive experience between parent and child. In addition, it did not engender the residual guilt feelings that can sometimes result from children's expressed hostility with ancillary adults, nor did it have the emotional repercussions that arise from the exclusion of parents from the therapeutic process.

Susan, through the discussions with the therapist, began to recognize that she had actually been banishing Aiden to his room in order to arrange a "time-out" for herself. The therapist asked several questions about how Susan envisioned Aiden's affective state when he was first in his room, and what she imagined contributed to his ability to calm down. They then shifted to a focus on Susan's own correlative experience: How did *she* feel at the outset of the banishment? Did she too calm down? To what did she attribute her capacity to regain sufficient composure in order to enter Aiden's room? In this way, Susan and the therapist were able to establish just how disruptive these episodes were for Susan herself. Following this consultative work, she began to be more explicit with her children, explaining that she needed to calm down after so much fighting. She was delighted at her own ability to shift sets. She was equally delighted at how startled her children were at the introduction of their mother's subjective experience. These interventions were so effective that the children were able, each time they were used, to make more fluid transitions to more cooperative behaviors. In addition to the changes in Aiden's interactive style, these playful moments brought great pleasure to Susan. She reflected on her own family, the ethos that had emphasized work and seriousness of purpose had simultaneously denigrated all play as childish. When these thoughts emerged in the consultation, the therapist helped Susan to view play not as frivolous and wasteful but as essential to the business of growth and development, and to realize that her play with her children could be useful and enriching. What followed in her parenting was a new inclination to engage in translating some of Aiden's unprocessed conflicts. She was able to see his aggressive behavior as an attempt to communicate, much as her adolescent depression had been. She was then able to provide the metabolizing function of discussing with him some of his rage and his sense of loss around the birth of his younger sibling and his mother's return to full-time employment.

This therapy served to consolidate some of the achievements from Susan's previous individual treatment. Her newly acquired playfulness with her children helped her to establish a sense of herself as an adult who could provide guidance for her son, partly because she could see herself as both identified with and separate from him. It is important to note, in reflecting on Aiden's aggressive behavior, that at school his teacher's concerns emphasized his anxiety and his tendency to withdraw, and even to be victimized by more aggressive peers. Susan reported that his school had contacted her to discuss a potential therapy referral for what they perceived as Aiden's extreme social anxiety. The therapist understood his behavior to be contextual and to have a multiplicity of meanings, many of which were interpersonally induced and created. She conceptualized his anxiety as a pervasive attempt to control affective expression. The aggression could then be seen as his reaction to the tension created by his own overcontrol of angry expression. Aiden's anger about his mother's return to full-time work, temporally coupled with his sister's increasing demands for parental attention, created a chronic fear of his own rage, because he had never known an acceptable outlet for the safe expression of negative affect. Like his mother before him, Aiden was able to manifest some of this tension through his aggressive behavior at home; in the context of the outside world, he had internalized his family's prohibitions against the expression of negative affect, and was thus overly reserved and anxious at school. The therapist intervened around the family ethos and psychic climate rather than the individual symptom. The idea was to liberate some of the general inhibition in order to relieve Aiden's tension.

In this context it becomes clear that behaviors have multiple meanings and manifestations, and that it is essential, in understanding individual behavior, to consider the particular meaning that is embedded in the relational context of the child's experience. This discussion has in no way exhausted the possible configurations of the meaning of aggressive behavior in children, but rather has demonstrated how multifaceted these behaviors can be in the light of a given interpersonal context. We have highlighted here only one aspect in the treatment of this family's concerns, for the purposes of explicating the usefulness of the parent therapy model.

Let us now look at some aspects of a family constellation which reflect patterns of *undercontrol* of a child's behavior, ultimately leading to aggressive acting out. We focus here only on an elaboration of dynamic themes in the relational dyad of a father and son, although many other relational issues are also at play. We will then return to the process of the consultation.

Julio was an 8-year-old whose parents were frequently contacted by his school with concerns about his conduct. He was reported to be persistently rude, obstreperous, and generally unmanageable. He left his seat at will, defied classroom rules, called out disruptively, and frequently failed to complete assignments. At the request of the school, Julio's parents brought him for a psychological evaluation. At the first meeting, Julio's father, Mr. J., was apprehensive about the evaluation process and about the school's estimation of his son's behavior. He considered Julio to be a lively, sometimes rambunctious youngster who exhibited the normal behaviors of a vigorous and independent child. He was, however, tentatively, willing to pursue an evaluation of his son. The following information was derived from the psychological assessment and a detailed inquiry into the family history.

The father's history seemed to be notable in elucidating certain aspects of his son's behavior. He was raised in a patriarchically organized family in which his own father had had an autocratic authority over his wife and children. Mr. J.'s father had undergone extreme hardships and had adaptively become accustomed to living independently of social rules in order to survive in a dangerous environment. After emigrating to the United States, he married, and later in life, when he became a father, he was a volatile, tough, and at times abusive parent to Mr. J. Julio's father had suffered much fear of and physical abuse from his own father; however, in a defensive identification with him, he came to idealize power and even unconsciously to see it as heroic. An aggressive and domineering character was what had made Mr. J.'s father's very survival possible, and he was, as a result of subsequent successes, quite revered by others. Iconoclastic power and the authority that was revered in his culture were also mythologized by the family in the service of self-preservation and self-aggrandizement.

Mr. J. was identified in his own family as being quite like his father, and it was this identification that freed him from his earlier intimidation and enhanced his self-esteem in adulthood. In this context, Julio's behavior, equated with power and efficacy, was unconsciously supported by Mr. J. The child who was able to defy authority received, at least covertly, admiration for his strength and virility. Moreover, just as Mr. J. had been likened to his father, Julio, too, was intensely identified with his father. From the beginning, he was considered to be temperamentally more like his father—intense, demanding, and needy of attention. This attribution was curiously absent from Julio's brother, who was not perceived as tough and audacious, but was considered socially poised and gracious. From a relational pont of view, this might be understood as the different ways in which projections of self representations and identifications evolve. Through a variety of factors, including appearance, temperament, and birth order, children identify with particular parental attributes, and parents potentially project different qualities onto each child.

Psychological testing revealed that beneath the surface of Julio's toughness there was considerable fragility, and his concealed feelings of vulnerability were thinly veiled over by his defensive bravado. It seemed clear that, at some level, Mr. J.'s disavowed feelings of humiliation and powerlessness, originally suffered under the authoritarian abuses of his own father's domination, were unconsciously understood by Julio. Not only did Julio need to defend himself from the anxiety of helplessness, he believed that he could gain approval from and symbolically rescue his father through adopting a powerfully defiant stance. However, what made this situation a difficult and conflictual terrain for Julio to negotiate emotionally was that the child's defiance was also sometimes turned toward the parents, and at these times became emotionally threatening to the father's tenuous sense of power. When Julio became belligerent with his father, he ignited the old feelings of frustration and impotent rage that Mr. J. had in childhood felt toward his own father. In this way, the child was placed in what might be considered a double bind: he found himself in the untenable position of attempting to preserve an attachment to his father through the assumption of defiant power, yet destroying the attachment because of the father's own need to assert himself. What ultimately brought things to a critical point was an indication that Julio might be asked to leave the school. The administrative and clinical staff felt that Julio might be in need of medication to control his behavior, which they believed most likely resulted from a neurologically based attention-deficit disorder.

Ultimately, these parents sought the counsel of the evaluating psychologist in order to comply with the school's requests. In the therapist's office, they described their son as exuberant and highly gifted, and disparaged the school's concern. What was at play in this view were the parents' narcissistic defenses; the need to ward off any negative evaluation of their child obscured from their consideration the anxiety and depression that underscored Julio's bravado. As he did in relation to his own father, Mr. J. rejected the school's judgment as foolishly authoritarian and oblivious to his son's special talents. He also felt rejected and unappreciated himself, since he had always made himself available for school events and felt that he had contributed significantly to the life of the school. When he was threatened by the external demands and judgments of the school, he reexperienced the tyrannical presence of his father and responded with defensive rebelliousness.

One major difficulty in the consultation was Mr. J.s inability to make fluid shifts from one feeling state to another, and this affected the constancy of his judgments and perceptions. He saw Julio as defenseless and victimized by the school's evaluations, or, alternatively, saw him as incorrigible when he was disobedient at home. Julio, in turn, was often poised between the two conflicting positions of defiance and compliance, and was unable to integrate the two into a more modulated response to authority. Like his father, he was trapped in a projected narcissism that, when injured by criticism, turned to humiliation and narcissistic rage.

The therapist first attempted to locate an intermediary space for the parents; because of the tenuousness of Mr. J.'s ability to remain in one intersubjective configuration regarding his child, the consultation had to be especially supportive. The school's pressure for Julio to be seen for treatment and/or medication was received by both parents with anxious hostility. The therapist supported the use of the evaluation as a useful intervention; it could produce measurable diagnostic results and help them generate a more reasoned disagreement with the school, and could also enhance their understanding of Julio's behavior.

The results of Julio's assessment were productive insofar as they indicated no attention deficit and no recommendation for medication. The parents felt bolstered by the evaluation and supported by clinical authority. The therapist was then able, through an alliance with them, to suggest something about Julio's subjective psychic experience and what might be some of the issues that were influencing his behavior. But most important was the therapist's encouragement of the parents' prerogative in establishing rules in their family for their own children. In pointing out Mr. J.'s identification with Julio as another victim of arbitrary authority, the therapist explained that Julio's rebellion gave them both a sense of power. She was able to create a bridge, a holding together, of previously shifting and irreconcilable states: the feeling that Julio was a misunderstood brilliant and gifted child, and that Julio was a "bad" insolent child. With these perceptions kept split apart from each other, the parents had only two equally untenable choices: they felt themselves to be either adversaries of the school or adversaries of their son's playfulness and creativity. The parent therapy helped them to see their child as both bright and charming, yet narcissistically vulnerable and defensive.

Julio's father, like Susan in our previous case, was so anxious about his son's difficulties and what they represented that, unlike with Susan, it was too great a struggle to address problems directly with him. With Susan, the therapist had been able to discuss, directly, the anxiety around her child's behavior. Julio's father, in contrast, oscillated between two opposing perceptions, making a more flexible understanding of his child more difficult and therefore requiring a different approach entirely. The therapist, in working with the parents and with Julio's school, became a transitional object between the various and conflicting perspectives: the parents and the school, the mother and father, and the father's identifications with his son's energetic, lively nature and his obstreperous defiance. In this case, the therapist emerged as the embodiment of a transitional space that could alleviate the tension between each duality. For Mr. J., whose affective transitions were especially brittle, simply participating in a process in which the therapist was able to maintain this cognitive bridge was a developmental step and an encouraging experience. He was able to soften his defensive stance sufficiently to recognize that although his son could be funny and entertaining, in some contexts his behavior was inappropriate and rude. He realized that the same behavior, depending on circumstance, has a variety of meanings and that, looked at from different perspectives, could have different interpretations.

These vignettes underscore the salient features in the development of some forms of aggressive behavior and the intrapsychic and interpersonal contexts in which they emerge. These patterns and events are necessarily oversimplified for the purpose of our discussion, and we have often alluded only to a single element of one parent's personal history in order to explicate the ways in which relational sequences may become established. Despite the fact that the significance of most behaviors cannot be explained so simply, this consultative paradigm can nonetheless effect major shifts in familial and individual experience. In this way it resembles the supervisory process in psychotherapy, during which not every issue in a particular treatment needs to be explored.

IV
Treatment Referrals

10
Divorce

*D*ivorce is an understandably difficult experience for children, and families are often particularly mindful of the resulting emotional repercussions. What is most ameliorative for the child's natural confusion, however, may be a matter of some ambiguity. What seems to be particularly problematic for youngsters who are experiencing their parents' divorce is the very pronounced concern that they are in some way, however indirectly, responsible for the rupture of the marriage. One 9-year-old girl, whose parents were divorcing, confided earnestly to her mother that she indeed felt personally implicated in the breakup. She stated, "I know that psychologists have this theory that children might feel that they caused their parents' divorce; but what if it's really true?" As in many anxious convictions, there is some truth to the child's concerns. What may exacerbate these concerns is the overzealous drive to place the child in psychotherapy, which, despite motivations to the contrary, may heighten the child's sense of having caused the divorce. The child may feel something bad has happened to him and he is therefore sent to a therapist. This may conceivably consolidate the feeling that something about the child himself has influenced the dissolution of the family structure. In this way, the child's already burdensome grandiosity, in regard to the divorce, is intensified by the nature of the treatment, which concomitantly may also replicate the altered relationship with the parents, who may both encourage the child's private or even secret communications with each of them. Often, psychotherapy may evoke the same internal conflict and ambivalence: a presumably benign adult is available to the child in order to facilitate the expression of feelings. However, this process may support a perception of the child as victimized and damaged by the parents' life decisions. Moreover, it may sacrifice the child's opportunity to generate a stronger individual relationship with each parent, insofar as psychotherapy is predicated on an exclusive relationship with an adult who stands outside of the family.

Individual child treatment often fails to solve one of the crucial problems that emerges between divorced parents. The animosity that is felt for the estranged spouse regrettably can often be projected or displaced onto the child. When this does occur, the parents become unconsciously invested in perpetuating the child's problems because those problems come to represent an indictment of the other parent. Highlighting the child's acting out or depression, through the child's individual treatment, may therefore serve to fuel each parent's repudiation of the other, and through a process of attribution each is seen as blameworthy. Both parents then attempt to cure in the child what is hated in the other parent, and one's own parenting then becomes an antidote to the "bad" parenting of the other. Moreover, in an attempt to disengage from each other, the parents can reverse all previously felt affection and denigrate the life and values that they had maintained as a couple.

One mother of a divorcing couple, who, for the sake of her marriage, had converted to Judaism and had become a vegetarian, immediately introduced meat into her children's diet, gave up all previously practiced Jewish ritual, and celebrated Christmas for the first time during the year following the divorce. Her drive to separate from her ex-husband and reestablish some autonomous experience left her children confused and divided between two powerfully demanding affiliations. The mother's actions were castigated by the father, who attributed the children's distress to her behavior, and the father's concerns were faulted by mother for their anxiety-producing overprotectiveness.

Too often divorced parents become competitive with each other, and in the drive to be the exclusive provider of good parenting unconsciously maintain a conviction about the "badness" of the other, which is then perceived as something symptomatic in the child. Through this unconscious need, not only is the child's symptom, or perceived symptom, perpetuated, but also there may be a prolongation of anxiety for the child. Some children, in their identification with the "condemned" parent, will internalize an aspect of the negative attribute in an anxious attempt to protect that parent. This can consequently create negative self representations for the child. Others will develop anxiety around feeling pulled into a condemnation of one parent, and still others will develop symptoms in order to ameliorate the tension and disputation of their warring parents.

One family came to a consultation about their 6-year-old son who was not yet fully toilet trained. The parents approached the problem in ways that bolstered their respective criticisms of each other. Thus, the father saw this developmental immaturity as a result of the mother's infantilization, and the mother attributed it to the father's pressure and his own constriction and rigidity. From the child's perspective, it is likely to be a way of constructing a compromise between the two major opposing forces in his life, and also a way of keeping them both present in a particular way. In other words, by keeping himself a baby, this child was able to sustain the fantasy that his parents would stay together; the act of preoccupying themselves on behalf of dealing with his symptom provided him with the illusion, or the actuality, that the symptom continued to bind them to each other since it required them to engage with each other on a daily basis.

Two of the effects of divorce that prove to be so deleterious to children's emotional comfort are the conflict between their parents and the loss of the noncustodial parent (Wallerstein and Blakeslee, 2000, Wallerstein, 1980). From this perspective it is safe to say that the alienation felt between the parents represents the greatest threat to the emotional life of the child insofar as it subjects the child to intense arguments, interpersonal tension, and considerable separation fear. One youngster, who was placed into therapy by conscientious parents who were in the midst of a divorce, revealed to the therapist that he felt okay about the divorce but what was deeply troubling to him was his fear that his parents would actually kill each other or do one another bodily harm. In cases such as these, the parent consultation is particularly advantageous, because it is a vehicle through which both parents can deconstruct their own fears about the other's hostilities, which, without external support, may threaten to create undue anxiety for the child.

In these situations it is important for the parent therapist to enter into an alliance with the protective parts of each parent in order to minimize this tendency for parents to aggrandize their own parental virtue by exaggerating the other's "badness." The goal, in part, is to create shifts in the particular relational matrices that have grown up through warding off the perceived aggression of the other parent. It is through the therapist's neutrality, or capacity to hold simultaneously two opposing views and affective experiences in consciousness, that each parent can feel fortified and relieved. Each parent is strengthened by the part of the therapist that is able to see his or her perspective, and in this way can be further motivated toward the best interests of their child. With the introduction of a neutral person, the parental disagreements can be reconfigured so that the approach of each parent can be understood as a desire to help the child, rather than criticized as a deficiency. When each parent is seen as earnestly attempting to do "good," the gap between the parents can be bridged. Thus, in the parent therapy paradigm, each parent's narcissistic needs can be mobilized in ways that are most beneficial for the child. Furthermore, because the divorced parent no longer has a partner, and because so much of parenting involves collaborative partnership, the parent therapist is able to perform certain functions similar to those of a collaborative helper, such as disengaging the parent from an intensely felt concern or vulnerability. Parents are then helped to think about their behavior in ways that they can see as beneficial for their children.

The consultative paradigm has another important advantage—the capacity to engage patients in multiple ways. Thus, when the gap between estranged parents is too great and does not seem amenable to easy repair, the therapist has the advantage of seeing each parent individually. This ability to shift from the dyad to the individual and back again expands the arena of therapeutic intervention and clinical possibilities. When the therapist works with the individual parent, it is often possible to elicit greater empathy for the ex-spouse because, in the absence of the rival, defensiveness can be diminished, and there is therefore less tendency to intensify and rigidify a particular position. The therapist's support of each individual may allow the parents to see the other more benevolently.

However, in the absence of this dynamic shift, when benevolence cannot be achieved, the consultative treatment model can actually capitalize on parents' competitive feelings with each other in the service of promoting more helpful parental behaviors. It is the flexibility of the model that allows the parent therapist to make alliances with each parent respectively, and to exploit the need for the preservation of a positive self-image. For example, one mother, reflecting on her parental attitude during the years subsequent to her divorce, acknowledged her own need to feel that she was the more virtuous parent. This need emerged in the context of a broader characterological pattern, but was additionally fueled by her guilt over having instigated the marital breakup. It often feels pressingly important for parents in this position to defensively ward off the anger that children might feel toward the parent who is perceived as responsible for the dissolution of family life. In these instances, the consultant can redefine "virtuousness" as the desire to facilitate a positive relationship with the other parent for the sake of the child. Many parents can be helped to understand that, ultimately, when their children mature, they too will recognize and appreciate this effort.

Let us look at the course of treatment in a traditional play therapy approach in which the therapist sees the child for regular weekly visits and supplements this with collateral visits with the parents. This individual treatment was eventually reorganized into a parent consultation in order to address the predominant relational issues in the child's life.

Hal, 7 years old, was referred for treatment by the psychologist at his school; he was repeatedly sent to the principal's office and was becoming a management problem. He was inconsolable when he felt unable to accomplish an assignment, and would become disruptive and aggressive as a result. He was the son of divorced parents who were rather contentious with each other and not only had very different parenting styles but also were critical of the other's approach. Hal's father and stepmother were committed to providing Hal with a structured and consistent environment that they believed would enhance his sense of security and decrease his acting out behavior. Routines and behavioral consequences became urgent considerations for them because Hal was often difficult to manage. Hal's mother traveled a good deal for her professional acting career and felt more flexible in her parenting style; she tended to be less committed to routines such as formal meals and set times for doing things. Both parents agreed that the mother was significantly better able to soothe Hal when he was distressed. However, Hal spent half of the week at his father's home, and when his moods were difficult to regulate his father would become distressed by the child's volatility.

Hal's course of treatment was dynamically organized play therapy; in his weekly sessions he repeatedly and obsessively acted out extremes of his anxiety, constructing dangerous and terrifying fantasies in which he was rescued by his own ingenuity and the assistance of the therapist. Rage against any ineptness on the part of the therapist was also continually expressed, and the slightest in-fraction, manifested by a minor variation in routine, was severely punished. Persistent attempts to project and then control his uncom-fortable internal experience were manifested by fantasy play in which he would poison or imprison the therapist. On one occasion the therapist made the interpretation that Hal wanted to put into her all of the badness he felt inside of himself, and, with exquisite under-standing, Hal agreed that that was correct; he confessed that what he wanted more than anything was to be able to feel "goodness" inside. However, despite his own ability to recognize some of the aspects of his distress, much of the parental conflict persisted and continued to have repercussions for his complex internal dynamics. Hal's already conflicted sense of self, exacerbated by the real divisions in his object world, remained a source of anxiety and confusion. Each of Hal's parents was earnest and devotedly loving, yet, despite this, they were unable to prevent the transmission of their own deeply felt anxieties, when Hal often needed them to see him as a separate person with his own unique anxieties.

Because of these particular dynamics it seemed to the thera-pist that a parent therapy model would be most useful and effective as a treatment modality for Hal. What was complicating for the family was the fact that the father had a younger sister who has suffered from a pervasive developmental disorder. In consequence he had often felt overlooked because of his parents' preoccupying concerns and felt pulled in conflicting directions by the press of his own needs and concern for his sister and parents. Ultimately he often had to contain his own anxiety with a precocious sense of maturity. Hal's lability and emotional distress thus became particularly disturbing for his father and, in the consultative sessions, the father was able to identify them as associated both with his sister's odd behaviors and with his anxiety and guilt around the transmission of "bad" genes. The consultant, in exploring the father's anxiety, wondered whether it was in part this anxiety that caused Hal to turn to his mother for comfort even when she was out of town or during stressful episodes when he was separated from her. It was further suggested that both parents were caught in internally driven projections to which Hal responded and perpetuated in his own way. At the inception of the therapy Hal's mother voiced her conviction that Hal could be easily soothed and her concern that his father was not sufficiently empathic; the intensity of her focus on her ex-husband's rigidity and empathic failures led the therapist to believe that these served some defensive function for her, allowing her to deny some of her son's problems. The therapist proposed this defensiveness as a possible obstacle to empathizing with the concerns that her ex-husband expressed. When the father, on the other hand, voiced his concerns about Hal's unruliness, the therapist suggested that he might sometimes magnify his son's problems, both as a criticism of his ex-wife's casualness, and in association to his own sister.

As the consultation evolved, the particular dynamics that emerged for Hal's father centered around his own previously unconscious conflicts. In the consultative relationship, the psychologist explored the father's feelings about his own position in the family matrix as it was now constituted. In reflecting on his affective experience, he spoke about his sense of being pulled in two different directions by powerful but opposing forces; what was further elucidated through the discussions was that this conflict was in part a replication of some of the tensions he had felt earlier in his life in a family dealing with the prolonged trauma of developmental impairment. His wife and ex-wife listened intently and became more empathic than they had previously been in regard to his hesitancy and indecisiveness. This empathic response served the purpose of shifting the emotional tenor in the room. The women even joked that they themselves were the powerful forces that he felt swayed by. Hal's father was then more explicit about his conflicts; he felt torn between his wife and Hal's mother, sometimes between Hal and his ex-wife, sometimes between Hal and his wife. What was emphasized by the therapist, and became a primary focus of the sessions, was that Hal felt much the same way. He also felt caught in the grip of unconscious but powerful interpersonal forces acting on him, not only in disregulating ways, but in ways that profoundly affected his sense of himself as integrated and cohesive.

The therapist explored the idea that when Hal was identified with his mother in his drive for flexibility, he felt bad about disappointing his father, and when he needed for his mother to recognize more of his psychic pain, he sometimes felt that he had to protect her in her desire to perceive him as just a normal kid. In addition, when he felt especially troubled, he became concerned that he was creating an anxious situation for his father and stepmother, and sought soothing from his mother. But this often pushed him into a self state of anxious dependency. The therapist was also able to clarify for the parents that, for Hal, what occurred was the emergence of an anxiety about being anxious; his anxiety was so distressing for each of his parents that they had difficulty in providing a holding environment for his multiple and conflictual self states and confusing feelings. His parents' concerns about each other had profound effects on Hal's capacity for self cohesion. The therapist believed that when Hal was criticized at school, for example, he was unable to call forth an internal sense of security and reassurance, which would have allowed him to maintain his equilibrium. He thus became affectively overwhelmed. The parental projections and their reservations about each other left Hal in a state of heightened disintegration and self-doubt. In addition, when he felt an attachment to and alliance with one parent, he was left with feelings of disloyalty in relation to the other, and vice versa.

For a child, maintaining a cohesion among multiple self states and object relations remains a difficult task, and the capacity to coherently organize self and object representations becomes a developmental achievement. In marital separations that are dominated by conflict, the heightened splits between the parents may lead to even greater experiences of self fragmentation in the child.

What was most effective in helping Hal to emerge as a more integrated and self-accepting person was for the therapist to meet with all three parents and engage them in an exploration of their concerns about Hal. The therapist asked them to discuss their disappointments and hopes directly with each other.

Hal's stepmother was able to share her belief that, although she felt deeply sympathetic toward her stepson, he often made their interactions difficult by making her feel like the wicked stepmother. She felt that she was an easy target, owing in part to the fact that she was not a biological parent, and his attachment to her was more tenuous and more ambivalent as it was charged with jealousy and guilt. However, when she married Hal's father she also entered this new family with her own expectations of family life. She had a daughter from a previous marriage who was quite compliant and self-contained, and she began, through her own parenting style, to introduce greater structure and discipline into the act of parenting.

Hal's mother expressed distress about the fact that she felt that her work schedule was an area of conflict in the family; she often felt humiliated by her sense that she was perceived as a bad mother. In her own defense she expressed the feeling that Hal's father and stepmother placed too much pressure on him and exerted too much control over him. She perceived her own approach as flexible and relaxed rather than negligent, and argued that what Hal needed was greater autonomy and self regulation. Hal's father expressed his feeling that structure and consistency were important for their son and felt that Hal benefited greatly when his mother was consistently available. Not surprisingly, the therapist stood equidistant between the extreme positions, but more importantly she understood that the parents tended to intensify their positions in opposition to each other and in defense of their own ideas.

Another way in which Hal's parents were polarized was in their respective levels of identification with their son. In the sessions each parent's particular identifications were explored. Mother realized that she felt so deeply identified with Hal that she was sometimes unable to establish an adequate perspective on his contentiousness with other people. She reflected on her own attitudes toward particular events, most notably some of his difficulties at school. She came to the conclusion that she frequently fortified his more defensive behaviors by feeling so protective that she tended to perceive problems, often, as externally driven and circumstantial, exactly the way Hal did, perhaps originally, in an identification with her. Following this, Hal's father was asked to reflect on his experience, and he expressed his feeling that perhaps he was underidentified with Hal; in this regard, he believed that he was so determined to be fair-minded, and was so concerned about his ex-wife's constant defense of their son's belligerent behaviors, that he was often left feeling unable to support Hal. In his own estimation, he was intent on promoting egalitarian values and wanted all sides to be explored. The parent therapy was able to effectively unravel and address many of these issues, as well as the persistent feelings of isolation and disapproval felt by both Hal's mother and stepmother as a result of their co-parenting arrangements.

The parent therapy was effective precisely because the therapist was able to assume a position that was simultaneously containing for all three parents. Each seemed to have a genuine interest in and empathy for Hal, and this was the most highlighted aspect of the interrelations in the joint sessions. Only when the mutually reproachful positions could be understood as expressions of anxiety, related to real concern for their son, were all three parents amenable to and prepared for reconfigurations of their roles. The therapist encouraged them to shift the particular ways in which they had become polarized. Their awareness of their identifications, explored and acknowledged in the consultative sessions, loosened their defenses and allowed them to attempt new approaches to their parenting. The mother then felt more comfortable in assuming a greater share of the discipline, and the father and stepmother felt encouraged to assume roles that were more supportive of Hal. While this work does somewhat resemble other types of work with families around divorce, it should be stressed that it was more consistent with the supervisory model. When the transition was made from play therapy to parent therapy, the framework was redefined to include the parents in a more fully collaborative role and to incorporate the idea that the parents, with support, would ultimately be the more effective therapists for Hal. This stance helped to promote an atmosphere of cooperation among the parents as they were, in effect, defined as being part of a treatment team.

One aspect of adult development bears on this discussion and on the choice of treatment plan for a youngster in Hal's position. For adults, the retrospective construction of childhood experience into a coherent life narrative can take place in the therapeutic setting; they can use the relational context of that situation to foster and facilitate self integration. But for children, who are locked in the immediacy of their affective experience, an integrated sense of self is far more difficult to achieve. A child who is disappointed and enraged with a parent, for example, may be unable to keep in mind that he may soon again experience that same parent as a reliably comforting or playful person. The sudden shifts in affect can feel unmitigated, and each affective state can feel like a permanent condition; it becomes the task of the environment to assist the child in maintaining a sense of coherence among these states. In the context of divorce, when the environment has been split, emotionally and logistically, it is even more difficult for the child to develop a sense of a cohesive self. Both the conflicting loyalties and attachments and the increased burden of attuning to the conflicted perceptions and demands of the parents make it that much more difficult for the child to direct energy toward the development of self integration. Children often express this felt disequilibrium through manifest anxieties about the concrete disarray in their lives: where their favorite clothes and toys are, where their homework was left, or who will be picking them up from school. In this regard it becomes essential for the therapeutic situation to serve as a holding environment for the parents. In the context of feeling understood and "held," the parents can extend their capacities for holding and caring empathically for their child, and can achieve a measure of awareness about what will be most manageable for their children.

Even in the most amicable marital separations, the child's object world will be markedly altered or disrupted. Younger children are particularly vulnerable to the confusions created by the shifts in marital status and in parent–child relations. At some point in divorcing families, the personal fulfillment of each parent will move into the foreground of family life, in ways that disrupt the child's sense of unitary and cohesive family priorities. For example, children can find it confusing and troubling when they become cognizant of their parents' marital dissatisfaction, as this puts into bold relief the individual needs of the parents. For children, who have previously felt their own needs to be central in family life, their parents' emotional and sexual satisfaction has now taken center stage. There may also be some competition between the separated parents around custodial responsibility for the children; the drive for greater freedom and flexibility of scheduling that accompanies a new and different social life for each parent may leave youngsters feeling that the parents are moving on to other, more preferred company, and that their own care is becoming increasingly precarious. This is often literally the case, as many divorced parents date and remarry, and have other children, sometimes without adequately integrating their older children into their new families. All of this intensifies children's awareness of their parents' subjective experience and of the aspects of their parents' lives that exclude them.

For children who are attempting to retain a maximal degree of constancy, these relational shifts may be greatly disturbing and disorienting. They may stimulate or reinforce fears of abandonment, or an overabundance of concern or guilt, depending on a child's age, temperament, and ongoing familial relationships.

One adult patient, reflecting retrospectively about his experience of family life during the years after his parents' divorce, poignantly described his predicament. Each time one of his parents developed a new romantic relationship, he found himself wishing that they would remarry. He explained how he longed to be in a family with a "mom and dad, my sister, and me." In some sense it did not matter to him who "mom and dad" were; the intense desire for family obscured any individual character of the parental figures. The patient elaborated on his recollections of childhood by adding that this longing created a profound sense of guilt in him, for as soon as he imagined himself to be a part of this idealized family life, he immediately thought of the *other* parent, "the lonely one, despairing and left out in the cold." He would then come to imagine himself as singularly responsible for that parent's happiness. He perceived his parents efforts to engage him in social activities as reflections of their own neediness, and he was thus unable to enjoy his relationship with either one of them when they were unattached. It felt deeply burdensome for this young child to feel that he had to take care of his mother and father in this way. His parents, sensitive to this distress, placed him into psychotherapy; however, this not only failed to ameliorate his anxiety and guilt feelings, but also reinforced his belief that he was the one who needed to resolve problems and address the concerns of others. In his adult treatment the burdensome feelings of responsibility persisted and, as would be expected, pervaded his other relationships. He longed to marry and have his own family, but this desire was often foreclosed by a continued preoccupation with his parents' circumstances and his concern for the stability of their lives. In some real sense, he was unable to relinquish the 5-year-old who felt the unshakable belief that his parents were lonely without each other. We can understand this as a projection of this boy's own loneliness and sense of loss. However, these feelings were not resolved by his therapy, in part because the parents' preoccupying concerns and conflicts did, in fact, often correlate with his concerns about them. This left him in a bind: on the one hand he was valued in part for his attentiveness to his parents emotions; on the other hand, he was expected to move on and not suffer emotionally himself. In either schema, the way in which he responded to his parents' needs simultaneously left other needs unmet. This patient's dilemma highlights the ways in which the individual's own preoccupations are inextricably entangled in a relational matrix.

In these cases, the parent therapy will focus on assisting parents to identify these issues for their children, and resolve some of the concerns about the modifications in each parent's new lifestyle. Clearly, this endeavor can be a difficult and contentious one, but a child whose parents are willing to attempt some resolution of their problems can feel supported in several ways. The child will be able to feel comforted by the fact that the parents are being cared for by someone else, and their disputes are being managed elsewhere. The child may be further comforted by the sense that the parents are working, on his behalf, to ease a traumatic life transition, and this also implies the parents' mindfulness of the impact on him of this transitional experience.

Ultimately, if the estranged parents can engage with each other, this anticipates positive future outcomes, since divorce is accompanied by changes in family structure that will continue to require parental collaboration. Often what is obscured is that, for children, divorce is not simply a transitional episodic event, but an ongoing, continuous, experience that evolves with developmental changes in a child's life. Therefore, issues implicated in the initial phases of the divorce will continue to change as family life evolves, and as the child's relationships within and outside of the family context develop. It is for this reason, most prominently, that placing a child in individual or family treatment at the time of the divorce will be less meaningful and less mutative than parent therapy. It is the parent consultation that can establish the collaborative parenting relationship, the usefulness of which will endure over time.

11
Referrals for Symptomatology

$\mathcal{W}$e have explored thus far some of the consequences of suppressed negative experience, including aggressive acting-out behaviors. Suppressed negative experience can also create symptoms that are common in childhood and resemble more phobic reactions. We can interpret the phobia of Little Hans (Freud 1909) in far more relational terms than Freud did from the perspective of oedipal theory. For Hans, the phobic object, the horse, became a representation of both the unbearable separation from his mother and a punishment for his own angry and aggressive feelings, generated by parental threats of abandonment and punishment. The phobic experience may be seen as one adaptive solution to the child's anxiety over his unacceptable rage and retaliatory wishes. There are many examples in which fear turns to aggression, as was partly the case with Julio (see Chapter 9), whose obstreperousness in school masked his feelings of vulnerability. There are other cases in which aggression, when it feels intolerable and must be denied, may turn to fear. This occurs because both phobias and aggression may serve as defenses against experience that is underscored by projective and identificatory processes, and that threatens to disrupt the cohesiveness of self experience or the experience around primary attachments. The following case describes a process in which rage was transformed into phobic feeling in order to preserve a cohesive sense of self, and an attachment to a parental ideal.

John was a 10-year-old from a rigidly organized family structure; his mother was kindly and permissive, and his father was somewhat more stern and given to outbursts of temper. In both the family and its subculture, respect for parental authority was generally expected; however, in the family in particular, male authority predominated and demanded absolute compliance. On the other hand, Mr. and Mrs. D. were also upwardly mobile and interested in their children's assimilation into the larger culture. Mr. D., though uneducated, was very bright and resourceful and had, on his own, built a successful business. He was eager to raise his children in more progressive ways from the ways in which he had been reared, but was also very concerned about providing a sound moral education for his son. In this regard he tended to condemn any signs of greed, self-aggrandizement, or hostility that he detected in John. He encouraged competition in sports and tournaments, but when John exhibited disappointment over a loss, he was advised not to be a "crybaby" and was encouraged to control any need for self-congratulation or grandiosity.

An incident that was salient in the dynamic life of the family involved one of John's peer relationships. John had befriended an emotionally troubled youngster in the neighborhood, and his relationship with him had become increasingly difficult for John to sustain. When the child visited John he was overly demanding, ruthless, and destructive, and, despite John's graciousness and reserve, he eventually lost patience with the child and retreated from the friendship. Mr. D. was extremely angry and disappointed in John's action and repeatedly castigated his son for discarding a friendship, behavior he believed to be morally reprehensible.

John was an avid reader and had read a rather frightening ghost story in which retribution for one's misdeeds was the predominant theme. John then developed a regressive fear of leaving the company of his parents. He had difficulty going to sleep, and was unable to remain in his bedroom alone at night. He became accustomed to having his mother sit with him until he dozed off, and if he awoke during the night, he would go into his parents' room and sleep on the floor. It was at this point that the parents sought advice from a therapist.

The therapist delayed starting a course of treatment with John individually; she first explored with the parents the structure of the family, the interrelationships, and the parents' perceptions of their son's problem. The consultation thus began with an examination of the parents' thoughts about their children and set the stage for generating ideas about their situation. They described their son as anxious, and their daughter as far more relaxed and less high strung. The therapist focused on this information and on the differences described, questioning the parents about how these differences might have developed. During this discussion the parents themselves began to review how they had been, and continued to be, significantly less demanding and less scrutinizing of their daughter's behavior. When the therapist paused to linger on the meaning of this observation, the parents were able to reflect on their family dynamics and the asymmetry in their approach to each of their children. They also described their daughter as less sensitive to disciplinary acts; she did not seem to feel humiliated or distressed and was not nearly so obedient as their son.

The consultant suggested the possibility that their son's compliant temperament and particular sensitivity to his parents' attitudes correlated with his anxious behavior. Mr. D. began to speculate further about these particular sensitivities and to think about John's response to his affective experience. During subsequent sessions, Mr. D. proceeded to think about ways in which John was identified with Mr. D.'s sense of tension and anxiety, how he tended, like his father, to constrict his feelings, and how he might consistently be straining to control his anger and distress. Following the father's reference to his own difficulty with anger and his tendency toward explosive outbursts, the consultant was able to point out that John might also, through an identification with his father and his desire to remain good and obedient, have considerable unvoiced anger. However, she explained, John had no one to explode at. At this point in the consultation, Mr. D. began to experience feelings of self-doubt and contrition about past incidents and errors he felt he had made in his treatment of his son.

It is important to pause here to consider the intricacies of the consultative moments in which parents express regret over mistakes they feel they have made. As in the supervisory setting, it is the willingness to engage in such exploration that is endorsed and serves to minimize the guilt and shame regarding their behavior. The parent therapist also supports the parents' benign motivations, as in this case in which she focused on Mr. D.'s desire to provide his son with deeply ethical values. It was emphasized that he would do well to continue to educate his son about this moral concern. However, he was also supported in remaining open to the feelings that John was not quite able to openly express, or perhaps to tolerate. Observing that the parents were open to reflecting on the underlying emotional components of their son's symptom, the therapist explained ways in which various feelings, when they are too frightening or disturbing, can convert into behavioral symptoms. She suggested the possibility that the ghost story had evoked for John the idea that the more negative, hostile, or aggressive feelings and impulses that he took pains to repress might be severely punished at some later time.

What seemed to have occurred was that the particularly critical evaluations of John's social and ethical behavior had left him in an extremely ambivalent situation; he was so dutiful and conscientious that he had few means through which he could discharge his less congenial attitudes. He was locked in a relationship in which the expression of a full range of affective experience was met with paternal disapproval. Moreover, his potential anger at parental authority made him especially concerned about his parents' well-being as well as his own. This idea is consistent with Bowlby's (1969, vol. 2) and others insofar as it suggests that separation anxiety is rooted in concern for the parent's safety or, alternatively, in an attunement with parental anxiety. With all of these ideas in mind, the parents were encouraged by the consultant to invite greater emotional expression from their son. Mr. J., in particular, was encouraged to accept an array of responses from him and to play with the idea of exhibiting a more flexible approach in response to the less gracious feelings and moods that John might display.

Many studies (Ainsworth et al. 1978, 1991, Bowlby 1969) have pointed to the correlation between parental rejection and anxious dependency, and the emergence of children's heightened anxiety as a consequence of parental threats to withdraw love. The high correlation between threats of abandonment and the emergence of separation anxiety leads to the theory that it is not the fear of the external object per se that causes phobic reactions, but rather something deeply embedded in the primary relationships in which the child is enmeshed. In other words, just as the horse was not the true object of little Hans's fear, it is, in general, some anxiety-provoking aspect of the relational matrix that eventually becomes anchored in the phobic object. In this regard, it is the expansion of the parents' knowledge and understanding, both of their own fearful reactions and of the projection of their fears onto their children, that can serve as a mitigating force in the phobia.

The exploration of the child's underlying need for parental reassurance can help to alleviate some of the fears that children may be experiencing. For example, the parent who has difficulty in allowing appropriate levels of separation, for numerous reasons such as neediness, loneliness, or social anxiety, may unwittingly create similar anxieties in the child as well. In these cases, the child often absorbs the parent's fears and may need to stay close to the parent in order to maintain a sense of security. Moreover, although the child is clearly implicated as an active participant in this schema, it is the parent's need and anxiety that require amelioration in order to alleviate the child's phobia. The consultative relationship is designed to help the parent resolve such issues, by loosening the fixed relational patterns and identifications in order to provide the child with the capacity to navigate his/her environment more adequately. When this is successfully accomplished, the child can feel free to engage in relationships and activities independent of the family, without a concomitant fear that doing so will result in damage to primary attachment figures or to attachment structures.

John's situation highlights only one of a vast array of dynamic family situations that can lead to phobic reactions in a child. Overall, John was not an unduly anxious child; his phobic symptom was time limited and did not generate difficulties in other areas of functioning, although it did have the potential to create an overall constriction of affective expression. A child with a more severe and chronic phobia would most likely suffer prolonged and multiple repercussions, as in cases of school phobia. In these cases, the separation anxiety, irrespective of etiology, has far-reaching implications that create ancillary problems, such as social humiliation for both child and parents, deepening failures of self-confidence, and disruptions in the academic setting that in turn create additional anxieties for families. In John's case we see a phase-specific anxious period in a child's life that was secondary to a sustained atmosphere of recriminatory attitudes. The paternal guidance here, although intended to promote exemplary ethical behavior, actually propelled the child into an anxiety state. We might predict that without some shift in parental attitudes, John would develop characterological traits of anxiety, guilt, repressed anger, and the potential for dissociated aggression.

More specific phobic reactions may also have far-reaching implications for the child's relational world. Little Hans's phobia can be viewed from many perspectives, and animal phobias continue to be prevalent in contemporary culture. Curiously, they are seen in treatment situations with less frequency than other, more disruptive, symptoms. In some ways, phobias retain an aura of social acceptability, and in many families the phobic symptom emerges in the service of a particular need, just as John's constriction was misconstrued by his parents as courteousness rather than anxiety, and was consequently consistent with the general ethos in the family. Moreover, phobic tendencies tend to create obvious dependencies in children, thereby keeping them close to their families. For many parents, this is not an entirely undesirable occurrence, and may actually satisfy a number of needs for the parents themselves. The dependency, arising from a child's anxieties, allows for an intensification of nurturance and care that often enhances the sense of parental devotion.

The causes of animal phobias are overdetermined, and can range from a single traumatic event such as a dog bite to the projective identification with a parent's fear. This is precisely why it becomes crucial to pursue the parents' attitude toward the phobic object itself, in addition to the relational issues or dynamic configurations that accompany a particular phobia. In many cases the phobia is sustained in part through a parent's identification with the child's fear. It is because the fear is so compatible with the parent's experience that it can be difficult to transform the phobic reaction. In consultations these parental attitudes are easily evoked, because parents often discuss their own childhood fears and anxieties, and sometimes find it difficult to perceive their children's experience as different from their own. Some parents, on the other hand, zealously strive to spare their children from replicating their own anxieties, but the intensity of their concerns, coupled with the conflicts created around them, make it difficult to shield the children from the parents' unconscious feelings and communications. The parent who is afraid of heights wants her child to be spared that fear. However, the sense that heights are actually dangerous is unavoidable because it is a compelling truth for the parent. Moreover, a parent who has difficulty grasping the fact that an acute fear of dogs inhibits or restricts the child's social opportunities may have a limited sense of the importance of unencumbered and uninhibited play, or may actually derive some unconscious comfort and reassurance from the child's anxious clinging. In parent therapy, it is often these underlying parental attitudes toward the child's symptomatology, rather than the symptom itself, that determine the course of treatment.

Because parent therapy focuses on the relational underpinnings of symptoms, rather than the symptoms themselves, we have attempted to explore symptoms in the context of familial relationships. Moreover, there are situations in which developmentally normative behaviors in children are perceived as pathological and, partly in consequence, may evolve into more problematic symptomatology. This is sometimes the case, for example, with children's phase-specific preoccupation with issues of cleanliness and the concomitant interest in messiness. This preoccupation, while common at certain ages, may manifest itself to a greater or lesser degree, depending on the attitudes in the household, as well as the inherent proclivities of the particular child regarding cleanliness and tidiness. The relational matrix surrounding the obsessive cleaning behavior is extremely relevant; whether the 2-year-old's messiness is seen as normal for toddlers, or the intense need for tidiness is pathologized, admired, or promoted, will depend on the parents' values, views, and unconscious predilections. It will also be influenced by the social support system and the roles that have been established in the family for carrying out domestic chores. The comfort that each parent experiences around these chores and around the division of labor may indirectly influence attitudes or generate fears about the children's tendencies toward obsessionalism or obsessive-compulsive disorders, or, alternatively, the inclination toward destructiveness and the subsequent tendency toward violence.

Because behavior occurs so predominantly within a framework that is both interpersonally and intrapsychically determined, a parent's anxiety about her own obsessive-compulsive tendencies may evoke a particular reaction to this phase in her child's life. It is typical that the toddler's intense interest in cleaning will occur in conjunction with the impulse to be messy and to make messes. Parents of toddlers are familiar with the affective and behavioral sequence of fussiness around soiling, and the need to have hands and the high chair washed, only to be followed by the exhilaration of throwing food and soiling. Parents who are already overtaxed by the responsibilities of housekeeping may overstate the degree of messiness, and parents who are frustrated by the child's continual need to tidy up and be washed may worry unduly about their child's compulsiveness. In these contexts, what becomes important is the capacity to place these behaviors in a developmental and relational context. The parent consultant can help parents locate and organize their own thoughts and feelings as well as their understanding of their child's behavior, in such a way as to diminish the emotional intensity about something that is a developmentally driven, phase-specific occurrence rather than a burgeoning characterological vulnerability.

Despite the fact that depression also seems so much a part of internal, intrapsychically generated experience, it very often occurs in and grows out of a relational context, through responses to existing familial reactions to ongoing events and through projective and identificatory processes. In regard to aspects of depression that are supported by relational experience, the treatment of Jennifer (see Chapter 2), the child seen in once-a-week individual therapy following the death of her father, proved to be less than optimal, primarily because her depressive reactions were inextricably tied up with her mother's self and interpersonal experience. Jennifer was understandably distressed over the death of her father; we know from studies on stressful life events that the death of a parent ranks as one of the most traumatic experiences that an individual endures (Alpert, et al. 1983). Nonetheless, in Jennifer's family, her depression, which had extremely debilitating repercussions for her development, seemed to be part of, and was kept in place by, a larger dynamic configuration.

The consultative sessions with Jennifer's mother were extremely valuable, largely because they led to an understanding of some of the parental reactions that were effectively sustaining Jennifer's symptoms. Ms. M. was understandably distressed and preoccupied during her husband's illness. Following his death, and the painful and anguished period of mourning, she once again turned her attention to her young and clearly sensitive and distressed child. She herself was a devoted and loving parent who subsequently became overwhelmed by her sense of guilt around what she realized had been her prolonged emotional unavailability during the critical early years of her child's life. Her general level of stress during this trying period, in which she had to endure her husband's death and simultaneously care for her family on her own, left her feeling emotionally depleted and therefore inadequate to sustain the energy necessary for daily child rearing. In view of this situation, she had immense difficulty in extricating herself and her daughter from an internal and interpersonal atmosphere of dejection. She was herself deeply depressed, not only over her husband's death but also over the plight of her young child. In consequence, she was unable to conceive of Jennifer's experience as anything but a painful and dreary one. This perception of Jennifer was influential in all of her interactions with her daughter. She felt so great a pity and compassion for her, and was so deeply identified with any of Jennifer's transitory experiences of distress, that she was often immobilized in her efforts to help her daughter to stretch herself—to expand her developmental capacities.

Ultimately, Jennifer was falling behind in school and was therefore increasingly withdrawing from daily activities in the classroom. This affected her social experience as well, and she began to engage in more regressive behaviors such as napping during the day and sucking her thumb continually. Thus, Jennifer's depression needed to be understood in the context of regressive tendencies that, though troublesome and painful, allowed the mother, through the projection of her own depression and guilt, to attempt reparations by infantilizing her child. Ms. M. perceived any achievement-oriented challenge as too strenuous for Jennifer, and she therefore did not demand that she do things such as household chores or daily homework. It was through this

dynamic that the depression was, to some degree, iatrogenically created; the child was, in effect, failing to thrive, had few activities that
were sufficiently stimulating, and was too often in a lethargic, nearly
vegetative state.

Curiously, Jennifer was most animated in the one activity that
was seen as pleasurable and therefore not demanding of her, and that
was her singing. She was intensely engaged in numerous music lessons
and performances, and she performed on stage with immense energy
and flair. Ms. M. and Jennifer both took such great pride in this
achievement that they brought performance tapes for the therapist to
view. This was an area of spontaneous activity in which Jennifer could
be freely expressive, owing in part to the fact that the creativity of
music was hers alone, and could not be impinged upon by any projective forces. In this endeavor she was seen as remarkably talented
and, more importantly, capable and competent. She was free to play,
to be a child, and to exert energy. Ms. M. saw the singing as Jennifer's
unique talent, and had no particular identification with it herself.
Because there was no mirror of depression and inadequacy here, it was
an arena in which Jennifer was able to flourish and excel.

In the consultative work, the therapist was able to provide support
and reassurance for the mother, so that, in feeling herself "cared for," she
was able to care for her daughter in a less lonely and depressed manner.
What was also crucial was the therapist's ability to see, through a more
distanced perspective, all of the vitality and competence that Jennifer was
capable of. By achieving different levels of identification and disidentification,
the therapist was able to forge a sense of separateness for mother and child.
When Ms. M. began to see Jennifer as separate from herself, she projected
less of the sense of inadequacy and depression onto her, and was able to
reintroduce vitality into their relationship.

We have approached symptoms, in general, in terms of the relational configurations that support or even create them. Our view of somatic
symptoms follows the same general theoretical presumptions as the other
symptoms we have discussed. In many cases, when children manifest distress somatically, the symptom may serve to express one aspect of a rela-

tionship. It is important, therefore, to examine the surrounding dynamic attributes of their lives. While classical psychoanalytic understanding of somaticization involves the idea that it is a symbolic manifestation of some intrapsychic conflict, this thinking led Freud, to some degree, to the unfortunate interpretation and treatment of Dora's catarrh. Such a position also leaves psychoanalysis in the realm of a one-person psychology. In assuming that the somatic symptomatology is primarily psychogenic or intrapsychic, the relational and interpersonal elements not only may be lost, but also may obscure the very issues that the symptoms are designed unconsciously to convey. In Dora's case, as in many others, the physical symptom was a direct outgrowth of the disturbed relationships in which she was involved.

A 9-year-old girl, for example, lived in a situation in which her brother, who was significantly older, was often left in charge with too much authority and without the judgment of an adult. The girl felt intimidated and abused by him. Eventually, she developed the symptom of picking continually at her skin until it bled. The staff at her school was quite alarmed at such an intense manifestation of anxiety, and indeed the child did suffer considerable internal distress. Nonetheless, this symptom was not simply an internally driven experience but was also a way of conveying unconsciously that she felt "picked on."

This particular kind of communication often occurs with cases of sexual abuse, where the child's terror of discovery and exposure is so great that the only path of communication is through the body. As Van der Kolk (1984, 1987) has pointed out, it is because the experience of sexual abuse is so often dissociated from conscious awareness that the only possible awareness is through body memory.

One young girl who was sexually abused by a family member developed pervasive somatic symptoms that eventually became a partly delusional concern about body damage. At first she complained of persistent stomachaches, which were believed by both school personnel and parents to be related to anxiety. When she began to fail at school, she was transferred to a class for learning-disabled children, where she began to claim that some body part must be broken, sprained, or bruised. She asked repeatedly for the nurse at her school to examine or treat the injuries with bandages, splints, and ointments. No one understood the meaning of her somatic symptoms because their focus remained, unfortunately, fixed on the internal life of the child, without reference to the relational context.

In families where children feel that aspects of a relationship cannot be exposed, the children may develop surreptitious ways of revealing the feelings they have about the experiences to which they are subjected. What occurs somatically, from the outset, is an interaction between physiological vulnerabilities and psychological and environmental occurrences. For example, when a baby is hospitalized and placed on a respirator because of immature lung development, parents will experience intense anxiety about the child's breathing, and this anxiety can persist long after the medical problem has been resolved. In this way, the psychological finds expression in, and also drives, the particular physiological predisposition. Thus, what compounds these situations is that families focus great attention on the manifest physical problems of their children, and the somatic then becomes the conduit for the expression of emotional distress. Ultimately, this distress becomes significant in the child's intrapsychic and interpersonal life. Many theorists have pointed to the communicative and symbolic meaning of somatic symptomatology. Bateson's (Bateson et al. 1956) communication theory, his concept of the double-bind and the schizophrenogenic mother, focused on the impact of a parent's unconsciously ambivalent communication on the psychological development of the child. Minuchin (1974) built on this theory and further addressed structural issues within the organization of families. Both theorists are prominent contributors in shifting the analysis of physical symptoms to the realm of the interpersonal. Minuchin, in particular, explored the hierarchical family arrangements, and the maintenance of boundaries along generational lines, in the emergence and treatment of somatic symptoms. Many others, such as Horney (1937, 1939, 1945), Fromm (1947, 1962), and Sullivan (1953, 1973, 1984), focused attention on the cultural derivations of symptomatology in general. They understood physical manifestations as representations of those feelings that were unacceptable or too frightening to be consciously expressed.

Relational child therapists, as well as family therapists, have long focused on the critical importance of the dynamic interrelations in families in the development of psychosomatic symptoms. Treatment technique is dictated by the theoretical underpinnings adhered to by its practitioners. Nonetheless, relationally informed thinking and systems theory are not always sufficient for optimal psychotherapeutic intervention. What distinguishes parent therapy is its attempt to locate and incorporate the role of the therapist in the relational schema in such a way as to intervene effectively, without further disrupting and impairing the relationships within the family.

Let's explore two cases of relationally informed treatment with adolescents that were ultimately ineffective because the choice of a treatment model had the unfortunate effect of iatrogenically exacerbating some of the symptoms it was enlisted to alleviate. Symptom formation is particularly prevalent in adolescence, a period during which youngsters can experience extremes of distress and confusion. The acting out that is so prevalent among teenagers is well documented in the literature (Blos 1962, A. Freud 1958) as a developmental norm. It can be seen in part as a reaction to the anxiety and ambivalence that is generated by the loss of the prerogatives of childhood and the anticipation of adult responsibility. There is therefore much confusion emanating from the tension between compliance and rebellion. Disobeying the parent and making one's own decisions can produce a sense of autonomy and a euphoric sense of one's own power; however, it also represents the surrender of a certain degree of parental protection, and this is accompanied by a frightening sense of loss. The experience of having one's impulses contained by adult authority is converted, in adolescence, to more mature self regulation. Young children look to the parent to help them contain their impulses, but later on, with the move toward internalizing this capacity, the teenager must relinquish both parental control and containment. The ambivalence that precedes or accompanies this stage is illustrated by the following incident:

A preadolescent girl, in the throes of this ambivalence, tried to solicit her mother's permission to use the profanity that had always been forbidden in the home. Her mother understood the girl's need to experiment with rebellious behavior, but also understood that granting permission would preclude the opportunity for her daughter to forge the necessary independence embodied in adolescent rebellion. This girl, only 11 years old, had not yet established a sufficiently autonomous capacity for practicing independent decision making.

Aspects of the intrapsychic world of the teenager are generally in flux, although, in contrast to earlier childhood periods, self and object representations tend to be largely stabilized. For this reason, choosing a therapeutic modality for the teenager presents a particular problem for the clinician. In attempting to make a prudent decision about an appropriate treatment plan, it is efficacious to consider the situation holistically, that is, to explore the relational issues that are most prominent and that appear to be most critical in the development and persistence of the symptoms. The same or similar symptoms may derive from substantially different relational contexts, may have significantly different meanings, and will therefore require different treatment approaches. It is in this framework that we will explore aspects of two cases in which teenage girls had many of the same presenting problems, with different underlying relational significance. In both cases there was a proliferation of symptoms and diagnoses, which included drug and alcohol abuse, school failure, and premature sexual activity. Both girls were embroiled in intense familial conflict and were, at various times and in various institutions, diagnosed with anxiety disorder, depression, and antisocial personality.

Fifteen-year-old Lisa was treated in family therapy, with two therapists, along with her father, brother, stepmother, and stepbrother. The degree of humiliation for Lisa in this particular situation, was intense; in the family sessions she had difficulty in forming an alliance with the two family therapists, owing to the fact that she was in the presence of her parents, by whom she felt controlled and dominated. Because of the conflicts with her parents, she felt unable to discuss any of her most intimate concerns while they attended these sessions. Her openness with the therapists occurred only when she was alone with them, at which time she revealed that there were many activities that she felt compelled to conceal from her parents. However, despite the problems with the family sessions, Lisa rejected the offer of individual therapy sessions. More often than not, the family sessions were so acrimonious and vituperative that Lisa would storm out of the room spewing curses at the adults. The remaining time was then spent in exploring strategies through which to reengage Lisa in the treatment process. This was an unfortunate aspect of the family-centered treatment paradigm: Lisa had become the identified patient, despite the theoretical premise of the systems approach to the contrary. In the family treatment she participated only insofar as she was able to use the sessions to condemn and admonish her parents. In this way, the family therapy became another medium through which she "acted out." Moreover, it was precisely this need to act out that precluded the choice of individual therapy. Her parents were also unable to make effective use of this treatment; their assumption that the therapists were the experts further robbed them of empowerment with their daughter, and perpetuated the contentiousness and contempt in the family.

Had the treatment been structured, from the beginning, as a parent therapy, many of these issues might have been circumvented, not because the dynamics of the family would have been understood differently, but because the conception of the treatment is different. In parent therapy the scrutiny of family dynamics occurs only in conjunction with an understanding of the impact of the therapist on those dynamics. It is in this way that the disempowerment of the parents is deliberately and carefully avoided, and therefore obviated. In this case, family therapy privileged the therapists and permitted further acting out on Lisa's part. Ultimately, a transition was made with Lisa's parents to parent therapy, and it was only through this modality that the parents eventually turned their attention to providing

greater structure for Lisa. With Lisa out of the room, the therapist was able
to commiserate with them while simultaneously engaging them in thinking
about their own parenting approach.

What became the focus of the parent therapy was not Lisa's behavior but the parents' ambivalence toward authority. When this emerged as
the central theme, they were able to explore their difficulty in structuring
Lisa's life in ways that were appropriate for her age. In their abhorrence of
authoritarianism, they had for many years provided too little parental guidance
for her. However, in response to Lisa's acting-out behavior, they reversed
this approach and became overly punitive and infantalizing. What underscored their approach to parenting was their deep affinity for the values
and ideals of their own late adolescent years. Both parents had been politically active in the civil rights movement of the 1960s. Each continued to
promote these principles in their work, and maintained self representations
that had derived from their social and political commitments. For this
reason they had difficulty in perceiving themselves as authority figures
against whom rebellious feelings and behavior would be directed. They had
assumed that an identification with them would produce a rebellion that was
outward directed and politically motivated, just as theirs had been. What
this reflected was their apparent failure to make an adequate distinction
between their own experience and their daughter's. But their daughter's
experience was informed by an entirely different set of circumstances and
cultural context.

It was only through the gradual unraveling of this couple's beliefs
about themselves, and their shattered expectations of their daughter, that
any improvement was possible. Through the support of the consultative
therapy, the parents began to impose stricter, more consistently outlined
rules. Despite Lisa's initial protest and the rejection of increased involvement with her mother and stepfather, a part of her seemed to welcome the
closeness that the increased supervision provided. The parents also had
difficulty in assuming new roles in relation to Lisa. Mother was especially
reluctant to surrender the image of a progressive parent and the self representation as a mother different from her own. Nonetheless, she was able
to use the parent therapy to retain an identification with her daughter by
redefining her maternal self as capable not only of understanding but also

of managing her daughter's adolescent struggles. The therapist helped her to reframe Lisa's behavior in ways with which she could identify. She was then able to understand that Lisa was motivated by the need to define herself in ways that were not simply compliant with authority. She grew increasingly comfortable with the idea that her daughter was constructing an autonomous self in much the same way that she herself had done. This new path toward identification, forged by the consultation, allowed the mother to see Lisa's behavior as her own form of rebellion—an identification with, rather than a rejection of, her mother. Lisa was then free to define her own adolescent experience; she could ultimately feel that she was seen as a person in her own right, separate from her mother.

Ashley was an adolescent who exhibited many of the same problems as Lisa, and her parents also sought psychotherapy for her.

Ashley was seen in twice-weekly therapy by a psychoanalyst who specialized in the treatment of adolescents, and she was a willing participant in this arrangement. Both of Ashley's parents had been previously married so that she and her sister lived with their parents and several half siblings from each side. The household was somewhat chaotic; at the center of it was the family business in which several of the older siblings were employed. Competition for power and promotion in the business, as well as for their father's approval, was pervasive in the family dynamics, and created considerable dissension for everyone. Ashley, unlike her siblings, consciously and deliberately shunned this behavior and was intent on making a different career choice after college. Her father's intense preoccupation with business matters, however, made it difficult for her to attract his interest and attention.

Ashley developed a strong attachment to her therapist and organized her efforts around receiving attention, support, and sympathy from her. In the service of enlisting attention from the therapist, she tended at times to greatly exaggerate her difficulties. With some frequency, she would telephone the therapist during their appointed session time and indicate that she was in a precarious situation from which she could not extricate herself; at other times she would reveal that she was in a hospital emergency room after having taken too many sleeping pills. She would implore the therapist to rescue her by implying that there was no one in her life who was sufficiently devoted to her to do so. The therapist felt deeply torn by her concern for the girl, and harbored persistent fears that the parents were neglectfully preoccupied with other concerns. This dynamic is not atypical in the treatment of acting-out adolescents, where the primary relationships often seem to be impaired, and the therapist feels troubled by the apparent irresponsibility of the parents. In Ashley's case this dynamic was extreme. Typically she would become incensed and envious about some commendation or gift with which one of her siblings was favored, and would protest to her mother. However, her mother was in a compromised position in consequence of her lowered status in the business, and was therefore unable to effectively assuage Ashley's distress. This was typically followed by behavior on Ashley's part that sufficiently alarmed the therapist to the point where she would bend the treatment boundaries in order to respond to the presumed crisis. Ashley would then berate her already exasperated mother for her inadequate nurturance and lack of attention, and, bolstered by the therapist's attitude, would attribute her emotional problems to her parents' neglect. These episodes, in turn, caused the parents to experience the treatment as ineffectual, and eventually they terminated it.

What was essential to grapple with in this case was the dynamic through which money was used as power in this family, and was often used as a substitute for attention and nurturance. The father was able to express interest and nurturance only through financial support, and would often withhold money in order to demonstrate his disapproval. The therapist also was made to feel deeply resentful, because the father repeatedly withheld payment for the therapy sessions. In this way she was swept up into the dynamic system of the family. Without being able to stand outside, at some therapeutic distance, she was rendered ineffectual and inept. Yet in this family dynamic, individual treatment for the girl could not have transpired otherwise and still retained the daughter's participation. The therapist, cognizant that her frustration with the parents was intrinsic to this treatment paradigm, referred the family for parent therapy.

The therapy was conducted with the mother alone, due to the father's refusal to attend. The therapist engaged the mother around her sense of helplessness and depression, and explored her difficulties in feeling effective as a parent. Whereas Ashley's therapist had become similarly disempowered and frustrated, in the way that this parent had been, and the treatment served to reinforce the cycle of anger and helpless protest, the parent therapist explored the problems created by the loss of parental authority. What was further revealed was the fact that the more depressed the mother became, the greater was her unavailability to her daughter. The therapist provided a holding environment for this mother and, in consequence, helped her to increase her involvement with Ashley. Turning attention to the needs of the parent, in this way, circumvents the violent exposure of parental deficits, and provides the hope of creating a different dynamic experience between parent and child. The parent consultation concluded with a psychotherapy referral for this mother who used the consultation to identify her own depression and need for therapeutic support.

We can see from the above two cases that parent therapy may be able to achieve treatment results that are unattainable through other treatment modalities. Individual treatment for children sometimes may have deleterious effects on the family dynamic system because it may have an insufficient impact on the hidden causes of behavioral problems and on parenting difficulties, and family therapy models may reinforce the sense of ineffectiveness that underlies some parenting failures. In contrast, in the parent therapy model, the relational configurations can be deeply explored, and the parents can feel supported and therefore collaborate more effectively in ameliorating the emotional difficulties of their children. As in the supervisory model, a primary emphasis is on the growth of the parents themselves, and it is through this growth that they can engage fruitfully with their children.

12
Learning Disabilities

 $\mathcal{W}$ e conceptualize learning disabilities as a complex dynamic interplay among multiple factors, including a number of bidirectional influences. Much research has explored the relationship between learning disabilities and the emotional environment of the family and has delineated the significant emotional repercussions of intellectual handicaps. A relational view emphasizes the interrelationship and reciprocal influence between psychological and cognitive development, with specific reference to familial dynamic patterns. It looks at the impact of organically based disabilities on the emotional life of the child and the family, as well as the impact of emotional concerns on the learning experience of the child.

Because learning disabilities have such a deleterious impact on both the child and the family, they often result in referrals for psychotherapy for the child. This is particularly common, in our experience, for bright children, whose school failure is felt as an especially powerful humiliation. Both parents and teachers, in their efforts to ameliorate the pain and stress created by the child's learning problems, may look to psychotherapy to provide a forum for the youngster to express the anger, frustration, and confusion associated with a learning disability. This benign impulse, however, may sometimes serve simply to reinforce the same feelings of shame originally generated by the disability.

The learning disabilities to which we refer here are cognitive difficulties that create problems in the child's overall academic experience. These difficulties are usually identified in the early grades of elementary school, in children of normal or average intellectual capacities, and are reflected in difficulties in the acquisition of basic reading, writing, language, or arithmetic skills. We are not addressing the very minor but common neurological anomalies that do not grossly interfere with school performance. For example, weak visual-spatial abilities in an otherwise competent learner will not unduly impair the child's overall school performance, although the child will be unlikely to excel in certain areas, such as geometry, and will ultimately be disinclined toward certain professions, such as architecture. Neither are we concerned with the child who has a proclivity toward math and science and less interest in the humanities. In general, children will have clustered strengths and weaknesses in their capacities and interests, which are usually overlapping, as the two are likely to reinforce each other. These normal inconsistencies in cognitive functioning do not constitute learning disabilities. In the absence of marked learning deficits, children who have areas of weakness are able, for the most part, to compensate for these discrepancies, and process sufficient information through other cognitive channels.

On the other hand, children who do experience pronounced difficulties in learning to read are at risk for experiencing a profusion of other, related problems; notably, they are unable to expand their fund of general knowledge at the same rate as their unafflicted peers, and the awareness of this fact, particularly for bright children, presents a painful addition to the other repercussions of their learning deficits.

Parent therapy attempts to assist the parents of these children to achieve a measured perspective on their child's learning issues and school performance, in order to help the child establish a manageable perspective on the problem. It proceeds, as always, on several levels. Often, by the time the consultation has begun, parents have been struggling with their children's school performance in ways that have profoundly affected the parent-child interaction. In many families, it is one parent who assumes the greatest share of homework supervision, and thus there is often a rift between the parents over the tensions that arise around this daily activity. Many factors are at play in determining parents' reactions to their children's learning failures: the parents' school histories; the value placed on achievement in the parents' families of origin; the differences between the parents regarding these issues; and the particular identifications that each parent has with aspects of the child's personality, talents, and weaknesses. For example, a mother whose narcissistic shame is rekindled when her child is struggling with reading, in the same way that she once did, may feel that she is to blame for transmitting a bad attribute. She may, in addition, be angry at the child or at the school, or at the spouse who cannot fully appreciate what it feels like to have a disability. The husband, in this situation, may feel angry because he does not experience the problem in the same way as his wife does. Since it is not part of his own history, he may find it perplexing in ways that make him doubt its significance. Then the father might feel that his son is lazy or that his wife is coddling the son. In this way, learning disabilities present a focal point through which a relational interplay occurs, as the multidirectional reverberations that surround a problem are enacted and lived out through the individual and intersubjective responses in the family. Assisting the parents in differentiating themselves from their child's learning problems becomes one of the fundamental features of the parent consultation and can alleviate some of the parents' narcissistic injuries. When their identifications are less powerful and compelling they can begin to think more dispassionately, and therefore more compassionately, about the subjective experience of their child.

The following excerpt from a parent consultation will serve to illustrate some of these points.

Tate's parents sought the advice of their family physician when, at the end of the school year, Tate's first-grade teacher suggested psychotherapy to help him deal with his learning disability. Tate was in a program for gifted children and had had, thus far, in preschool and kindergarten, very positive school experiences. He was an amiable, alert youngster who had affectionate relationships with his parents, both of whom reported much pride in their son's previous enthusiasm for learning. They were quite unprepared for the difficulties he developed in the first grade, and found it difficult to comprehend that reading problems had developed in a child for whom learning had seemed to come so easily. Psychological testing revealed pronounced weaknesses in visual sequencing in an otherwise very superior intellectual profile. The psychologist's report suggested, in addition to cognitive recommendations, the implementation of play therapy as a way of alleviating the inevitable feelings of frustration and shame. However, the family physician presented the idea that play therapy was not the only therapeutic form of play and, on his advice, they sought a consultative meeting.

In the consultation, the parents, who were highly successful in creative professions, easily disclosed their disagreements about managing Tate's predicament. Mother had assumed a more stringent position with Tate, and attempted to impose a rigorous structure for schoolwork and to limit his extracurricular activity. Father felt this was too restrictive for a 6-year-old, and he felt ambivalent about the pressure that was being exerted by the school. Both parents were clearly distressed over the dampening of their son's enthusiasm, and they shared the perception that the painful battles over homework were unproductive and were burdening the family with an atmosphere of strife and dissension. As is frequently the case, the anxieties in the family about the persistent nature of Tate's problem began to dominate family life. Tate's younger sister was often relegated to the care of a baby-sitter so that mother and son could together struggle with the academic problems at hand. The sister was resentful of this and openly expressed her concern that Tate's books were "all that my parents seemed to care about." This intensified the mother's guilt and generated greater anger toward Tate.

The consultation focused on the homework situation, Tate's school experience, and the complex play of intrapsychic and interpersonal dynamics within the family. What emerged was the startling realization that Tate was being given almost no opportunity to engage in play activity. The gifted program, overwhelmingly preoccupied with intellectual achievement, had no recess during the school day; instead, the students had an indoor lunch, which was followed by a brief educational film. Because of the intense anxieties that had grown up around homework, Tate's after-school activities had also been significantly curtailed. The social and creative activities, which were previously enjoyed by everyone in the family, were now considered ways of indulging Tate's resistance to work, rather than experiences that could promote cognitive, emotional, and physical growth. What became significant in helping these parents achieve some distance from their subjective anxieties was the consultant's engagement around the simple routines in the family's life. The parents' responses to questions about when Tate could play with friends and what activities he had previously enjoyed at home and before bedtime, such as mutual storytelling, helped to consolidate their awareness that almost all creative and social play had become dramatically restricted. In the consultation room, they were able to think about the effects of this deprivation on their son's experience. They explored with the therapist the possibility that their preoccupation with his disability would be internalized as a character trait, obscuring Tate's perception of himself as a vital, bright, and imaginative youngster.

As is often also the case in the supervisory setting, it may be sufficient for the parent therapist simply to provide the impetus that allows parents to explore and expand their own thoughts; in this case, the consultation created the necessary space for the parents to think about Tate in a different light, removed from the pressures of the school authorities, as well as the induced pressure to exert their parental authority. The parent therapist is able to share his expertise without becoming another authority figure, and it is through this unique relationship that parental defensiveness can be diminished. Following the consultative therapy Tate's parents were able to move more comfortably into arranging plans for the following school year. It was decided that Tate would receive resource room services, that teachers would be exclusively the ones to assist him with his schoolwork, and that family life would shift away from the intense focus on school. When they were able to delegate his schoolwork to the academic setting, and defer to the school staff regarding educational issues, they were also able to reestablish their identities as the experts on their child as a person. The therapist supported their decisions, and encouraged their inclination to return to social and play activities for their son—activities that could then foster a more mutually enjoyable relationship. Though they had temporarily become rigidified in their approach to their son's intellectual growth, they came to recognize, in the therapy, the value of engaging in other life-enhancing activities. They allocated some of Tate's weekly schedule to sports activities and returned to the playful and creative games to which they had previously been accustomed. Subsequent to this, Tate's mood shifted significantly, and the family tensions substantially abated. Because Tate was a creative and talented child, he was able to reestablish his sense of himself as a competent person; he could see himself as diligent instead of lazy, active instead of passive, and successful instead of deficient.

The primary challenge in this case was to help the parents overcome the anxiety and guilt they felt when they became more relaxed and less demanding of academic rigor from their son. This loosening of standards leaves many parents feeling irresponsible or insufficiently conscientious about their children's intellectual growth and self-discipline. In his teachings, Ghent (1995) has eloquently addressed the psychic expansiveness of play and its power to enhance growth on many levels. For children in distress, play not only becomes instrumental in relieving tension and anxiety, but also is often vital in nourishing children's intellectual lives. In addition to cultivating the creative fantasy life of the child and fostering symbolic representation, play can nurture actual learning. Learning in the school setting functions in the service of developing the child's skills for lifelong pursuits. School provides the most pragmatic setting for this to occur, but learning can take place in several other arenas. The parent who cooks and bakes with a child, for example, is able to foster numerical reasoning through measurement. Making cookies together also enhances multiple capacities for children: anticipatory functions, delay of gratification, the pride taken in a process that they know will ultimately culminate in a pleasurable end, the attention to detail, and the concentration required to follow sequential directions. All of these capacities can also be fostered in a variety of classroom activities. However, for the learning-impaired child, whose experience has often precluded certain types of learning, these activities may provide an ancillary context in which to develop important skills. Similarly, engaging in sports can promote the development of multiple cognitive and relational capacities; besides en-hancing visual-motor coordination, participatory games can help the child to establish a sense of interpersonal boundaries. Being assigned to a particular position on a team, for example, can assist a child with the demarcation of self from others, in the context of functioning with a community and maintaining a collective effort. Moreover, an interest in a particular sport can encourage curiosity about numerous other endeavors, such as reading about the history of the sport, and acquiring geographical information or even arithmetical information, as teams travel around the country or the world and into various time zones. Thus, it is vitally important to encourage play, not as something that exists outside of the realm of learning, but as an activity that is essential to developmental and academic growth.

As children with learning disabilities grow, their sense of failure and frustration tend to be internalized as relatively stable characterological features. Negative self representations and family dynamics, although secondary to the learning problem, are likely to predominate in therapy, and compound or even obscure, for both parents and clinicians, the significance of the learning disability. Many such children develop attendant emotional distress, and thus they may become depressed or withdrawn, or act out aggressively in the school setting. Educators and clinicians then confuse learning problems with the child's emotional reactions.

One highly intelligent youngster, for example, stuck one of his classmates with a pencil, and consequently was sent to a therapist. After several sessions of play therapy, during which the child was gracious and fair-minded in his play, his father inquired about how he was discussing his problems in school and his unfortunate aggression for which he had been temporarily suspended. The child replied, "I didn't discuss it; why should I tell a nice stranger all about my problems?" This poignant remark reflects the drive that so many children develop, during periods of stress and humiliation, to preserve some experience of dignity and self-respect. It further illustrates how problematic it sometimes is for children, who are already pained about their failures and embarrassed by their peers, to subject themselves to the scrutiny of a clinician. Despite the benign motivations of parents, then, it is often counterproductive for children to enter a treatment process that intensifies their shame and where they may be reluctant to reveal their sense of failure. Also, for children with visually based disabilities or pragmatic language deficits, there is a significantly greater potential for misreading social cues. In the classroom setting, it is these perceptually based confusions that often have the unfortunate consequence of leading to aggressive behaviors. In this context, it becomes particularly important for the consultant to assist parents in understanding this phenomenon, in order to alleviate their anxiety that their child is emotionally unstable or hostile.

Thus, the learning situation is one in which the entire family, not only the child, is implicated in an intersubjectively organized system. Many researchers have pointed to the idea that learning problems can be, at times, a function of family conflict and the poor resolution of familial problems. Children with learning failures often feel helpless to reverse their experience, and parents may have difficulty in conceiving solutions to the school problems. Moreover, they may be unaware of the unconscious projections and anxieties that help to keep these problems in place. In some cases, underlying issues in the intersubjective experience of parent and child may create manifest problems in academic functioning.

Some children are intensely sensitive to their parents' internal reactions and respond to the learning experience with a confluence of mild and subtle cognitive deficits that are influenced by emotional factors. In this way, what occurs in the child's academic life and achievement strivings is complexly layered; it is a synthesis of the cognitive and the emotional, neither of which individually would necessarily create disabilities. This was the situation in the following case:

> Isabel, a 6-year-old, was referred by the psychologist at her school for a suspected learning disability that the staff believed was disguised by social difficulties. Her disruptiveness in class was interpreted as one way in which she deflected her anxiety about her learning problems. The school staff also believed strongly that Isabel should begin therapy for her emotional lability and difficulty in getting along with other children.
>
> When Isabel's parents solicited therapeutic intervention and advice, the psychologist first explored their perceptions of their child's difficulties and the context of their family life. They described their daughter as dependent on others and often intrusive with other chil-

dren, acting out in ways that thwarted the possibility of harmonious interactions in her class. The parents were deeply concerned about Isabel's social difficulties; they were especially interested in her capacities in the social sphere, owing in part to their overvaluation of independence and adjustment in the outside world.

Both parents were intensely engaged in high-powered professional lives outside of the home, and were often busy and preoccupied when they were at home as well. They were therefore not always available for sustained involvement with Isabel, and were rather intent on raising their daughter to be so precociously mature that she could be consistently self-sufficient. They both left home early in the morning, before Isabel awoke, leaving her in the care of a nanny who accompanied her to school and picked her up at the end of the school day. The parents reported that when they returned home after work, Isabel excessively sought their attention. She wanted their help with homework, but the parents, experiencing this as infantile, rebuffed her requests. They related this to the psychologist with distress, conveying their idea that Isabel was falling behind at school, and was immature and overly demanding of their time. When they decided to punish her for what they perceived of as excessively demanding behavior, they did so by banishing her to her room, and when she protested they became irritated. When Isabel eventually emerged, she was eager to be comforted. However, since her parents continued to feel annoyed by her behavior, they were loath to soothe her with affection.

In the consultation, the psychologist listened with particular attention to indications of the particular attachment style and values that had apparently developed in this triad. As many theorists and infant researchers have pointed out, parents and children develop attachment patterns that influence a child's relational patterns outside of the family constellation (Ainsworth 1991, Ainsworth et al. 1991, Main et al. 1985). It is through the filter of the self/other representation, established through the parent-child relationship, that the child experiences the outside world and adjusts to the social sphere at the school level. The consulting psychologist began to conceptualize the problems in terms of the attachment issues that seemed to surface in the parents' description of Isabel and set out to ascertain how the learning and the emotional issues might be interactive.

When Isabel's parents were questioned about their marriage there was an uncomfortable tension and a marked diffidence about expressing any emotional or subjectively felt attitudes. They had been profession-ally ambitious, were prominent in their fields, and seemed to be primarily interested in companionship with each other rather than deep intimacy or passion. This seemed to be confirmed by their distant manner with each other. In the consultation they revealed that, in their own childhoods, neither of them had had much soothing care that they could remember. This salient information was emphasized by the consultant, who suggested the possibility that they might be afraid of indulging in their daughter what they had managed to repudiate in their own relationship.

Subsequent to the initial consultation a psychological as-sessment was done that indicated that Isabel had a relatively mild weakness in the capacity for categorizing and conceptualizing com-parative phenomena. The psychological results also pointed to Isabel's depression and sense of isolation and loneliness, both of which were tinged with a sense of guilt about her own neediness. The con-sultant further explored the idea that the parents' disavowal of dependency was internalized by Isabel as self-deprecation for her childish needs. The therapist saw this as a salient feature in Isabel's intellectual life as well as her social behavior. First, in her friendships she appeared to be acting out, simultaneously, both her need for connectedness with others and the repudiation of those needs, thereby reflecting the intersubjective life in the family. The interaction with her parents was one of approach and rebuff—the very same interac-tion that was observed in her classroom. Isabel's anxious attachment, developed in her primary relationships, thus had marked ramifications for her outside friendships. In the intellectual sphere, the area that seemed to be significantly affected was her capacity to perceive re-lationships, to make links between different but related things. It was the idea of a "common bond," a shared relatedness, which, deficient in her emotional experience, was also missing from her cognitive repertoire.

The therapist explored with the parents the particular attachment issues that dominated Isabel's psychic or mental life and invaded the learning process itself. She further suggested the possibility that Isabel became disruptive in the classroom, not primarily because she was unable to do the academic work, but because her need for assistance was continually being played out, as was her unconscious depression over feeling isolated and abandoned. When they reflected on the child's behavior in the classroom, the parents could see the connection that the therapist had made; they understood that Isabel seemed to be soliciting the aid of her teachers in the same way that she attempted to gain the attention of her parents. Through this realization, and the acknowledgment of their own defensive experience, they were able to establish greater distance from their projected fears and to develop an image of their daughter that was closer to the child's subjective experience.

Peter Fonagy (1991) has written extensively on the importance of the reflective function; his work has emphasized the importance of a parent's capacity to appreciate the internal life of the child and to recognize the child's experience as separate from one's own. This empathic experience allows the parent to recognize the subjectivity of the child and to provide a necessary holding environment for the child's emotional concerns. When internal experience is not sufficiently reflected upon, it can be projected outward in relatively crude ways, resulting in a wholesale and unmitigated projection of personal anxieties onto one's child.

With Isabel's parents, the therapist helped to establish more reflective awareness of the internal but disguised needs of their child. This was accomplished through the therapist's inquiry into the subjective experience of the parents. The parent therapy helped to unravel the parents' own attachment experiences. They were able ultimately to reflect on the aspects of their own childhoods, which had been isolating and emotionally depriving, and recognized in their marital life the foreclosure of a more intimate and nurturing stance. During the deepest interactions with the therapist, the parents revealed that they felt each other's unavailability and lived with a fairly continual striving to ward off their dissociated need for more affectionate contact. The therapist here made the connection that the repudiation of their own needs, and the perception of them as bad, served to create an image of their child as voraciously demanding and emotionally indulgent. Therefore, what became necessary in the consultative relationship was to create a holding environment for the parents that allowed them to acknowledge and tolerate their own need for more intimate and soothing care. Through this process they were able to recognize their daughter's needs and distance themselves from the contemptuous feelings they had previously maintained as a defense against their own self-criticism.

Samantha had a very pronounced neurologically based learning disability. She was diagnosed with dyslexia and gross deficits in motor functioning, which included fine-motor problems, problems with laterality, and problems with encoding and written expression. She attended a special education class for learning-disabled children. In school she also had problems in negotiating free time and peer interactions, and got into frequent altercations with other students. She had a contemptuous attitude and tended to become intermittently castigating of other students. These social difficulties in part were related to the fact that she was verbally astute and precocious in many ways, and her deficits were therefore a source of narcissistic humiliation for her. Her parents wanted her to see a therapist to ease her anxiety and enhance her self-esteem.

During the initial meeting with Samantha's parents there was much tension and disagreement. Her mother reported that she herself had been, and continued to be, dyslexic, and had suffered greatly as a result of both her disability and the failure of her family to recognize and address it. She had felt deeply distressed and abandoned for much of her childhood and school life. She also revealed at this time that her relationship with Samantha and with her husband was often very contentious. She had recently been at a party with Samantha and had been deeply hurt and embarrassed by her daughter's public tantrum and her insults to several people including her mother. On the other hand, she was persistently angry with her husband for demanding too much from Samantha and failing to sufficiently acknowledge his daughter's painful struggles with her massive cognitive problems.

The father was a successful physician who had always done well in school, and had excelled without much effort. He was a strong, independent man who also had received great commendation for and prestige from his accomplishments and had little need of external assistance and support. He was demanding of Samantha and, although intelligent and cognizant of her learning problems, often got into battles with her over her academic work that ended in frustration. He revealed in the initial phase of the consultation that he sometimes had the irrational conviction that she was lazy and just wasn't trying hard enough. The consultant first reassured the father that this was a common thought among parents of learning-disabled children. However, she also suggested that his need to see Samantha in concordance with his own self representation of a powerful, dynamic person, might cause Samantha to try to master tasks and interactions with a false bravado.

In the consultation, the parents and consultant explored a dynamic in which Samantha seemed to be caught between two parental projections, with little room for her own autonomous sense of self. Her mother often felt rejected by Samantha's identification with her father and was injured by her daughter's critical attitude, which to some extent echoed her husband's dismissive and condescending manner toward her. In addition, she tended to see Samantha as more fragile and deficient than she was in actuality, in consequence of her own projected self-doubt. The parent therapist helped the mother to see that she continued to feel the pangs of humiliation over her childhood failures and, in consequence, she was unable to gain sufficient distance from her daughter's disabilities.

The persistent ruminations about the insult at the party were used, by the mother, as a paradigmatic interaction that rekindled her sense of humiliation, generated earlier in her own personal history. The therapist pondered, with her, other ways of looking at the same incident: one could perhaps see Samantha's insulting manner as a way of deflecting attention away from her own deficits. If other people

were the target of criticism, she could be, at least temporarily, lib-
erated from her own sense of inadequacy. Viewed from this perspective the event took on a different flavor for the mother.

The transformative value of this idea creates a space in which new
identities can exist; in this case, she was able to see Samantha, not simply
as an incarnation of familiar figures or of her husband's contempt, or as
fragile as she felt herself to be, but as someone in her own right, with a
different set of problems. In this way, transitional or intermediary positions
can be achieved because the new perception allows for a flexibility that was
foreclosed by the representation of Samantha as a cruel humiliator or a
fragile and deficient child. We can thus see Samantha's school behavior, at
least in part, as a reflection of her attempt to respond to her father's
expectations of a strong, socially competent youngster, and her mother's
fantasy of a fragile, wounded child.

Each of these cases might be treated with a different approach;
however, the parent therapy model is especially compelling for work with
learning disabilities. As in the supervisory paradigm, in which consultations
assist therapists who may feel derailed in their work, the parent therapist
assists parents in a manner that is relationally informed. In supervision, the
supervisor and therapist, acknowledging their own skills and capacities,
assess, in a mutually created way, what will be most fruitful for the progress
of the treatment. This is not based, necessarily or exclusively, on a particular
problem of the patient, but rather on the therapist's subjective experience
as well. Specific knowledge may be offered when it is needed, or transference and countertransference issues may be deconstructed and reworked.

The parent therapy model proceeds similarly: in the case of Isabel,
who suffered from a very subtle cognitive weakness, the primary focus
involved the ways in which the internal representations of the parents held
sway over many of the child's manifest behaviors. The consultation here
focused, not on behavioral advice, such as counseling the parents about
more appropriate time-out methods, but engaged them instead in a process
that could help them to accept the idea that their own developmental needs
had been stifled, and they had, in consequence, been threatened by their
daughter's emotional cravings. This is not unlike much analytically informed

ancillary work with parents. In Samantha's case, there appeared to be both a mismatch in the parents' reactions to their child's disability, and an ongoing marital conflict that Samantha had internalized in a complex and discordant series of self representations. Here the therapy focused on helping the parents create a space that could contain their own concerns and look more impartially at their daughter's subjective self. In this way, the work resembles psychodynamic systems work with families.

For Tate's parents, the therapy enabled them to identify and take control of their anxieties in such a way as to allow them to reestablish their roles as the authorities in their family. It was through this more confident authoritative position that they were able to reinstate creativity and vitality into their family. This was a more directive and supportive therapeutic approach. However, what is common to all of these approaches is the creation of a holding environment for the parents, the provision of a space that can expand their capacity to mentalize, and therefore both separate from and attune themselves to the subjective experience of their child. It is not the specific content but the relational paradigm of the parent consultation that has mutative value.

What distinguishes the parent therapy approach is that, unlike other paradigms, it is not a relational analysis of family dynamics, or an analysis of the child's intrapsychic and interpersonal experience, but a modality through which the parents, like therapists in supervision, can be held and invigorated by the relationship with the therapist. It is this relationship, which takes place separate and apart from the intensity of the manifest problems, that creates shifts in perspective and enables parents to creatively engage problems, and to repair and revitalize their relationship with their child.

Attention-deficit disorders have become such a ubiquitous part of contemporary clinical thinking about learning disabilities that we did not address them as a separate problem. Research has suggested that the use of stimulant medications affects brain functioning in such a way as to suppress children's need for play activity or mental relief. This may create permanent neuronal change (Panksepp 1998), and therefore obviate the need for parents and schools to adjust to a wide but normal range of temperamental variation. We have focused, alternatively, on the value of play as an integral determinant of both psychic and cognitive growth. In this regard, consultation for a child with an attention deficit would proceed in a similar manner as that of other learning problems. Its focus would be on assisting parents in understanding their child's temperamental proclivities, and in tolerating and managing the range of temperamental variation that can exist among different children. It follows the same course as the three cases considered in this chapter. Whether a child has suffered an insult to the central nervous system, or has trouble concentrating in school because of anxious preoccupations, or displays a normal range of restlessness in school, school performance, and the capacity for sustained attention is likely to be at issue. How the parents conceptualize the issue, and what that conception dictates in their parenting, will be relevant factors in conducting the consultative work. Ultimately, the aim is the creation of a supportive environment in which overidentifications or real impediments to progress, such as a mismatch between the child's capacities and the school's demands, can reach resolution.

V
Special Situations

13
School Consultation

$\mathcal{S}$chool consultation is predicated on the idea that each school, like each family, has developed its own culture and dynamic life, and that each member of the culture is embedded in a complex intersubjective set of experiences (Alpert, 1995a). It is consistent with a relational perspective insofar as it maintains that individual experience is functionally related to the systemic life of the culture in which it is embedded. It further rests on the assumption that change is a systemic phenomenon and that individual behavior, therefore, is dependent in part on the relationships that surround it. Shifts or revisions in the behavior and emotional life of the child can be created by modifications in the intersubjective life of the family and in the particular relationships in which children are engaged, especially at developmentally charged moments. Similarly, the interrelationships in the school setting are vitally linked to the school life and education of the child.

A relational view of school-based learning focuses not simply on the child but on the interactions between students and teachers, between teachers and parents, and between teachers and other staff. It assumes that there is a complex set of interpersonal and cultural factors that facilitate or impede learning. Exploring and understanding these interrelationships and the intersubjective nature of classroom experience is what constitutes a consultative engagement in the context of children's academic experience. Reflection on children's social and emotional behavior and on the teacher's reactions to this behavior can lead to a significantly enhanced understanding of and amelioration of academic problems.

Much of the school consultation literature forms a compatible correlate to the parent therapy paradigm. The fundamental premise is one that rests on the understanding that anyone who intervenes in an established system is necessarily a part of that system, while simultaneously attempting some degree of distance from systemic problems in order to be maximally effective. Thus, the consultant to a teacher or parent must assume an integral position in the life of the family or school system, must generate feelings of trust, and must understand the "existing regularities" (Sarason 1971) that are inherent in, and are maintained by, any given dynamic system. That is, the consultant must be mindful of the underlying assumptions that function to bind a family or school relationship. Thus therapy in the school optimally involves the school authorities as well as the parents in an exploration of the community's traditions and values and in expanding existing channels of communication to foster interdependence and collaboration. Consistent with the premise of the parent therapy model, the ideal relationship between clinicians and school personnel is composed of interdependent, interrelated parties pooling their knowledge in a collaborative endeavor.

The consultative model may be understood on a variety of levels and in a variety of configurations in the school setting. There are several relationships that may be effectively employed as focal points for consultation: the teachers and administrators may be seen as surrogate parents and thus are often subject to the same or similar dynamic interactions with their students as parents are with their children. The amount of time spent in the classroom and the emotional investment in the students are likely to leave teachers and administrators feeling vulnerable to many of the same projections and transference experiences as family members. As a consequence, group dynamics in the classroom are frequently governed by the ways in which teachers respond to each child as well as to the group as a whole. It is precisely for this reason that some children's behavior can shift dramatically from one class to the next and from one school year to the next.

Behavior is at least partially constructed through interaction. Even children with attention-deficit disorders may, under optimal classroom and relational conditions, manage to sustain adequate levels of attention for both social and academic purposes. Both neurologically based and anxiety-related inattention may often be ameliorated by a relationship that provides the tolerance and the structure necessary to bind a child's anxiety, thereby decreasing the child's distractability. The relationality in this perspective suggests that it is the particularity of the teacher–student relationship, just as it is the particularity of the parent-child relationship, that so powerfully influences the behavioral patterns of children in the classroom. The parent consultation model, therefore, may be effectively used in the classroom setting in the same way that the exploration of dynamic configurations in the family may be used therapeutically to alleviate children's emotional problems. In addition, teachers are often in a position to provide expert advice to parents and, in this capacity, may serve as consultants themselves. This chapter explores the ways in which the tradition of consultation, once esteemed for both teachers and clinicians, has been unfortunately largely subverted by therapies that have an exclusively individual focus, and much of the collaborative effort of parents, educators, and clinicians has been lost. This chapter demonstrates how this tradition can be effectively restored in the school community, through consultative work with teachers and parents, where the teacher is the consultant, and through consultative work where the teacher is the consultee.

Let us look at the latter case first—at a relationship between a consultant and a teacher. The consultant engages with the teacher in much the same way as a clinician attends to parents in parent therapy. As in the consultant–parent relationship and the supervisor–therapist relationship, the consultant's task is to understand the situation from the viewpoint of the teacher. This incorporates the teacher's conscious experience in an exploration of the more conflictual and unconscious material that may indirectly influence the relationship with students. This is the delicate balance that consultation ideally strikes: listening to aspects of individual experience while hoping to look at other possibilities and ameliorative interventions. Establishing a trusting relationship is paramount in any consultative paradigm. Just as in the parental experience, offering early and peremptory advice can undermine the teacher's authority and confidence. Rather, an exploratory approach to clarify and understand the subjective experience of the teacher is the most effective course of action. The same types of phenomena we see in parents with their children, such as overidentification and transference distortions, will constitute some of the content of the consultation. These factors are significant and come into play in the classroom as well as in the larger school environment.

In the field of school consultation, it is assumed that each behavior is constructed in a complex social context and occurs in a specific sequence of events, antecedents, and consequences. It is important to explore what events precede the child's behavior and what the reactions are to that behavior. The purpose of consultation in the school and in the classroom is to enhance the teacher's effectiveness, in part through the enhancement of self-confidence. In this way it is analogous to assisting parents through a process of restoring their sense of self-sufficiency, competence, and control. This may, at times, result in a relaxation of unrealistic or unattainable goals as well as in a sensitization to the capacities of each child. Contextualizing behavior within an understanding of developmental issues and normative functioning can expand a teacher's tolerance of, and appreciation for, the wide range of behaviors he or she may encounter. This can pave the way for strengthening the teacher's capacity to help students build on existing skills and, in doing so, can curtail the tendency to focus on their deficits. Redefining a particular behavior by placing it in the context of the child's overall development can also reduce the tension within the teacher–student relationship, just as it can between parent and child or therapist and patient.

Children's classroom behaviors can change fairly dramatically by means of mild interventions that emerge out of the consultant's classroom observations. Information sharing may be sufficient to reorganize the particular teacher–student or peer relationships that have been established. A clinician can bring a teacher's attention to the particular events or experiences in a child's life that are relevant to the child's classroom behavior. This was the case with Isabel (see Chapter 12), for example, who became disruptive in class whenever feelings of depression and isolation emerged; her outbursts served to elicit contact from an adult who provided the solicitousness and attention that she so intensely needed, despite feelings of disapproval about her behavior. Identifying, for a classroom teacher, some of the internally generated causes of overt behaviors can be immensely productive. When the consultant discussed with Isabel's teacher some of the emotionally salient issues that seemed to be generating her disruptiveness, the teacher astutely linked some of these themes to observations that she herself had made but had not fully integrated into a cohesive framework. Connecting some of her perceptions of Isabel's behavior with the more organized picture that the consultant presented helped the teacher to see the ways in which she might address some of Isabel's needs—needs that were thinly disguised by her demandingness in the classroom. The presumption is that through collaborative reviewing of history and other data, the picture of the child can be revised, expanded, and deepened. In this case, the teacher became amenable to providing greater support, in part because she was able to recall from her own previous observations interactions between Isabel and her parents that she had not previously connected to the attention-seeking behaviors. Moreover, this teacher had in her repertoire of feelings the empathy and affection available for this rather needy child, and she was able to call upon them with the support and assistance of the consultant. One can assume in this case that the teacher's own capacities were not unduly taxed by the child's neediness, whereas another teacher might have had a more difficult time in attempting to modify her teaching style to accommodate Isabel's emotional state. Nonetheless, one point is essential: the consultation evoked and strengthened the ability of the teacher to be more open to addressing Isabel's very specific needs.

One little boy who was quite anxious about his own capacities in school became extremely distraught when he anticipated failure of any sort. He had particular difficulty in collecting himself and modulating affective states, and this proved to be a disruptive force in the classroom. The teacher was somewhat rule bound and, with this child in particular, used criticism of his behavior rather than offering positive suggestions for improvement. She informed the child that his behavior was unacceptable, adding that he was very smart and certainly could accomplish the assigned classroom tasks. The parents of this child were concerned that his anxiety and frustration were escalating as a result of the teacher's approach, and so they contacted the school's psychologist for a consultation. The psychologist engaged the teacher in a discussion of the boy's behavior and, while she supported many of the teacher's perceptions and sympathized with her sense of frustration, she also suggested ways in which the approach with the child could be modified. The idea that the teacher could encourage a positive outcome by making specific suggestions about how the child might approach his work had not occurred to the teacher in any systematic way, and this constituted much of the consultative advice. Encouragements from the teacher such as, "You can do it if you try it this way," or "You might want to try this," while constituting only a minor change, proved to be a useful approach for this child, as it decreased his feelings of humiliation when he was in a state of agitated frustration. The increased structure of the teacher's suggestions helped the boy to make the affective transition to a calmer and less disruptive state, much as the consultant's suggestions to the teacher helped her achieve greater balance with the child.

In the case of Julio (see Chapter 9), whose aggressive acting-out behavior was in part unconsciously fostered by his father's deep ambivalence around aggression and control, the consultation with a psychologist was multifaceted: it engaged the parents, the teacher, and the school administrators. This situation emerged, in part, because attempts by school personnel to constructively engage the parents had been largely unsuccessful, primarily because neither the personnel nor the parents were able to empathize with the position of the other, and seemed to adhere staunchly to a sense that the other was frustrating and thwarting their best efforts toward the child. The school found the parents unrealistically defensive and therefore unwilling to obtain the services necessary for Julio. The parents felt that the school was remiss in its efforts to assist their son and unable to recognize and appreciate their own dedication to Julio. Additionally, in their efforts to bolster their own sense of competence, neither side was able to perceive the child as being difficult for the other to handle. The failure of empathic feeling led each party to an overcritical evaluation of the other. The consultant here had to grapple with the teacher's transference, the school's frustration with the child and with the perception of the parents' uncooperativeness, and the parents' defensiveness about their child, all of which had to be sorted out in an extremely complex and emotionally charged system.

While Julio's father was easily threatened by his son's obstreperousness, he also unconsciously encouraged it as a mark of strength and competence. In the family Julio thus experienced something of a double bind; his oppositionalism was, on the one hand, valued, but it was also repudiated when it was directed toward his parents. At school he was treated in much the same way as he was at home. The school was notably liberal in its philosophy; teachers were called by their first names and there was considerable freedom and mobility for students. Thus, children were permitted a great deal of discretion regarding their own behavior, and were expected to negotiate the school's system with considerable independence and autonomous decision making. This was problematic for a student like Julio, for numerous reasons. The unconscious directives to be tough and powerful left him ill-equipped to know when to curtail his independence and willful bravado. Just where autonomy ended and the overstepping of boundaries began was, for Julio, a matter of some confusion. The school, like his parents, encouraged mutuality up to a point, but recoiled at Julio's inappropriate behaviors and rudeness to adults. As is generally the case, independence was valued, but only in the context of courteous deference to authority. Thus, Julio encountered the same confusion and lack of external control that he did at home. The looseness or casual structure of the school replicated the undercontrol that eventually contributed to Julio's aggressiveness.

It should be emphasized that this kind of school orientation is ideal for many students, especially those with well-developed self-regulatory capacities. However, it is problematic for students who are struggling with conflicts between autonomy and compliance. Had the culture of the school been less casual in its approach, and provided a different kind of structure and guidance, the situation with Julio may never have escalated to the problematic level that it did. For this reason, the relationship between the school and Julio required intervention in order to address the temperamental mismatch between them. The parents eventually arranged for a psychological evaluation that they believed would exonerate their child and their parenting. The school anticipated that the results would confirm their perceptions. The evaluating psychologist used the information from the assessment to create a bridge between the school and the family.

As the consultant, the psychologist had numerous tasks, all of which involved negotiating a complex terrain of interrelationships—those between Julio and his teacher, Julio and his peers, the teacher and the administrators, the parents and the teacher, and the parents and the administrators. What had emerged in the consultation with the parents was their conviction that the school was remiss in its failure to make greater efforts in providing a solution to their son's problem in the classroom setting. In an effort to ward off guilt and anxiety about Julio's behavior at school, they tended to blame the teacher for her passivity and lackadaisical handling of classroom behaviors. Julio's mother consistently referred to a morning when she brought Julio to school and found several students running about the room throwing things. She was equally affronted by the administrative failure to resolve these matters. Additionally, she felt unappreciated for what she believed to be valuable contributions that the family made to the school, particularly in the area of recruitment of other Latino families. The parents believed that their being from a different cultural background may have contributed to the school's lack of motivation and ineptness in dealing more effectively with them. The consultant observed Julio in his class, met with the parents and the school staff separately, and eventually met with everyone together, including the teacher, school administrators, the school's learning specialist, and the school psychologist.

The consultant began with the understanding that both the administrators and the teacher shared a view of children as capable of mature and decorous behavior and seemed to have difficulty with a student like Julio, who deviated from this expected demeanor. Thus they appeared to have relatively few tools at their disposal with which to implement behavioral change. From the school's point of view the parents had been neglectful in not providing adequate social direction for their son and in denying his serious social and emotional problems. This situation necessitated, for the consultant, the creation of a terrain on which the parents and the school could achieve some common ground. The first task was to position each of these participants in a more receptive mode. The consultant explained the results of the evaluation in a way that elicited greater empathy from school personnel for Julio's internal conflicts. His bravado and rudeness were interpreted as a defensive mask for his insecurity. The consultant emphasized such relevant factors as Julio's being somewhat small for his age and his self-consciousness about his speech, which retained the residue of a Spanish accent. Some of his clowning and provocativeness were thus explained as a defensive attempt to deflect attention away from his shame, as well as his efforts to fit in socially. At the meeting, the teacher's responsiveness to these interpretations suggested an attitude that already seemed as if it would generate potential shifts in her approach with him in the classroom. As we find in any setting—in the office with parents, in the school with teachers, or with the therapist in supervision—a refocus onto the internal, subjective experience of the child, student, or patient can often elicit an empathic response that diminishes angry feeling and creates the potential for new interactions.

The consultant encouraged the parents, and the parents in collaboration with the school administration, to consider whether this was, in fact, the best school for Julio. The idea of brainstorming together about what kind of environment would be best suited to elicit Julio's strengths and his sense of comfort achieved multiple goals: it removed the onus of the parents' shame and guilt about Julio's behavior, reframed the situation to include ways in which the school might not be equipped to adequately serve this child's needs, and initiated a collaborative discussion about how the school might rethink the ways in which their program could better assist Julio.

The collaborative efforts continued and, together with the consultant, the school staff was able to generate numerous ideas about how to shift Julio's attitude and enhance his social and academic behaviors. One idea was to assign an assistant to help him negotiate assignments that required considerable preparation. A floating teacher aide could intermittently monitor his transitions throughout the school day. Underlying this notion was the idea that supportive contact would alleviate some of Julio's anxiety, which often propelled him into a state of narcissistic vulnerability and defensive oppositionalism. A holding environment to contain his emotional experience would diminish the need for this defense and create greater fluidity and flexibility in his social behavior. The other suggestion, provided by the learning specialist, was to create a program of greater structure and reinforcement so that Julio was not left to carry out so many independent tasks, and so that he was aware beforehand of precisely what was expected of him. The psychological evaluation was thus utilized by the entire school team to generate ideas about how to work most effectively with Julio.

The final area to address was Julio's relationship with his teacher. For the particular cultural values established at the school, this teacher was exemplary. She was a very gracious person with a quiet demeanor. Her classroom persona was one of contained and considerate understanding, and she served as a helpful resource in a harmoniously functioning classroom environment. She saw herself as a facilitator among interested, engaged, and motivated students who could conduct themselves with relative independence and resourcefulness. Since she was a young woman who had recently begun her teaching career and was intent on establishing a positive image with her administrative superiors, she had an especially adverse view of Julio's behavior and how it might reflect negatively on her classroom management. However, there were also personal reasons for her difficulty with his obstreperous behavior, and this is what became significant in the ensuing consultation with her. In reviewing the particular distress that the teacher felt, the consultant learned, in a private meeting with her, that she had grown up with three brothers and was consistently dominated and often humiliated by their control. She had developed, over time, an adaptive restraint that both concealed her anger and gained approval from others, as it had earlier with her parents. In light of this background, which she freely shared with the consultant, there was an ongoing dialogue about the particular ways in which Julio's behavior often reminded her of her brothers', making it more personally offensive to her. The consultant first and most importantly listened to the teacher's perceptions about Julio's disruptiveness. She supported the idea that Julio's behavior was disruptive and that his cavalier attitude was difficult to tolerate. She then shared some of her own observations about his classroom behavior, noting, for example, that he was often more disorganized and subsequently disruptive when he was left on his own, particularly with a difficult assignment. The teacher was able to use the consultation to reflect on her own attitudes, and moreover was able to recognize Julio's need for greater structure in the classroom.

A consultation can take into account the influences of both the parents and the teachers when endeavoring to understand a child's experience. Parents are the primary influence in a child's life, but an overwhelming part of each day is spent with the teacher, so this confluence of separate and sometimes different approaches often needs to be addressed. Specifically, when there are gross inconsistencies in parenting and teaching style, children may experience difficulties that are not necessarily inherent in their characters, but emanate from the interrelationships that govern their daily lives. When parenting and teaching styles conflict significantly with each other, the child can be misunderstood. We saw with Julio that the undercontrol of his parents' style came into notable conflict with the undercontrol of the school setting and the teacher. Each expected the other to be in greater control. In other situations, particular combinations can be equally deleterious to a child's functioning as, for example, when there is parental overcontrol and teacher undercontrol. In such cases the parent consultant must take into consideration these powerful influences on the child's behavior.

A 5-year-old boy who had never attended school was enrolled in a kindergarten program that was somewhat disorganized. The teacher, who was kindly and well meaning, had marked difficulty in establishing an adequate degree of authority and was unable to facilitate an organized and stable atmosphere in her classroom. The boy's parents were strict and highly authoritarian and he was thus accustomed to a great deal of external structure. When he engaged in classroom activities, he expected to receive considerable direction from the adult in the room. However, his teacher was often preoccupied and sometimes flustered by the activity and noise level in the room. Although she endeavored to handle each child's questions and requests, she was unable to adequately integrate the many disparate occurrences into a harmonious whole. Under these circumstances, the child floundered; the disorganization agitated him and, as a result, he became aggressive with other children. In his attempt to negotiate the situation, so that he felt less disorganized, he got in the way of others and this tended to cause friction. When the teacher evaluated his behavior, she tended to see him as somewhat unruly and, in her failure to contextualize his behavior, she reported his unruliness to the boy's parents.

What the teacher was not sufficiently aware of were the aspects of her behavior that influenced her students in very particular ways. Her comments regarding this child created much concern for his parents who became even harsher with him at home. A consultation was initiated with the school psychologist, at the teacher's request, and ultimately was designed to increase her awareness of the impact of her classroom approach. She was quite amenable to discussing ways in which she could assist the student in becoming better organized. The teacher and consultant together arrived at the idea that the child would benefit from micromanagement in the classroom, as he had not yet developed the greater independence that this teacher was accustomed to. She was able to structure him more effectively because, while a more structured teaching style was not consistent with her self-image, the motivation to help her students was. The psychologist had engaged in the consultation with the explicit presumption that the teacher was open and flexible. Again, in this way, the consultant circumvented the teacher's potential feelings of inadequacy and defensiveness by conveying her confidence in the teacher's benign motivations.

In addition to the practice of consultation with teachers, teachers often act as consultants to parents; they are clearly in a position to observe in the most direct and consistent manner the daily life of the child. In fact they have, historically, performed consultative functions, including providing intermittent feedback to parents about their children's academic progress and social interactions. They have traditionally also been purveyors of current thinking about child development. Particularly in the child's early years, when developmental issues are most salient, nursery school teachers serve some of the same functions as the clinician, at the same time that they must assume the role of a surrogate parent. With the advent of child guidance clinics and nurseries, preschool teachers can be prominent figures in the relational matrices of the child's life. Teachers working in therapeutic nurseries often have specialized training to implement programs designed to address the needs of autistic, emotionally disturbed, or neurologically challenged children, and parent consultation will necessarily be a significant component of these programs.

Commonly this type of teacher involvement engenders a degree of anxiety in parents who anticipate that their children, and by extension their parenting, will be "graded" by school personnel. Consultation between teachers and parents thus takes place in a complex relational field. For example, teachers can be much younger than the parents with whom they are working and may not yet be parents themselves. This particular configuration may create its own tensions, especially if there is friction in the interaction to begin with. Parents' defensiveness can be heightened by minor hints at criticisms from teachers who, for their part, can be self-conscious and concerned about how competent they appear to others, both to parents and to school administrators. We saw this dynamic at play in the case of Julio, in which all participants—parents, teachers, administrators, learning specialist, Julio, and the psychological consultant herself—were sensitive to potential criticisms from others. It may, at times, be difficult for teachers to remain mindful of this, particularly in the course of the average school day.

To highlight this point, consider the mother who admitted that she had relatively little trouble with her 4-year-old when they were at home, and they managed together quite harmoniously. However, when confronted with what she perceived as the competitive climate in her child's school community, she often became worried and dismayed by her child's natural exuberance and intensity. She was especially self-conscious when she brought her child to school, where she felt scrutinized by the observations of her child's teachers. At the anticipation of each school day, she worried that her daughter might be seen as unruly.

The following vignette illustrates more extensively this self-consciousness and the anxieties typical in parents' reactions to authority figures, in relation to their children.

A young mother reported having taken her 3-year-old daughter, her only child, to be evaluated for admission to a private school. Upon completion of the assessment session, the evaluator met briefly with the girl's mother. She informed the young mother that her daughter had been unusually self-possessed during the course of the evaluation. She added that this quality must have been particularly difficult to manage when the child was 2 years old, a time when she would have been starting to individuate from her mother. The mother, somewhat startled by the comment, assented that, indeed, they had had a very trying time together during that developmental period. The evaluator went on to observe that the mother had clearly done a wonderful job with her child, as this was evidenced by the girl's exemplary behavior that day. The young woman wept as she listened to this comment; it was profoundly meaningful to her that someone, and especially a person in this position of authority, could both recognize the interpersonal difficulties she had had with her child and at the same time praise her skill and fortitude in parenting. She was sensitive about the nature of her relationship with her child during that period, and was powerfully relieved when their interaction had regained its harmonious quality. This exchange with the evaluator was powerful in two ways: it was an acknowledgment of the difficulties this mother had had with her daughter, and it was a recognition that, despite this, she was still a "good enough" mother. In this way, the evaluator had sensitively used the power of her position to empathize with the mother in a way that did not vilify the child, and, by extension, the mother's parenting.

Sometimes teachers who work with children over the course of years are in the best position to counsel parents, as they have had the opportunity to know a family under a variety of circumstances.

One young boy, Eric, was undergoing a psychiatric evaluation to ascertain whether he had attention-deficit disorder. His behavior in his classroom in an urban school was grossly disruptive. It is a common phenomenon for children who present management problems in the classroom setting to be referred for assessment of this disorder, particularly in larger classes in which psychostimulant medication can seem like a useful management aid to the teacher. The preliminary results of the evaluation suggested the existence of attention deficits in the child.

The child's mother was concerned about the potential harm of the diagnosis and the likelihood that pharmacological intervention would be prescribed. She began to discuss the situation with her son's Sunday school teacher, whose class he had been in for two successive years. This teacher, whose class contained a smaller number of children, also found Eric to be a disruptive force and often felt rather irritated with him herself. Yet, at the same time, she felt quite a good deal of compassion for this mother, who had previously confided to her that she too felt overwhelmed by Eric's activity level.

In their discussion, the Sunday school teacher listened attentively as the mother discussed the preliminary findings of the evaluation. She explained to the teacher that, while the report did not resonate with her own view of her child, the diagnosis could explain why his teachers found him difficult to manage. The teacher suggested to Eric's mother that she convey to the psychiatrist some of the different views of Eric. She herself found one aspect of his behavior to be the most problematic—his habit of calling out answers in class. While it was true that this could be a sign of the impulsivity associated with attentional deficits, what was more noteworthy to this teacher was that Eric seemed to accurately recall everything she mentioned in class even from the previous school term. She believed that his attention, at least in regard to the absorption and retention of information in an academic setting, was unencumbered. Thus, despite the fact that she concurred that he had difficulty in containing himself, she was able to distinguish between his attentional capacities and his impulsivity.

The exchange of information and the teacher's specific response to Eric's mother was part of, and linked to, an informed effort designed to strengthen this parent's ability to advocate for her child. Because the teacher had known the mother over a period of years, she was also aware of the woman's timidity and her tendency to defer too easily to authority figures. Moreover, she knew the child in the classroom context, and while she did not wish to undermine a clinical assessment that might be useful to the family, she nonetheless encouraged the mother to rely, in part, on her own perceptions, and to seek further evaluative data. Ultimately a cognitive assessment revealed that Eric was a highly gifted youngster, and when he was later placed in a class for gifted children, he began to thrive in the more challenging setting.

Not all children's problems have such fortunate solutions. The relationship between this mother and the Sunday school teacher permitted a reliably open discourse and incorporated both people's perceptions of Eric. In her consultative role, this teacher was able to offer impressions that the mother was able to use in the most optimal way because they felt so deeply supportive and corroborative of her own experience. And in the teacher's personal and sensitive relationship with this mother, she knew that it would be useful to encourage her to become a more assertive participant in formulating plans for her child.

14

Consultation in the Physicians's Office

The special knowledge by means of which he was able to interpret the remarks made by his five year old son was indispensable, and without it the technical difficulties in the way of conducting a psychoanalysis upon so young a child would have been insuperable. It was only because the authority of a father and of a physician were united in a single person, and because in him both affectionate care and scientific interest were combined, that it was possible in this one instance to apply the method to a use to which it would not otherwise have lent itself.

*—Sigmund Freud (1909, p. 5) on the treatment of
Little Hans by means of parent consultation*

A child leaves for school in the morning with an anxious concern about how he will be able to contact his mother should he need to do so. He anticipates an anxiety-provoking event at school, perhaps a tryout for a sports team. This is particularly stressful, as he has never attempted to participate in organized sports activities before. He is worried about the possibility that he will not be able to locate his mother in the event of an unanticipated catastrophe. The mother also seems to demonstrate her own anxiety by way of her overzealous reassurances that nothing bad will occur and that she will be easily located. Once at school, the boy asks to go to the nurse's office in order to telephone his mother. He has some difficulty concentrating in class, but eventually becomes absorbed in his work, until the end of the day, when he again repeatedly asks to go to the nurse's office.

This sequence of events is repeated in various degrees of intensity, throughout this child's school years, and is more or less manageable at various times. We could say that intervention would most likely be helpful for this family, that the bidirectional nature of the anxiety should be explored, and that attachment issues are most likely highly relevant. How the family has managed crises in the past, and what constitutes a crisis would also be pertinent in exploring the boy's anxiety and anticipation of disaster. We might also want to explore the impact of this anxiety on the boy's social relationships and on other aspects of his development.

Now, suppose this boy has asthma. The clinical picture is immediately transformed. The nature of the mother–child relationship is more understandably fraught with anxiety, particularly around the phenomenon of separation. This is what one would expect under circumstances in which a family lives with a potentially life-threatening condition. Indeed, if the child's asthma did not generate considerable anxiety, one might even more actively question the nature and quality of the attachment. In this case we can see that the attachment is characterized by the child's experience of the mother as a reliable presence whom he calls on at times when there is the anticipation of increased risk, such as an instance of increased physical exertion.

Asthma is a chronic medical condition caused by swelling, inflammation, and spasms of the air passages in the lungs. It is the single most prevalent chronic disease among children, afflicting about five million children in the United States. It is the number one cause of school absence, and poor inner-city children are affected at disproportionately high rates (Center for Disease Control and Prevention 2001). The precipitant for an asthma attack is the exposure to such indoor environmental factors as cigarette smoke, cleaning solvents, perfumes, dust and mold, and such outdoor factors as cold weather and ozone. Behavioral factors include strenuous exercise, emotional excitement, and anxiety. All of these factors imply for parents that leaving their asthmatic children in the care of others requires greater and more vigorous supervision than for most families. For all of these reasons, poorer families are at greater risk: the environmental activators and settings are more difficult for them to control, and they have fewer options for child care. National health authorities recommend that child care providers, including school personnel, maintain a health file on each asthmatic child in their care and that emergency contact with the child's physician and parent be easily accessible. Asthma is an illness that requires the coordination of multiple services from multiple spheres. It is a medical condition that has profound implications for a child's emotional life. Asthma is an illness that exemplifies the usefulness of the biopsychosocial model of medical management, which, at its best, incorporates an understanding of the specific ways in which health problems are intertwined with and affect the intrapsychic and interpersonal lives of children.

Psychologically minded physicians have frequently noted the correspondence between asthma and separation anxiety in children, and relationally oriented clinicians focus on the bidirectional nature of the separation issues that are frequently involved. Asthma thus provides a useful illustration of the role that the physician can assume as a parent consultant. The physician can assist parents in establishing ancillary services and plans for the child's school routines or when the child is in someone else's care. Pediatricians and family practitioners have usually known their patients over long periods of time, and therefore are in a position to assist parents in organizing and controlling circumstances in which the asthmatic episodes can be minimized. They can also help to deconstruct the secondary anxieties that typically occur in families in which a serious medical condition exists. Often, the physician will have been a participant in the initial diagnosis of the condition and will already be an integral part of the family's experience with the illness. Thus shared knowledge and history will be an already established part of the physician–family relationship.

Physicians do parent counseling, which is a form of parent therapy. They are often the first to be consulted when parents have concerns about their children's behavior and development. Parent consultations with the family doctor or pediatrician about normal, as well as problematic, development focus on issues and concerns about breast-feeding, eating and sleeping habits, and the developmental difficulties of adolescence.

The auspicious tradition of psychoanalytic work began, largely, through patients' consultations with their physicians about their "nervous" disorders. Winnicott began his career as a pediatrician whose interest in the relationships between parent and child forged his transition into psychoanalytic theory and child therapy. He continued to be solicited for child guidance in his books, lectures, and radio addresses (Winnicott 1971, 1993). More recently, many other physicians, including Benjamin Spock (1989), T. Berry Brazelton (1983, 1986, 1989, 2000), Stanley Greenspan (1989, 2000), and Richard Ferber (1986), have been prominent as providers of advice on child rearing practices.

The best kind of doctor–patient relationship incorporates a comprehensive integration of medical, psychosocial, and familial factors, and can be achieved through the context of the relational structure of primary care. A holistic approach that is not confined to one discipline but incorporates a broader and deeper and more encompassing view of the patient provides the most fruitful and effective strategy for intervention. The renewed emphasis on the integration of the psychic and the somatic has enhanced clinicians' sensitivity to both the social experience and the internal life of patients. This biopsychosocial model was introduced into medical thinking in order to achieve a greater awareness of the interplay of social, biomedical, and psychological forces. It enables physicians to examine somatic problems contextually, and nowhere is this more relevant than in work with children.

This chapter reviews numerous problems that confront the physician–patient relationship, examining some of the cultural underpinnings that stand in the way of a more collaborative and equitable relationship, and demonstrating how medical expertise and ordinary parental sensitivity and awareness can be successfully combined to benefit both parents and children.

What considerably complicates the position of the medical practitioner is the great value that our culture places on health care and medical information. Physicians regularly engage in consultations with their patients and they are in a unique position to collaborate with them. What presents a radical obstacle in developing greater collaborative alliances, however, is the fact that medical training emphasizes an empirically based "correctness," and consequently many doctors feel pressed to maintain their status as the exclusive experts of specialized knowledge. In this regard, their opinions can feel unassailable to parents. In parent therapy, as we have defined it, it is essential to achieve a shift in this relational balance so that decisions made by parents and doctors are more collaborative than unidirectional. This does not diminish the need for the particular training and expert knowledge that are in the domain of the medical doctor. However, just as in the psychotherapy supervision paradigm, where the therapist, not the supervisor, has actual and sustained experience with the patient, the parents, who live with the child, understand something about the unique ways in which their child functions. The physician can prescribe effective medications, but a parent will know whether the child is more amenable to taking medications in liquid or pill form. Good medicine attempts to treat the whole person, with adequate sensitivity to idiosyncratic experience, and thus the familiarity and understanding of parents are invaluable for the physician's diagnostic and treatment considerations.

One of the great virtues of Winnicott's attitude toward parents was his firm conviction that the most effective guidance distills from ordinary parental behavior that which allows parents to feel more secure in what they do. Rather than instruction, Winnicott believed in support. His idea that "any propaganda, or telling people what to do, is to be deplored" (Winnicott 1993, p. 2), reflects the weight that he gave to the personal knowledge and wisdom of the average parent. Winnicott often emphasized that ordinary maternal care has a seamless quality that should be, for the most part, left undisturbed. In working with families, therefore, it is extremely important to realize that parents are sensitive to the evaluations and judgments of authority figures; the natural inclination toward self-consciousness about the adequacy of one's parenting is heightened in the face of authority, in general, and can be especially pronounced with medical authority, in particular.

One parent, during a regular medical check up for her 2-year-old, was discussing general developmental and medical issues. The child was an active, alert toddler, enthusiastically engaged in social activities and normally responsive to his environment. The pediatrician, however, suggested that the child should have acquired greater language skills by this time. Despite the fact that the mother was a child psychologist herself, especially skilled in the assessment of developmental delays, she began to feel intense anxiety about her son's language acquisition.

All aspects of his language readiness were intact—his receptive vocabulary being quite extensive—yet this mother spent months in worried preoccupation until her child became more verbally expressive. This highlights the power that the medical community has over the lives of parents. In this case, the influence of the physician was so powerful that, combined with the natural parental predisposition to worry about developmental progress, it obscured this psychologist's otherwise expert developmental knowledge and understanding. This mother, under other circumstances, without her own parental anxieties, might have felt more prepared to understand her physician's medical authority as an attempt to review developmental norms. In a different context, the physician, with concerns about a child's language development, would ordinarily defer to the psychologist's greater expertise in this area. The physician might have established a more collaborative interaction and diffused the mother's anxiety by simply phrasing her concerns with a statement such as, "We should pay attention to Robbie's speech development over the next six months."

Physicians feel pressured to be expert, accurate, comprehensive, and unequivocal in making diagnostic and treatment determinations. This pressure leaves little room for collaboration and for process over product. In such a climate, collaboration becomes a complicated and difficult task for both doctor and patient. In the physician's efforts to be rigorous and comprehensive in her developmental evaluation, she failed to consider the totality of the child's developmental situation: that is, the interaction of his social engagement and linguistic understanding. For a collaborative effort to ensue, there should optimally be an exploration and integration of multiple spheres of influence; in most cases there is a confluence of issues at play, so that behaviors are likely to be overdetermined. Clinicians who are overconfident about the psychological aspects of behavior can miss the more subtle but essential medical elements of a case.

Consider the plight of the 2-year-old boy who was in the process of toilet training. He easily mastered urinary control but was experiencing undue distress around his attempts at defecation. His body-to-brain signaling appeared to be in place—he was aware of when it was that he needed to use the toilet; however, he seemed so anxious at the prospect, that he developed the tendency for fecal retention, which resulted in severe constipation and concomitant abdominal pain. This situation generated further anxiety in the family, with the parents worrying about possible dangerous repercussions to their child's health. They consulted their pediatrician, and together they came to the conclusion that the boy's problem was a phase-specific, internally driven conflict around the relinquishing of power. The physician had interpreted the child's behavior as a willful, although not conscious, withholding of bowel activity as an attempt to reestablish some of the earlier, and now lost, control over his parents. And, indeed, the behavior did seem to be powerfully controlling, directing enormous attention and concern toward the symptom. Nonetheless, despite their desire to remain open to psychological explanations, the parents had great difficulty in tolerating their son's distress. They also had lingering doubts about the validity of this explanation, since they saw their son as relatively calm and anxiety free in regard to toilet training. They had acquiesced to the pediatrician's advice largely out of deference to her expertise.

After some time, they decided to solicit the advice of their own family physician, who advised them that, while issues of power, control, and autonomy can indeed come into play around toileting, the degree of their child's pain and distress seemed beyond the normal range of toilet training issues. He, in fact, suspected some physical vulnerability, and on examination, the physician discovered the existence of rectal fissures, which were causing the child acute pain. This condition was medically treated to relieve the painful experience of defecation.

What is significant here is that their own physician had assumed the presence of a physiological problem, not because of a theoretical belief, but as a result of his familiarity with these people as parents. He trusted, as part of his long history with them, that their dissatisfaction with the initial interpretation of the child's behavior, and their persisting skepticism, reflected a strong possibility that the diagnosis was incorrect. Thus, the parents' feeling that the diagnosis was inconsistent with the ways in which they perceived their son provided a sufficient impetus for further medical exploration.

The tendency for some physicians to overpsychologize may represent an important attempt to incorporate salient psychological variables into their largely biologically based discipline. However, for some, it may also be a way of maintaining the established order, the status quo, in the relationship between physicians and patients. Thus, when the apparent limits of medical understanding have been reached, a diagnosis of stress trends to become a ubiquitous substitute for an otherwise undiagnosed, and therefore improperly treated, condition. The implicit attribution of the patient's psychic responsibility may exonerate the doctor or, at the least, mitigate the impact of the failed diagnostic and treatment situation, but it also leaves the patient feeling guilty and frustrated. Following the discovery of the rectal fissures, the parents, in collaboration with the physician, sought a consultation with a psychologist to reestablish the family equilibrium and to offset some of the conflicts that had developed around the stressful toileting situation. In this case, the medical condition had psychological consequences because the delay in appropriate treatment interfered with the accomplishment of a normal developmental milestone.

Another example is pertinent here:

A 10-year-old girl was performing adequately in her daily school routines but was failing consistently on larger, standardized exams. Intermittently she complained of blurred vision and vibrating images when attempting to read things. Her very conscientious parents took her to their ophthalmologist for an eye examination. After determining that the child's visual acuity was adequate, the doctor decided that her visual discomfort and reading dysfluency were stress related. The parents, with much insightful knowledge of their daughter, were not satisfied with this explanation, particularly since they saw their child as happy, socially engaged, and not likely to manifest anxiety in this somatic form. A parent therapist met with them and advised that they pursue further assessment.

A psychological evaluation revealed that this very bright and well adjusted child had an acute but discrete learning disability in the area of visual scanning and left/right discrimination. Looking at an array of visual symbols was a significant problem for her that, undetected, had been causing her great visual discomfort and pronounced problems in a particular visual medium, such as computer-generated exams and blackboard work at school. The ophthalmologist had accurately tested her vision, but visual scanning is primarily a brain processing function. He had also accurately ascertained that the child was tense about this; however, had the doctor been in a position to elicit more detailed information from the parents, and had they been assisted in reflecting on their own observations and their daughter's, he might have strengthened their confidence and enabled them to make better use of the information that was at their disposal.

One obstacle to employing a more interdisciplinary, biopsychosocial model here was the fact that the ophthalmologist is a subspecialist, in contrast to the family doctor with whom the parents would have had an ongoing relationship and who would therefore have been more likely to explore a variety of ancillary issues—to attend to the larger picture and incorporate interpersonal information as well. This brings to mind the old parable about the three blind men who came across an elephant and tried to determine the nature of the creature. The first leaned against the elephant's side and thought that it was a huge stone wall; the second got hold of its tail and believed it to be a rope; the third embraced the elephant's leg and had the idea that it was the trunk of a tree. The significance of the parable is that looking from a narrow, circumscribed perspective tends to obscure the fuller and more integrated view of things—to miss the forest for the trees. It is for this reason that an enduring relationship with parents of young children can yield a multi-faceted understanding of a child's problems.

We must distinguish between attempts by physicians to explore, holistically, all avenues of influence on the somatic and behavioral life of the child, and the facile psychologizing of some clinicians. Thus, the precipitous, theory-driven conclusions to which we have referred, even though they are presumably attentive to psychological factors, do not give sufficient weight to, and do not sufficiently explore, a variety of relational issues in conjunction with medical phenomena. This brings to mind Freud's (1910) caution about "wild" analysis, and his exhortation to clinicians that they base their interpretations on careful consideration in the context of an enduring relationship with patients. Freud believed that intervention should be predicated on sustained contact with a patient. "Attempts to 'rush' [the patient] at first consultation by . . . telling him the secrets which have been discovered by physicians are technically objectionable" (Freud 1910, p. 226). Freud's remarks capture the powerful impact of medical authority by which many patients are intimidated, and through which they lose their own capacity to participate in the assessment of their problems. He also clearly warned that premature or exclusively theoretical interpretations tend only to be disruptive for the patient and significantly compromise the doctor–patient relationship.

Another example of a domain in which pseudopsychological theory has held sway over a more empirically driven dissemination of information is in the area of infertility. Until recently, infertility had a largely unknown etiology, and in the absence of identifiable and treatable factors, patients were often told that the underlying cause of the infertility was stress. This overlooked the fact that the condition itself was a great cause of stress, making for a coincidence of variables, and that stress has not generally been known to have precluded conception. In keeping with this idea, that stress was an underlying etiological factor in causing infertility, conception and successful pregnancies that occurred subsequent to adoption were considered to be a consequence of the postadoption shedding of anxiety (Brazelton 1989). However, when this theory was tested empirically, research indicated that successful conceptions and pregnancies, for couples who adopt, occur at the same rate as infertile couples who do not adopt but actively continue in their attempts to conceive (Shapiro 1998). The faulty logic persists in the medical community, in part because it obscures, for both doctor and patient, the fallibility and limitations of the physician's knowledge. It may still be difficult for physicians to acknowledge the apparent gaps in existing medical knowledge.

Thus the medical establishment maintains a sense of invulnerability. Its knowledge is either difficult to challenge or unassailable. The doctor–

patient relational structure can be powerfully injurious to the strengthening and enhancement of parental skills, skills that we believe are better augmented through the process of collaboration. On the other hand, there are many areas in which medical knowledge has been successfully integrated with relationally organized psychological theory, both in the primary care of families and in specifically targeted areas. In the area of international adoption, for example, which has immensely expanded in recent years, there are medical practitioners who have adopted a consultative model that makes use of the principles of collaboration and reflection on the multiple medical, psychological, and cultural factors.

Adopting children from foreign countries is fraught with anxiety for prospective parents. The application process requires much scrutiny by various governmental agencies that assess the applicants' suitability as parents. Agencies are well equipped to counsel people through the vicissitudes of the process. However, when the parents must decide whether to accept a particular child for adoption, a new set of uncertainties and anxieties arises. In many cases there is insufficient information about the child's history, including genetic, pre-, and perinatal conditions, and early infant care. Parents may be given a brief videotape of the infant accompanied by some demographic, medical, and diagnostic information. It is at this juncture that the physician can serve most usefully as a consultant as the parents think about their own capacities. Consultation can help them reflect on the anxieties and difficulties they may anticipate. A physician can present an array of potential medical consequences and developments based on the available information, and through this counsel, parents can anticipate future developments and eventualities. They can then contemplate whether or not they are prepared to manage particular health problems or developmental delays. Many physicians do parent consultation specifically for adoption, and they use a collaborative model of pooling information to assist parents in making decisions and in planning for future contingencies. The physician functions similarly to the psychotherapy supervisor by capitalizing on and expanding the parents' anticipatory functions.

Physicians are increasingly being trained to incorporate their patient's social experience and psychological character into the planning of medical treatment. This integration of environmental factors and temperamental traits contributes invaluable information to the treatment setting, and enhances the usefulness of the biologically based medical knowledge. There are situations in which a doctor's expertise is most effectively executed in conjunction with the parents' social and psychological circumstances. The physician as consultant can assist parents with the coordination of services at school, with child care, and, in conjunction with therapists, with managing their children's anxiety. The physician who has an ongoing relationship with a family is in the most advantageous position to serve as a consultant. Like the therapist's relationship with a supervisor who is familiar with the individual vulnerabilities and concerns of both the therapist and patient, parents can make use of the relationship with their family doctor, consulting on a variety of issues. The doctor can maintain a perspective on the nature of a particular parenting approach. The time spent with parents, like a supervisor's ongoing knowledge of a therapist, will yield information about what kind of help they need: advice for first-time parents grappling with the vicissitudes of toddlerhood, soothing reassurance for anxious parents who tend to catastrophize, or referrals when deeper psychological intervention is called for.

As consultants, physicians can create the holding environment that is so beneficial in working with parents. One way in which this space can be created is through the collaboration of therapist and physician—a collaboration that addresses the interplay between medical and emotional issues. This approach is similar to that employed in mental health centers and hospitals when staff members meet to exchange information so that care can be effectively coordinated. The difference in parent therapy is that the parents are included as part of the treatment team. The framework is thus twofold: professional clinicians share their views and elicit information from parents, which in turn creates an atmosphere of candor, demystifying the special knowledge of the professionals. The professionals become one part of a team that endeavors to enhance a child's emotional and social experience.

Physicians who are inclined to reflect on psychological processes might regularly consult with psychotherapists when they believe that psychosomatic issues are of significant relevance for the patients they are treating. In the case of a condition such as anorexia, the underlying causes are decidedly psychological. This is a condition that is biopsychosocial, and while its etiology is, seemingly, purely psychological, it is physiologically compromising to the patient. Patients with anorexia, most commonly adolescent girls, can be seen as having a psychological disorder in which the predominant feature is compromised nutrition, which ultimately may be fatal. However, the anorectic condition has social implications for the patients and their families. Because of the emphasis on the etiology of this condition in the determination of a treatment plan, physicians are relatively adept at incorporating families into the treatment process. Curiously, psychotherapists are sometimes not as facilitative in this way, perhaps because issues of adolescent privacy and separation from parents occupy such a central position in psychoanalytic therapy. Thus psychotherapy for the anorectic often takes place in a climate of marked familial tension.

One mother of an anorectic girl confided in her family physician that her daughter's therapist had informed her that, although she could not be at all involved in the girl's therapy, she should be aware of the fact that her daughter was deeply angry at her. This punitive communication only served to heighten the tension in the family by increasing the mother's already intense anxiety and self-recrimination about her daughter's condition. The cases of the two adolescent girls, Lisa and Ashley (Chapter 11), both of whom had had episodic eating disorders, are similarly illustrative of the problems that are inherent in treating these conditions. The physician becomes, in this context, not only an invaluable resource, but a reasonable and vital component of the parent therapy process. As in the school setting, physicians can work in conjunction with the parent therapist, or can serve as the primary consultants, particularly when they are psychologically sensitive to their patients' needs. Even when this occurs, parents may derive the greatest benefit from a more collaborative effort by a team of clinicians.

A psychologist who works extensively with anorectic patients, in consultation with a physician, was asked to comment on the utility of the collaborative process. "The collaboration works to reduce the anxiety of the therapist. We tell ourselves that it's to support the parents—to create a holding environment for them, and it certainly often does achieve that." Coordinating an ongoing, evolving treatment strategy with families that confront this overwhelming situation creates some emotional containment for parents and for the anorectic youngster, despite the fact that anorectics, confronted with a united treatment team, often complain that everyone is "ganging up" on them.

One psychotherapist-physician team working with the parents of a hospitalized anorectic girl discussed the efficacy of collaborative work and recognized that the management of the clinicians' anxiety was integrally connected to their capacity to effectively care for the family. The compromised physical health of these patients makes their condition both psychologically and medically critical. However, too frequently psychotherapists work individually, separate from other treatment providers, creating an undue, excessive burden for themselves in their attempts to treat patients whose lives depend on the success of the treatment. Under such conditions, the intense anxiety of the therapist may be projected outward, resulting in greater tendencies to blame the parents. This cycle has clearly deleterious effects on the relational atmosphere in the family, and in the treatment as well.

Similarly, physicians who treat anorexia may reasonably feel themselves to be out of their depth with regard to the psychological and familial aspects of the disorder. It is for this reason that they can greatly benefit from collaborative work with a psychotherapist, whose area of expertise provides support in areas in which they may feel relatively deficient. Often, the messages within a family regarding nutrition, weight, and food can be highly ambiguous and layered; clinicians must be able to maintain sufficient calm and resolve to be able to understand, interpret, and deconstruct complex and contradictory communications.

One patient who came to therapy in part for her concerns about an eating disorder reflected on the fact that she had never known her mother to eat anything without some anxious or embarrassed self-recrimination. In fact, this patient developed pervasive anxieties about ingesting almost anything; she was even preoccupied with the toxicity in the air. Physicians treating patients with eating disorders, particularly anorectics, are concerned with medical ramifications, which is their area of expertise. However, as was the case with this patient, many aspects of her family life, and the sometimes subtle but influential prohibitions around eating, were best explored by the psychologist. Therefore, combining the expertise of the physician with knowledge of the patient's internal and interpersonal experience can provide the most informed picture of patients' needs.

In another case of a hospitalized anorectic patient, each clinician, working alone in their particular discipline, was feeling hopeless about the girl's prognosis. The team was only able to confront the ambiguous communications of the parents of their anorectic patient when they were all in a conference together. When the parents were alone with the psychologist, they seemed to misunderstand the physician's counsel about the girl's weight, and when they were with the physician alone, they expressed concern about the wisdom of the psychologist's views. These parents were genuinely and deeply anxious about their daughter's well-being, yet in their attempts to ward off the terrible guilt they felt over her grave illness, they unconsciously and unwittingly attributed some of her present condition to the ineptness of the treatment providers. Only when the psychologist and physician met together with the parents did the clinicians feel composed enough to confront this very significant problem, and only through the confrontation were the parents able to approach their massive feelings of desperation and fear in a more productive way. With the achievement of this team support, which both released and contained their overwhelming fears of exposure, the parents felt empowered to be effective treatment providers themselves, and were able to use the clinicians for the reassurance they so desperately needed. The team then became composed of the psychologist, the physician, and the parents, with the clinicians acting more as supervisors in collaboration with the parents' therapeutic interactions with their daughter. The "supervisors" supported them through their inevitable mistakes, and as the parents' anxiety diminished, their sense of competence increased.

For information sharing and for emotional holding, the collaborative paradigm and consultative process not only offer the most coherent picture of a child's medical condition, but also can address the most salient needs of the patient. A more circumscribed view, while often expert, has the disadvantage of missing some feature of the relational structure that may be essential to a full understanding of a symptom. Like the family with toileting problems or the girl with the visual disability, the expert diagnostic conclusion lacked the more contextual and encompassing view, which could be derived only through sufficiently intimate and enduring knowledge of the child. The contention here is that a more intimate knowledge of the child both presupposes and incorporates the parents' knowledge and expertise.

15
Consultation in the Mental Health Center

Work in the mental health center presents the clinician with challenges that are unlike those faced in private practice. The rigors of treatment in the public sector have been eloquently chronicled by Altman (1995), who has applied psychoanalytic thinking to the dynamics of working with the urban poor. Mental health facilities are riddled with problems that stem, in part, from the structure of the overarching social system. Care in these facilities is thus subject to the many stresses that characterize the provision of services in the public sector in general, a sector that typically serves poor, overburdened, and disenfranchised people. Unlike in private facilities, there are multiple financial stresses created by politicized issues that affect funding.

Much of the structure of the mental health center replicates the more damaging and demoralizing power inequities that disenfranchised people confront in their daily lives. An expert—more educated, more privileged, and thus more self-assured—is in an authoritative role with a less knowledgeable parent. In this schema, young women who are having difficulty in managing their children may experience the authority of the mental health clinic as just one more derogation of their already fragile sense of themselves as capable and competent in the care of their children.

To illustrate some of the ways in which a parent consultation can begin to address this problematic paradigm, we focus here on a patient and the attempts made to increase her self-confidence as a parent. This case highlights the flexibility of the parent therapy model and its advantage in accommodating the wide range of needs that parents have in their efforts to promote their children's growth.

Let us return to the consultation with Frances (Chapter 7), the teenage mother who initially sought treatment for her daughter Angela, whom she had referred to as a "monster" child. This consultation proceeded over the course of nearly a year and ultimately made significant shifts in the relationship between Frances and her children. Frances attended the initial interviews with both of her children and agreed that in the next session the family members would be videotaped interacting together. After the taping, Frances would meet with the parent therapist alone while the children were cared for by their great-grandmother. There were several reasons to organize the treatment plan in this way. What was considered of primary importance was the working collaboration between Frances and the clinician, and it was felt that this could best be facilitated if the videotaping was conducted without the additional presence of the treatment provider. In this way, what would become most salient would be the collaboration and mutual reflections of the therapist and the parent around strategies for improving the family dynamics. It was felt that for Frances and the clinician to watch the videotape of the mother–child interactions together, rather than the more traditional parent report, would facilitate a containing relationship for this adolescent mother and furthermore would help her formulate ideas about her own mothering. The goal, in part, was to encourage her own observation of her children's behavior and to help her develop greater capacities for self-reflection. Videotaping the session would be helpful because Frances had demonstrated considerable difficulty in the capacity to hold in mind a range of ideas about behavior in the abstract.

As we discussed earlier, the initial interview set the stage for Frances to begin to collect her thoughts. She had not thought of doing so prior to the first meeting, but felt only that her children were exhibiting gross problems that needed immediate attention. She had fully expected to present her children to doctors in order to have their disorders diagnosed and treated by them. The interview questions explored the children's behavior but emphasized more of Frances's interior experience—her thoughts and feelings about her children, and her understanding of herself as a parent.

The interviews revealed that Frances felt overwhelmed by the demands of her children. She did not realize that being a single, unemployed, teenage mother was inherently stressful and demanding; rather, she felt that only her children were problematic. She disclosed to the therapist that she felt abandoned by the father of Angela, her older daughter, who had severed all ties to them, and was more modestly disappointed in the father of her younger daughter, Keisha, who played only a minor role in their family life. Frances expressed the belief that Angela, whom she perceived as physically resembling the father exactly, had also inherited his willful, uncompromising nature, and, moreover, that father and daughter most likely shared a mental illness that accounted for many of the problems in the family. This was rather confusing for Frances, because as she reviewed her concerns about her older daughter with the interviewing psychologist, she realized that Keisha was exhibiting many of the same behaviors as Angela had at this age. This gave Frances pause, since it was difficult for her to reconcile her belief in the genetic transmission of the problem in a child with a different father. Two possibilities occurred to her: either the problems had been inherited from Frances, herself, or they were not genetically determined, suggesting that the environment might be a significant factor in Angela's problems. This was a question that lingered throughout much of the parent therapy, until the pathological behaviors began to subside.

The therapist worked with Frances in weekly sessions. They often began with a review of the week's events and the significant occurrences or upheavals that took place in the family, before turning their attention to the videotape. Discussions included topics such as interpersonal conflicts with the social worker who was administering her social service benefits, behavioral issues with her children and her relationships with their respective fathers, the discomforts she suffered with her current pregnancy, and her general sense of loneliness and isolation. Ultimately, when this pregnancy resulted in miscarriage, the sessions focused on her feelings about that loss. By this time in the therapy Frances was able to acknowledge that another child would not have been likely to improve her family situation but she was, nonetheless, saddened by the loss of an anticipated "good" baby.

The consultative sessions would then eventually give way to reviewing the videotaped interactions with Frances, Angela, and Keisha. The video

consisted of three segments. First, Frances and her daughters were to wait
in the consulting room and Frances, aware of the video camera, would try
to manage them until she received more explicit instructions. During the
second segment, Frances was asked to engage Angela, the older child, in
an activity that would absorb her, and yet could also involve her younger
child Keisha. In the third segment, Frances was asked to engage Keisha in
an activity and to provide Angela with her own activity that would require
only minimal or intermittent supervision.

The directions to Frances followed a typical consultation insofar as
they focused her attention on the kinds of issues that parents are usually
asked to comment on during initial consultative interviews. More typically
we have the option of asking parents to report on what occurs when they
are together with their children, how behavior might change when one or
another child is given greater attention, what kinds of activities seem to be
most engaging, and how family dynamics change when children's activities
are more or less structured. In this way, we can collect information about
children's difficulties and parental attitudes about particular relationships
and, through this kind of exploration, also begin to expand parents' perspectives on what may be alternative courses of action. Learning from these
meetings how parents conceptualize their children's issues significantly
determines the direction of the consultation. For Frances, who had difficulty
in imagining a variety of interpersonal scenarios, or even mentally calling
forth new possibilities, questioning her about her interactions with her
children proved to be far too great a challenge, both cognitively and
emotionally. Thus, in lieu of asking her to discuss, from memory, the quality
or shape of her interactions with the children at home, the instructions for
the videotaping served to organize an interaction and then to have Frances
reflect on it. In this way the therapist was able to create a dialogue with
Frances that resembled that of parents with greater organizational resources.
These instructions, and the subsequent queries about the interpersonal
exchanges viewed on the tape, constituted the initial phase of the consultative intervention. It was designed, as any parent therapy is, to engage the
parental capacity to reflect on a familial situation, and in doing so, to
consider alternative approaches to maladaptive behaviors. For Frances, whose
general level of emotional equilibrium depended prominently on moment-

to-moment experience, reflecting and considering issues hypothetically was very difficult. Reviewing the videotape together with the therapist, however, served to concretely contain the interpersonal exchanges with her children in order to make these relationships more tangible and accessible for discussion, since she would not otherwise have been able to keep them in mind. Frances was not yet able to think about one state of mind while being in a different state of mind.

Reviewing the tape with Frances was designed to serve an additional function for her: she was able to look, together with the therapist, at the same material from multiple vantage points. The video created the opportunity for her to explore her own perspective on her behavior and affective state at a given moment; this expanded both her reflective capacities and her capacity to look more fluidly at the intersubjective aspect of the relational dynamics on the screen. Through this process she could focus on Keisha's responses to an interaction between herself and Angela, then shift to discuss her own affective experience during that segment and then shift yet again to contemplate Angela's feelings during those same moments. This enterprise created the possibility of considering each of them from the vantage point of their own subjectivity, as well as considering their roles as objects for the others. The therapist's question, "What do you think it was like for Angela when you were playing with Keisha?" gave way to, "How do you imagine Angela felt toward you in that moment?" These questions began to expand her capacity to mentalize and to develop a more empathic stance toward her children. The therapy focused on her assessment of the children's internal states, without causing Frances to feel that her own concerns were being dismissed in favor of her children's. Simultaneously, she was able to feel that there was someone else who attended to and appreciated *her* experience. Finally, the therapist was able to use the evolution in the mother's perceptions to chart the progress of the treatment, and it would thus prevent the clinician from feeling overwhelmed by the chaos in Frances's life.

The videotaped session revealed a young mother with dramatically underdeveloped organizational skills and anticipatory functions regarding her two toddlers. Indeed, the children appeared to rapidly overwhelm their mother in their demands for attention and need for continuous guidance.

Angela, the "monster" child, had few behavioral controls. She immediately began taking items from the desk and shelves in the room where they waited. The room was equipped with toys as well as office supplies, and Keisha was initially drawn to the toys. During the first segment of the taping, when Frances was waiting for further instructions, she provided no guidance for the children nor did she offer any suggestions for their behavior. She was able to admonish them and verbally tried to curtail behaviors with threats of punishment. Apart from these outbursts, Frances remained passive and did not exhibit any initiative even in terms of observing them. Rather, she waited patiently for the therapist to reappear with an assignment for her.

During the second segment, Frances was asked to engage Angela, her 2-year-old, in an absorbing activity. Frances chose to read a story to Angela while Keisha played near them on the floor listening and looking up occasionally. Although Angela quickly lost interest in the activity, Frances persisted in her reading; this was the activity that she had chosen, and she seemed determined to accomplish the task. She continued to read her children's book, fully engaged, and compliant with the directions that had been provided for her. The therapist watched, with a sense of poignancy, as Frances read to herself and Angela desperately but ineffectively tried to obtain her mother's attention by breaking objects in the room.

In the final segment, Frances played with the toys together with Keisha, the 1-year-old, and tried futilely to control Angela. Occasionally Keisha became frustrated when she was unable to accomplish something; at these moments, Frances would become angry and Keisha would cry. Frances was able to engage Keisha at times and, on tape, appeared to feel relieved that she was still able to care for one of her daughters in a way that was satisfying for both of them. At the conclusion, Frances seemed pleased to have had this last episode documented. Most importantly, she seemed pleased that the psychologist was taking an interest in her, and felt, moreover, that her children's difficulties were now evidenced and could therefore be addressed.

It should be mentioned here that passively watching the videotape was a painful act of restraint for the therapist, who, at several junctures, had an overwhelming impulse to enter the room and intervene. Of course, this would have proved to be more damaging than helpful, to all parties and to the therapy itself. Like the consultants in Fraiberg and colleagues' (1975) "Ghosts in the Nursery," who longed to soothe the crying baby of Mrs. March, who was too depressed to comfort her child herself, the consultant here recognized that the children would only be truly helped by a mother who could become more adept at caring for them. For Frances, like Mrs. March, if the therapist were more knowledgeable, active, and effective with the children, this would only have confirmed and intensified her self-doubt, and would have precluded the opportunity to develop more effective parenting. While this experience may be somewhat more common when working with a population typically seen in mental health centers, the same issues are relevant in a variety of settings and modalities in which there are similar impulses to intervene, and which the therapist is then obliged to suppress.

The therapy proceeded over the course of a year, and Frances sustained a consistent interest in the process. It was a fluid process, with Frances and the psychologist sharing with each other their different views and perspectives on what occurred in the room. One of the most salient events in these exchanges, and one that paved the way for significant affective shifts, was the therapist's perception that Angela appeared to be very much like her mother. This was an idea that Frances had never considered, as she was so intensely committed to the notion that her older daughter resembled her father, exclusively. During one session, the therapist asked Frances to hold a photograph of herself up to the video screen and to compare it to a still shot of Angela, in order to consider a possible resemblance. This intervention could have occurred only after sufficient time had elapsed so that Frances could feel that the therapist could also see what she saw. We are reminded here of the playful but powerful exchange in which Bromberg (1998) describes changing seats with a patient in order for each of them to see the other's perspective. And indeed, despite her previous investment to the contrary, Frances was able to see the close physical resemblance between herself and Angela, as she was beginning to appreciate other similarities between them.

The therapist organized the early phases of the treatment around the development of an empathic identification with Angela, with whom

Frances appeared always at odds. Angela did seem to be, for her age, unusually impulse ridden and in great need of reassuring guidance. Yet, for *her* age, we might describe Frances similarly. The underlying feature of Angela's overtly rageful and oppositional behavior seemed to be the lack of a strong, containing presence, so she, like her mother, acted in ways that received negative attention. After several meetings that focused on the videotaped reading of the story, Frances was asked to talk about who had read to *her* when she was a child. This question evoked, for her, the deepest sense of longing, which, though unmet in her past, had in some visceral way never been relinquished. The therapist realized that each of Frances's pregnancies had held out for her the promise that this repressed longing would be fulfilled, and that the demands of parenting further intensified her profound sense of deprivation. It was through the empathic engagement of the therapist that Frances began to develop greater empathy for herself—an empathy that could then be translated into greater empathic feeling for her daughters. Through the continued clinical work, she began to identify some of Angela's behavior as expressions of the same deep longing for emotional and physical contact. The similarity in their family histories—Frances was raised by an overburdened young mother and no active father—precipitated an emerging warmth toward Angela that Frances had not felt since the child was a newborn.

This new empathic experience created the opportunity to focus the consultation more directly on the relationship between Frances and Keisha. This relationship had been described by Frances as having been a welcomed respite from the often burdensome demands of Angela, who was about 1 year old when Keisha was born. Yet Keisha, too, was now increasingly difficult to manage, which further damaged Frances's already fragile sense of competence in parenting. When she and the therapist explored what had felt positive in her first year with Keisha, Frances was able to identify the ways in which she had relished the warmth of the early physical contact with the baby. This coincided with the time that Angela was beginning to take her first steps away from her. Interpretations to Frances then became interwoven with information about basic developmental issues, and thus explanations about children's capacities were integrated with discussions of what might have been Frances's unrealistic expectations of Angela and

Keisha. Significant also was the therapist's decision not to interpret Frances's desire to be nurtured by her children, but, instead, to discuss how painful it must have been to watch her younger daughter make the transition from a cuddly baby to an active toddler. At the same time, these developmentally normal growth periods were discussed as positive reflections on Frances as a mother.

Like a motivated therapist in supervision, Frances used the consultative sessions to absorb information about her transference in relation to her children. Her increased ability to attend to Angela and Keisha was enthusiastically and positively received by the children and was reflected in their behavior. Of course, their more conciliatory engagement further elicited Frances's nurturance, and what developed became part of an enhanced relational cycle. When Frances's emotional needs were met in the treatment process, she became less needy and demanding of her children, and the relationships with them became more gratifying. She could now see them as both needful of her care and simultaneously, less burdensome. Like Mrs. March in "Ghosts in the Nursery" (Fraiberg et al. 1975), the compassion that Frances felt from the therapist, released the feeling for her children that had been buried in the dissociation of her own affective need.

16

Preservation of the Autonomy and
the Integrity of the Parent

*T*he most vital feature of the parent therapy model is the flexibility it provides in treating children's problems. In tailoring the work to the specific needs and propensities of parents it considers relational structures to be an essential and predominant influence in development, and also to be the most fruitful point of intervention. Although children's problems may vary with temperamental proclivities, characterological differences, and multiple environmental and familial circumstances, the predicates of the model remain constant: that children's relational experience is largely composed of the interpersonal interactions and intersubjective life of the family. This suggests that change can occur through transformations in that intersubjective arena. Our contention is that while this can occur in clinical work with the child, with families, or with parents alone, it is most successful when parents are supported in establishing or maintaining their own self-esteem. The paradigm makes central, in therapeutic work, the creation of a containing space in which parents can think about their children and think about their experience with their children.

Let us return momentarily to Sophie's parents (Chapter 7), the couple who experienced both internal and interpersonal conflict over the weaning of their baby. They had several sessions in consultation in which they discussed their thoughts about Sophie's developmental progress. At that point, when most of the issues around nighttime waking had been resolved, the parents brought a videotape of the family to a session. This can be seen, in a sense, as a reflection of the parents' comfort with the therapist and, from another perspective, as a way of sharing their "work" with her. Curiously, in discussing her experience of the consultation, Sophie's mother reflected that, despite the fact that the therapist had made no concrete suggestions, nor offered any explicit parenting guidance, she felt that the therapy had been invaluable in helping her to feel better about what she was already doing with her child. This in turn promoted greater confidence to continue her own parenting approach less ambivalently, which ultimately resulted in more fluid interactions with Sophie. At the point when the video was viewed, the parents experienced the therapist's admiring remarks as genuine reflections on their successful work, much as a therapist might feel when he has shared with a supervisor a meaningful moment from a therapy session. In this way the therapist can convey an aspect of his own work that he feels the supervisor can appreciate and he believes emerged out of the collaborative effort with the supervisor.

The therapy with Sophie's parents served primarily to contain their anxieties about their parenting, as they had already developed in abundance the capacity to mentalize. What was altered was their capacity to attend more sensitively, not to Sophie, but rather to their own needs as parents. In contrast to the use of the video with Frances, as a device through which the therapist created a containing space, Sophie's parents used the video as a reflection of the containment that they had experienced with the consultant. For Frances, the video contained, in a literal way, the data on which she needed to reflect. Both of these consultations were based on an assessment of each parent's needs as well as their capacities to respond to the consultative process. In every parent therapy, however, one thing remains paramount and that is the preservation of the autonomy and integrity of the parent. Fraiberg and colleagues (1975) describe how difficult and painful this therapeutic position sometimes can be. Yet they eloquently explain why it is so vitally important for therapists to resist attending themselves to a child at risk. In explaining how the therapists, referred to in "Ghosts in the Nursery," refrained from picking up the crying baby of a depressed mother, they states "If they should yield to their own wish they would do the one thing they feel must not be done. For [the mother] would then see that another woman could comfort the baby, and she would be confirmed in her own conviction that she was a bad mother" (Fraiberg 1975, p. 392).

References

Ainsworth, M. S. (1985). Patterns of attachment. *Clinical Psychologist* 38(2):27–29.

———. (1991). Attachments and other affectional bonds across the life cycle. In *Attachment Across the Life Cycle*, ed. C. M. Parkes and J. Stevenson. New York: Tavistock/Routledge.

———. (1993). Attachment as related to mother-infant interaction. *Advances in Infancy Research* 8:1–50.

Ainsworth, M. S., and Bell, S. M. (1970). Attachment, exploration, and separation: illustrated by the behavior of one-year-olds in a strange situation. *Child Development* 41(1):49–67.

Ainsworth, M. S., Bell, S. M., and Stayton, D.J. (1991). Infant-mother attachment and social development: "socialisation" as a product of reciprocal responsiveness to signals. In *Becoming a Person: Child Development in Social Context*, vol. 1, ed. M. Woodhead and R. Carr. Florence: Taylor & Francis/Routledge.

Ainsworth, M. S., Blehar, M.C., Waters, E., and Wall, S. (1978). *Patterns of Attachment: A Psychological Study of the Strange Situation*. Hillsdale, NJ: Lawrence Erlbaum.

Ainsworth, M. S., and Eichberg, C. G. (1991). Effects on infant-mother attachment of mother's unresolved loss of an attachment figure, or other traumatic experience. In *Attachment Across the Life Cycle*, ed. C. M. Parkes and J. Stevenson. New York: Tavistock/Routledge.

Alpert, J. L. (1995a). *Psychological Consultation in Educational Settings: Casebook for Working with Administrators, Teachers, Students.* Northvale, NJ: Jason Aronson.

———. (1995b). Some guidelines for school consultants. *Journal of Education and Psychological Consultation* 6(1):31–46.

Alpert, J. L., Richardson, M. S., and Fodaski-Jacobs, L. (1983). Onset of parenting and stressful events. *Journal of Primary Prevention* 3(3):149–159.

Altman, N. (1995). *The Analyst in the Inner City: Race, Class, and Culture Through a Psychoanalytic Lens.* Hillside, NJ: Analytic Press.

———. (1997). The case of Ronald: oedipal issues in the treatment of a seven-year-old boy. *Psychoanalytic Dialogues: A Journal of Relational Perspectives* 7(6):725–739.

Aron, L. (1996). *A Meeting of the Minds: Mutuality in Psychoanalysis. Relational Perspectives Books*, vol. 4. Hillsdale, NJ: Analytic Press.

Aronson, S. (2000). Reestablishing holding in families of divorce. *Journal of Infant, Child, and Adolescent Psychotherapy* 1(1):39–52.

Bateson, G., Jackson, D. D., Haley, J., and Weakland, J. H. (1956). Toward a theory of schizophrenia. *Behavioral Science* 1:251–264.

Beebe, B., Jaffe, J., and Lachmann, F. M.. (1992). A dyadic systems view of communication. In *Relational Perspectives in Psychoanalysis*, ed. N. Skolnick and S. Warshaw. Hillsdale, NJ: Analytic Press.

Beebe, B. and Lachmann, F. M. (1988). The contribution of mother-infant mutual influence to the origins of self and object representations. *Psychoanalytic Psychology* 5(4):305–377.

———. (1998). Co-constructing inner and relational processes: self- and mutual regulation in infant research and adult treatment. *Psychoanalytic Psychology* 15(4):480–516.

Bernstein, I., and Sax, A. M. (1992). Indications and contraindications for child analysis. *Child Analysis and Therapy*, ed. J. Glenn, pp. 67–109. Northvale, NJ: Jason Aronson.

Bettelheim, B. (1967). *The Empty Fortress: Infantile Autism and the Birth of the Self.* New York: Free Press.

Bion, W. R. (1984). *Attention and Interpretation*. London: Caranac.

Blos, P. (1962). *On Adolescence, a Psychoanalytic Interpretation*. New York: Free Press of Glencoe.

Bollas, C. (1987). *The Shadow of the Object: Psychoanalysis of the Unthought Known*. New York: Columbia University Press.

Bowen, M. (1978). *Family Therapy in Clinical Practice*. New York: Jason Aronson.

Bowlby, J. (1969). *Attachment and Loss*, 2 vols. New York: Basic Books.

Brazelton, T. B. (1983). *Infants and Mothers*. New York: Dell.

————. (1986). *In Support of Families*. Cambridge: Harvard University Press.

————. (1989). *Toddlers and Parents*. New York: Dell.

————. (2000). *The Earliest Relationship*. New York: Perseus.

Bromberg, P. M. (1993). Shadow and substance: a relational perspective on clinical process. *Psychoanalytic Psychology* 10:147–168.

————. (1994). "Speak! that I may see you": some reflections on dissociation, reality and psychoanalytic listening. *Psychoanalytic Dialogues*, 4:517–547.

————. (1996). Standing in the spaces: the multiplicity of self and the psychoanalytic relationship. *Contemporary Psychoanalysis*, 32:509–535.

————. (1998). *Standing in the Spaces: Essays on Clinical Process, Trauma, and Dissociation*. Hillsdale, NJ: Analytic Press.

Caligor, L., Bromberg, P., and Meltzer, J. D., eds. (1984). *Clinical Perspectives on the Supervision of Psychoanalysis and Psychotherapy*. New York: Plenum Press.

Center for Disease Control and Prevention. (2001). *Grants Awarded to Implement Inner-City Asthma Intervention*. Press release, February 5, 2001. Available from World Wide Web: *www.cdc.gov/health/diseases*.

Coates, S. W. (1998). Having a mind of one's own, and holding the other in mind: commentary on paper by Peter Fonagy and Mary Target. *Psychoanalytic Dialogues: A Journal of Relational Perspectives* 8(1):115–148.

Cohn, J. F., and Tronick, E. Z. (1983). Three month old infants' reaction to simulated maternal depression. *Child Development* 54:185–193.

———. (1987). Mother-infant face-to-face interaction: the sequence of dyadic states at 3, 6, and 9 months. *Developmental Psychology* 23:68–77.

———. (1989). Specificity of infants' response to mothers' affective behavior. *Journal of the American Academy of Child and Adolescent Psychiatry* 28(2):242–248.

Cohn, J. F., Tronick, E. Z., Connell, D., and Lyons-Ruth, K. (1986). Face-to-face interactions of depressed mothers and their infants. In *Maternal Depression and Infant Disturbance*, ed. E. Z. Tronick and T. Field, pp. 31–44. San Francisco: Josey-Bass.

Emde, R. N. (1989). The infant's relationship experience: developmental and affective aspects. In *Relationship Disturbances in Early Childhood. A Developmental Approach*, ed. A. J. Sameroff and R. N. Emde, pp. 33–51. New York: Basic Books.

Emde, R. (1988). Development terminable and interminable. I. Innate and motivational factors. *International Journal of Psycho-analysis* 69:23–42.

Erikson, E. H. (1963). *Childhood and Society*. New York: W. W. Norton.

Fairbairn, W. D. (1974). *Psychoanalytic Studies of Personality*. New York: Routledge.

Ferber, R. (1986). *Solve Your Child's Sleep Problems*. New York: Simon & Schuster.

Ferenczi, S. (1931). Child analysis in the analysis of adults. In *Final Contributions to the Problems and Methods of Psycho-analysis*, pp. 126–142. London: Hogarth.

Field, T. (1977). Effects of early separation, interactive deficits and experimental manipulations on mother-infant face-to-face interaction. *Child Development* 48:763–771.

———. (1987). Affective and interactive disturbances in infants. In *Handbook of Infant Development*, ed. J. D. Osofsky, 2nd ed. New York: Wiley.

————. (1995). Infants of depressed mothers. *Infant Behavior and Development* 18:1–13.

Field, T., Healy, B., Goldstein, S., et al. (1988). Infants of depressed mothers show "depressed" behavior even with nondepressed adults. *Child Development* 59:1569–1579.

Fonagy, P. (1991). Thinking about thinking: some clinical and theoretical considerations in the treatment of a borderline patient. *International Journal of Psycho-Analysis* 72:639–656.

Fonagy, P., Moran, G., Steele, M., and Higgitt, A. (1991). The capacity for understanding mental states: the reflective self in parent and child and its significance for security of attachment. *Infant Mental Health Journal* 13:200–217.

Fonagy, P., and Target, M. (1998). Mentalization and the changing aims of psychoanalysis. *Psychoanalytic Dialogues: A Journal of Relational Perspectives* 8(1):87–114.

Fraiberg, S., Adelson, E., and Shapiro, V. (1975). Ghosts in the nursery. *Journal of the Academy of Child Psychiatry* 14:387–421.

Frankel, J. B. (1998). The play's the thing: how the essential processes of therapy are seen most clearly in child therapy. *Psychoanalytic Dialogues: A Journal of Relational Perspectives* 8(1):149–182.

Freud, A. (1958). Adolescence. *Psychoanalytic Study of the Child* 13:255–278. New York: International Universities Press.

————. (1967). Introduction to psychoanalysis: lectures for child analysts and teachers 1922–1935. In *The Writings of Anna Freud*, vol. 2. New York: International Universities Press.

Freud, S. (1905). Fragment of an analysis of a case of hysteria. *Standard Edition* 7:7–122.

————. (1909). Analysis of a phobia in a five-year-old boy. *Standard Edition* 10:5–148.

————. (1910). Wild psychoanalysis. *Standard Edition* 11:219–227.

Fromm, E. (1947). *Man for Himself, an Inquiry into the Psychology of Ethics.* New York: Rinehart.

————. (1962). *The Art of Loving*. London: Allen & Unwin.

Ghent, E. Personal communication.

Gilligan, C. (1982). *In a Different Voice: Psychological Theory and Women's Development*. Cambridge: Harvard University Press.

Gilpin, D. (1994). Psychotherapy of the oppositional child. In *Clinical Faces of Childhood*, vol. 1, ed. E. J. Anthony and D. Gilpin, pp. 87–97. Northvale, NJ: Jason Aronson.

Glenn, J. (1992). General principles of child analysis. In *Child Analysis and Therapy*, ed. J. Glenn, pp. 29–66. Northvale, NJ: Jason Aronson.

Glenn, J., Sabot, L. M., and Bernstein, I. (1992). The role of the parents in child analysis. In *Child Analysis and Therapy*, ed. J. Glenn, pp. 393–426. Northvale, NJ: Jason Aronson.

Greenspan, S. I. (1989). *Development of the Ego: Implications for Personality Theory, Psychopathology, and the Psychotherapeutic Process*. Madison: International Universities Press.

————. (2000). *Building Healthy Minds: The Six Experiences that Create Intelligence and Emotional Growth in Babies and Young Children*. New York: Perseus.

Greenspan, S. I., ed. (1987). *Infants in Multirisk Families: Case Studies in Preventive Intervention*. Madison: International Universities Press.

Greenspan, S. I., Pollock, G. H., eds. (1989). *Course of Life: Infancy*. Madison: International Universities Press.

Haley, J. (1971). *Changing Families: A Family Therapy Reader*. New York: Grune & Stratton.

Horney, K. (1937). *The Neurotic Personality of Our Time*. New York: W. W. Norton.

————. (1939). *New Ways in Psychoanalysis*. New York: W. W. Norton.

————. (1945). *Our Inner Conflicts, a Constructive Theory of Neurosis*. New York: W. W. Norton.

Karen, R. (1994). *Becoming Attached: Unfolding the Mystery of the Infant-Mother Bond and Its Impact on Later Life*. New York: Warner.

Kay, P. (1992). Gifts, gratification, and frustration in child analysis. In *Child Analysis and Therapy*, ed. J. Glenn, pp. 309–354. Northvale, NJ: Jason Aronson.

Klein, M. (1948). *Contributions to Psycho-analysis, 1921–1945*. London: Hogarth.

———. (1949). *The Psycho-analysis of Children*, trans. A. Strachey. London: Hogarth.

———. (1957). *Envy and Gratitude, a Study of Unconscious Sources*. New York: Basic Books.

———. (1975). *Love, Guilt, and Reparation and OtherWorks, 1921–1945*. New York: Delacorte Press/ S. Lawrence.

Levenson, E. A. (1995). *The Fallacy of Understanding: An Inquiry into the Changing Structure of Psychoanalysis*. Northvale, NJ: Jason Aronson.

Mahler, M. (1975). *The Psychological Birth of the Human Infant: Symbiosis and Individuation*. New York: Basic Books.

———. (1979). *Separation and Individuation. The Selected Papers of Margaret S. Mahler*, vol. 2. New York: Jason Aronson.

Mahler, M. S., and Furer, M. (1968). *On Human Symbiosis and the Vicissitudes of Individuation*, vol. 1. New York: International Universities Press.

Main, M., Kaplan, N., and Cassidy, J. (1985). Security in infancy, childhood, and adulthood: a move to the level of representation. *Growing Points of Attachment Theory and Research in Child Development*, ed. I. Bretherton and E. Waters, serial no. 209, vol. 50, nos. 1–2, pp. 66–104.

Minuchin, S. (1974). *Families and Family Therapy*. Cambridge: Harvard University Press.

Minuchin, S., Rosman, B. L., and Baker, L. (1978). *Psychosomatic Families: Anorexia Nervosa in Context*. Cambridge: Harvard University Press.

Mitchell, S. A. (1998). *Relational Concepts in Psychoanalysis: An Integration*. Cambridge: Harvard University Press.

———. (2000). *Relationality: From Attachment to Intersubjectivity*. Hillsdale, NJ: Analytic Press.

Mitchell, S.A., and Aron, L., eds. (1999). *Relational Psychoanalysis: The Emergence of a Tradition.* Hillsdale, NJ: Analytic Press.

Mitchell, S.A., and Greenberg, J. R. (1990). *Object Relations in Psychoanalytic Theory.* Cambridge: Harvard University Press.

Napier, A., and Whitaker, C. (1978). *The Family Crucible.* New York: Harper & Row.

Panksepp, J. (1998). Attention deficit hyperactivity disorders, psychostimulants and intolerance of childhood playfulness: a tragedy in the making? *Current Directions in Psychological Science* 7(3):91–108.

Pantone, P. (2000). Treating the parental relationship as the identified patient in child psychotherapy. *Journal of Infant, Child, and Adolescent Psychotherapy* 1(1):19–38.

Pick, I., and Segel, H. (1992). Melanie Klein's contribution to child analysis: theory and technique. In *Child Analysis and Therapy*, ed. J. Glenn, pp. 427–449. Northvale, NJ: Jason Aronson.

Sameroff, A., and Emde, R. N., eds. (1989). *Relationship Disturbances in Early Childhood: A Developmental Approach.* New York: Basic Books.

Sander, F. M. (1979). *Individual and Family Therapy.* New York: Jason Aronson.

Sarason, S. E. (1971). *The Culture of the School and the Problem of Change.* Boston: Allyn & Bacon.

Scharfman, M. A. (1992). Transference and the transference neurosis in child analysis. In *Child Analysis and Therapy*, ed. J. Glenn, pp. 275–307. Northvale, NJ: Jason Aronson.

Schwarz, H. (1950). The mother in the consulting room: notes on the psychoanalytic treatment of two young children. *Psychoanalytic Study of the Child* 5:343–357. New York: International Universities Press.

Seligman, S. (1998). Child psychoanalysis, adult psychoanalysis and developmental psychology: introduction. *Psychoanalytic Dialogues: A Journal of Relational Perspectives* 8(1):79–86.

Shapiro, S. (1998). Psychological consequences of infertility. In *Critical Psychophysical Passages in the Life of a Woman: A Psychodynamic Perspective*, ed. J. Offerman-Zuckerberg. New York: Plenum Medical.

Spock, B. (1989). *Dr. Spock on Parenting*. New York: Pocket Books.

———. (1997). *Baby and Childcare*. New York: Pocket Books.

Srouf, A. L. (1988). The role of infant-caregiver attachment in development. In *Clinical Implications of Attachment*, ed. J. Belsky and T. Nezworski. Hillsdale, NJ: Lawrence Erlbaum Associates.

Stayton, D. J., Ainsworth, M. S., and Main, M. B. (1973). Development of separation behavior in the first year of life: protest, following, and greeting. *Developmental Psychology* 9(2):213–225.

Stern, D. N. (1971). A micro-analysis of mother-infant interaction: behavior regulating social contact between a mother and her 3-1/2 month old twins. *Journal of the American Academy of Child Psychiatry* 10(3):501–517.

———. (1985). *The Interpersonal World of the Infant: A View From Psychoanalysis and Developmental Psychology*. New York: Basic Books.

———. (1995). *Motherhood Constellation: A Unified View of Parent-Infant Psychotherapy*. New York: Basic Books.

Stern, D.N., Hofer, L., Haft, W., and Dore, J. (1985). Affect attunement: the sharing of feeling states between mother and infant by means of inter-modal fluency. In *Social Perception in Infants*, ed. T. Field and N. Fox. Westport, CT: Greenwood Publishing Group.

Sullivan, H. S. (1953). *The Interpersonal Theory of Psychiatry*, ed. H. S. Perry and M. L. Gawel. New York: W. W. Norton.

———. (1973). *Clinical Studies in Psychiatry*. New York: W.W. Norton.

———. (1984). *Personal Psychopathology: Early Formulations*. New York: W. W. Norton.

Target, M., and Fonagy, P. (1996). Playing with reality. II: the development of psychic reality from a theoretical perspective. *International Journal of Psychoanalysis* 77:459–479.

Tracy, R. L., and Ainsworth, M. S. (1981). Maternal affectionate behavior and infant-mother attachment patterns. *Child Development* 52(4):1341–1343.

Tronick, E. Z. (1989). Emotions and emotional communication in infants. *American Psychologist* 44(2):112–119.

Tronick, E., Als, H., and Brazelton, T. B. (1977). The infant's capacity to regulate mutuality in face-to-face interaction. *Journal of Communication* 27:74–80.

Tronick, E. Z., and Cohn, J. F. (1989). Infant–mother face-to-face interaction: age and gender differences in coordination and the occurrence of miscoordination. *Child Development* 60(1):85–92.

Tronick, E. Z., and Gianino, A. F. (1986a). The transmission of maternal disturbance to the infant. In *Maternal Depression and Infant Disturbance*, ed. E. Z. Tronic and T. Field, pp. 61–82.

Tronick, E. Z., and Gianino, A. F. (1986b). Interactive mismatch and repair: challenges to the coping infant. *Zero to Three. Bulletin of the Center for Clinical Infant Programs* 1–6.

Van der Kolk, B., ed. (1984). *Post-Traumatic Stress Disorder: Psychological and Biological Sequelae*. Wasington, DC: American Psychiatric Press.

———. (1987). *Psychological Trauma*. Washington, DC: American Psychiatric Press.

Wallerstein, J., and Blakeslee, S. (2000). *The Unexpected Legacy of Divorce: a Twenty-Five Year Landmark Study*. New York: Hyperion.

Wallerstein, J., and Kelly, J. B. (1980). *Surviving the Breakup: How Children Cope with Divorce*. New York: Basic Books.

Warshaw, S. C. (2000). The contribution of attachment research to my clinical work with patients of school-aged children. *Journal of Infant, Child, and Adolescent Psychotherapy* 1(1):3–18.

Weinberg, M. K., and Tronick, E. Z. (1997). Maternal depression and infant maladjustment: a failure of mutual regulation. In *Infants and Preschoolers: Development and Syndromes. The Handbook of Child and Adolescent Psychiatry*, vol. 1, ed. J. D. Noshpitz, S. Greenspan, S. Wieder, and J. Osofsky. New York: Wiley.

Wilson, A., Passik, S. D., and Faude, J. P. (1990). Self regulation and its failures. In *Empirical Studies in Psychoanalytic Theory*, vol. 3, ed. J. Mesling. Hillsdale, NJ: Lawrence Erlbaum.

Winnicott, D.W. (1965). *The Maturational Process and the Facilitating Environment; Studies in the Theory of Emotional Development*. New York: International Universities Press.

――――. (1971). *Playing and Reality*. New York: Basic Books.

――――. (1975). *Through Pediatrics to Psycho-analysis*. New York: Basic Books.

――――. (1993). *Talking to Parents*. Reading: Addison-Wesley.

Index

About the Authors

Carol Wachs and Linda Jacobs were both trained as child psychologists and received their psychoanalytic training at New York University's program in psychoanalysis and psychotherapy. They credit the flexibility of their analytic training, which did not demand loyalty or adherence to any particular clinical orthodoxy, with their interest in developing a treatment paradigm that worked most effectively for them. They have, through their training, felt the intellectual freedom to explore and reformulate ideas.

Linda Jacobs is an associate professor at Long Island University where she teaches graduate students in the School Psychology Program. She has a private practice in New York City and has worked with parents and children and teachers in the school system for many years.

Carol Wachs has a private practice in New York City. She has worked in the public mental health sector and also works in collaboration with physicians in New York.